The Gershwin Style

THE GERSHWIN STYLE

New Looks at the Music of George Gershwin

• • • • • Edited by Wayne Schneider • • • • •

New York   Oxford   •   Oxford University Press   •   1999

Oxford University Press

Oxford   New York
Athens   Aukland   Bangkok   Bogotá
Buenos Aires   Calcutta   Cape Town   Chennai   Dar es Salaam
Delhi   Florence   Hong Kong   Istanbul   Karachi
Kuala Lumpur   Madrid   Melbourne   Mexico City
Mumbai   Nairobi   Paris   São Paulo   Singapore
Taipei   Tokyo   Toronto   Warsaw

and associated companies in
Berlin   Ibadan

Copyright © 1999 Oxford University Press, Inc.

Published by Oxford University Press
198 Madison Avenue, New York, New York 10016

Oxford is a registered trademark of Oxford University Press

Library of Congress Cataloging-in-Publication Data
The Gershwin style: new looks at the music of
George Gershwin / edited by Wayne Schneider.
p. cm.
Includes bibliographical references and index.
ISBN 0-19-509020-9
1. Gershwin, George, 1898–1937—Criticism and
interpretation.
I. Schneider, Wayne Joseph, 1950– .
ML410.G288G49   1999
780'.92—dc21   97-50590

Permission has kindly been granted to reprint
Charles Hamm's essay "Towards a New Reading of Gershwin,"
first published in *Musica/Realtá* 25 (April 1988): 23–45.

Illustration on p. iii by George Gershwin.
Self-portrait. Oil on canvas board, 39.9 x 29.8 cm, 1934.
National Portrait Gallery, Washington, D.C. U.S.A.
Courtesy of Art Resource, New York.

1   3   5   7   9   8   6   4   2
Printed in the United States of America
on acid-free paper

Permissions

Contents

of the show music Gershwin wrote has ever been published: the complete list of published works in this category comprises piano-vocal scores of only four Gershwin shows and only selected songs from all the shows. Fewer than fifty songs are currently in print. Only two show librettos have been printed. The piano-vocal score of *Porgy and Bess* has been published, of course, but not the full score. The instrumental works have fared somewhat better, but often the published editions are corrupt versions—reorchestrated and arranged.

Gershwin's life, like his music, is well-known, too, the stuff of legend, almost a part of American folklore: his Horatio Alger–like rise from Tin Pan Alley songster to opera composer and his success in popular and art music have been told many times. On the one hand, his show business career—song plugger, rehearsal pianist, songster, composer of shows and songs for films—provided Gershwin with considerable income and formed the basis for that public adulation so unprecedented for an American composer within his lifetime. Yet, again, public memory for popular music is short, and most of the shows and much of the music are forgotten. Notwithstanding his tragic early death, Gershwin would be no more remembered or revered today than his fellow tunesmiths, say, Cole Porter, Vincent Youmans, or Irving Berlin, had it not been for his art-music compositions. Here is a different Gershwin—a voracious Gatsby-like student and learner, often insecure about his abilities as a "classical" composer but never doubtful about his muse. Periods of study with teachers from a wide range of compositional thinking—Charles Hambitzer, Edward Kilenyi, Rubin Goldmark, Wallingford Riegger, Henry Cowell, Ernest Hutcheson, and Joseph Schillinger—bore fruit strange for a Tin Pan Alley songster: instrumental works and operas. Many, but not all, of these are very familiar and widely performed: *Lullaby* for string quartet (ca. 1919); *Blue Monday* (1922); *Rhapsody in Blue* (1924); Concerto in F and *Short Story* (1925); Preludes for Piano (1926); *An American in Paris* (1928); *Second Rhapsody*, *Cuban Overture*, and *George Gershwin's Song-Book* (1932); *"I Got Rhythm" Variations* (1934); *Porgy and Bess* (1935); *Catfish Row Suite* (1936); and half a dozen short pieces for solo piano. The two different educations and compositional paths in the music of Gershwin and the fascinating crossovers between them have been subjects for much musical debate since *Rhapsody in Blue*'s first performance.

Even the debate is familiar. If numbers mean anything, Gershwin must be the most biographied composer of the twentieth century. When I occasionally mentioned to colleagues and friends that I had been putting together a book on George and Ira Gershwin, I was often met with the response: "Another Gershwin biography?" Indeed, the first Gershwin biography was written when the composer was in his early thirties. Countless newspaper and magazine interviews and essays from the 1920s and 1930s recounted his life story, a hagiographical set of essays was published in the year following his death, Hollywood produced a respectful biopic in the 1940s, at least one biography has been written for young adults, and the Gershwins continue to fascinate biographers into the 1990s. The list of English-language biographies is impressive:[1]

Isaac Goldberg, *George Gershwin: A Study in American Music* (1930; revised with supplements by Edith Garson in 1958)
Merle Armitage, ed., *George Gershwin* (1938)
David Ewen, *The Story of George Gershwin* (1943)
David Ewen, *A Journey to Greatness* (1956)
Merle Armitage, *George Gershwin: Man and Legend* (1958)
Edward Jablonski and Lawrence D. Stewart, *The Gershwin Years* (1958, 1973)
Robert Payne, *Gershwin* (1960)
Robert Rushmore, *The Life of George Gershwin* (1966)
Robert Kimball and Alfred Simon, *The Gershwins* (1973)
Charles M. Schwartz, *Gershwin: His Life and Music* (1973)
Florence Stevenson DeSantis, *Gershwin* (1987)
Edward Jablonski, *Gershwin: A Biography* (1987)
Alan Kendall, *George Gershwin: A Biography* (1987)
Deena Rosenberg, *Fascinating Rhythm: The Collaboration of George and Ira Gershwin* (1991)
Edward Jablonski, *Gershwin Remembered* (1992)
Joan Peyser, *The Memory of All That: The Life of George Gershwin* (1993)

The literature on Gershwin in essays, reviews, and even dissertations is equally large.

Problematic in this literature, especially the biographies, is the omission of frank, rigorous discussion of the thing that makes Gershwin matter: his music. The handful of famous songs, the instrumental works, and the operas receive attention—often reduced in the biographies to points of historical reference for the telling of Gershwin's life story—but only recent scholarly research has begun to paint a fuller picture of the compositional thinking of this American master.[2]

This book, *The Gershwin Style*, then, is not another recounting of Gershwin's life: names, places, love interests, parties, personal or psychological successes and failures, reviews, and tragic illness. This book is about Gershwin's music: what makes Gershwin's style his own, what makes it tick, and how that style has been received and passed on. The idea is to investigate this familiar man and music and assess his legacy as an American artist. The contributors to this book come from a wide variety of backgrounds and training—musicology, journalism, performance, and collecting. But each is a Gershwin fan, and each offers a new look at this famous composer's famous music.

The essays concern analysis and manuscript studies, reception, and performance practice. Charles Hamm's opening essay reviews Gershwin scholarship and suggests new approaches for Gershwin research. Wayne Shirley, Steven E. Gilbert, Larry Starr, John Andrew Johnson, and I have contributed analysis and manuscript studies on *Porgy and Bess*, the late songs, the operetta overtures, *Blue Monday*, *Rhapsody in Blue*, and *An American in Paris*. Issues of reception are considered by Charlotte Greenspan, Susan Richardson, and André Barbera on topics as far-ranging as Hollywood's hagiographic biopics, rock and roll, and jazz. Michael Montgomery and Artis Wodehouse tackle the issue of Gershwin as a pianist and discuss influences on his musicianship from piano rolls—a medium in which he recorded extensively. Finally, distinguished Gershwin scholar and writer Edward Jablonski rounds out the roster with a lively survey of the art of Ira Gershwin, George's brother and chief lyricist, whose poetry was an essential ingredient in Gershwin's song style. Taken together, these essays offer a kind of alternative biography that I hope will enliven future discussion of the music of George Gershwin.

No introduction is complete without acknowledgments. First, clearly this book is made possible by contributions from various authors. My debt to them is enormous. Putting together an edited volume such as this one takes time, and my contributors have been nothing if not extremely patient. Any inconsistencies in the final text are mine, not theirs.

The following libraries and their staffs gave invaluable assistance: Music Library and John Hay Library, Brown University, Carol Tatian and Rosemary Cullen; Bailey-Howe Library, University of Vermont; Champlain College Library, Champlain College, Paula Olsen; Music Division, Library of Congress, Wayne Shirley; Manuscripts and College Archives, Bryn Mawr College, Leo M. Dolenski. Bradford Pousland of the University of Vermont's Academic Computing Services and Rod Hunsicker, Barbara J. Heath, and Robert Wigness of UVM's music department helped in matters computer. Christine Hammes, Penny Souster, and Bill Austin encouraged me during early stages of the book. Susan Day, Sheldon Meyer, Sarah Randall, Jessica Ryan, and Brandon Trissler at Oxford University Press shepherded the book through permissions and production to publication. To all my thanks.

Finally, I thank Paula for her patience and support in a project that, as usual, took longer than I expected.

Notes

1. Foreign-language biographies include the following:

René Chalupt, *George Gershwin, le musicien de la "Rhapsody in Blue"* (1948)
Rosey E. Pool, *Een nieuw lied voor America: Het leven van George Gershwin (1898–1937)* (1951)
Maria Vittoria Pugliaro, *Rapsodia in blue: L'arte e l'amore nella vita di George Gershwin* (1952)
Bob Schoorl, *George Gershwin* (1952)
Brigitte Schipke, *George Gershwin und die Welt seiner Musik* (1955)
Lev Grigořevič Grigořev and Jakov Michajlovič Platek, *Džordž Geršvin* (1956)
Antonio Mingotti, *Gershwin: Eine Bildbiographie* (1958)
Mario Pasi, *George Gershwin* (1958)
Christian Longolius, *George Gershwin* (1959)
Wolfgang Schwinger, *Er komponierte Amerika: George Gershwin, Mensch und Werk* (1960)
Lucjan Kydryński, *Gershwin* (1962, 1967)

2. Steven E. Gilbert's *Music of Gershwin* (New Haven: Yale University Press, 1995), impressive and rigorous, is the best of the recent lot.

The Gershwin Style

1 • Towards a New Reading of Gershwin

CHARLES HAMM

The United States has not produced a more famous composer than George Gershwin, who died half a century ago, on 11 July 1937. Many of his popular songs became standards or "evergreens" throughout the Western world from the 1920s through the 1950s, and some even survived the evolution of popular-music style from Tin Pan Alley to rock. Jazz musicians have always found his songs particularly suitable for improvisation, and much of the bebop repertory is built over the chord changes of several of them. His concert pieces, particularly *Rhapsody in Blue*, *An American in Paris*, the Concerto in F for piano and orchestra, and the Preludes for piano, are among the most widely performed "classical" works of the twentieth century, and his *Porgy and Bess* has become the most popular opera of the century. He is said to have written popular classical music and classic popular pieces. A large literature has grown up around his music and his life, much of it dealing with the latter point.

Given all this, it might seem strange to suggest that Gershwin is in any sense an unknown composer; it seems likely that more people know *something* about Gershwin than about any other composer of recent times. In fact, however, there has been a remarkable absence of disciplined theoretical, analytical, or historical discourse on Gershwin and his music. Much of what we think we "know" about him and his music is based on popular, journalistic literature, much of it highly problematic in theory and

3

method. As a result, in a very real sense certain aspects of Gershwin have indeed remained unexplored, obscure, even unknown.

My intent in what follows is to identify and confront several factors that have contributed to this situation and to suggest possible ways to correct the problem.

Donald Grout states at the beginning of the preface to his *History of Western Music*[1] that "the history of music is primarily the history of musical style," then offers a reading of music history as a succession of chronological "style periods," each defined by melodic, formal, rhythmic, tonal, contrapuntal, and timbral elements unique to compositions of that particular era. One style "progresses" to another, and evaluation of composers and individual pieces is based largely on their contribution to this inexorable forward march of musical progress. Of course Grout was not the first scholar to construct a history of music around an examination of stylistic elements of selected compositions and to suggest a linear progression of style periods: the notion was developed in the nineteenth century and has dominated the thinking of mainstream musicology, at least in the United States, ever since. I mention Grout's book only because, as the most widely used text for academic courses in music history in the English-speaking world, it both reflects and reproduces this ideology. One encounters a similar view of music history wherever one looks in the standard literature, particularly in the United States. Selecting at random, Rey M. Longyear's *Nineteenth-Century Romanticism in Music*, one of six books in a series "present[ing] a panoramic view of the history of music of Western civilization, divided among the major historical periods—Medieval, Renaissance, Baroque, Classical, Romantic, and Twentieth-Century," deals with "Romantic" music by stylistic analysis of selected compositions making up the "panorama of mountains, some in shadow, separated by mist-shrouded valleys," as he sees the landscape of nineteenth-century music.[2]

Acceptance of the concept of historical style periods as the proper framework for the study of Western music has the immediate effect of defining the arena in which discussion and analysis of this music will take place. That is, the study of individual composers and pieces of music will tend to focus on the ways in which they do (or do not) conform to the stylistic parameters of the style period within which they fall, and value judgments will be based on such analyses.

Thus, an examination of certain pieces by Beethoven has suggested that they contain stylistic details not found in the music of earlier composers; a similar examination of compositions by certain composers younger than Beethoven has suggested that they drew on elements of his style; as a result, Beethoven is seen as an "important" composer, whose music is then worthy of even more intensive study. But Louis Spohr, highly esteemed by his contemporaries and as prolific and widely performed as Beethoven, has been relegated to near oblivion by musicologists, since "despite a capacity for free expression, he adhered to the discipline of Classical form and only occasionally exceeded its limits in experimentation"[3] and "[he] rejected most of Beethoven's music from the Fifth Symphony onwards."[4]

Charles Ives, whose music was virtually unknown during his lifetime, is now thought to be "the first great American composer of concert music, and unarguably the most original and significant one of the late 19th and early 20th centuries,"[5] largely on the basis of his experimentation with polytonality, multirhythms, and free atonality at a time when these devices were not in the vocabulary of most composers. But the music of Sergei Rachmaninoff, "the last great representative of Russian late Romanticism," whose creative life overlapped that of Ives, has been of little interest to musicologists since "it has not had any important lasting effect on the development of Russian music."[6]

Music history is taken to be linear and "progressive," and in line with the importance assigned to individualism in bourgeois culture, each composer has been judged on his ability to create pieces different from, and more "advanced" than, those of earlier composers.

Judged in this way, Gershwin's compositions have proved to be highly problematic and, at best, marginal. At a time when Schoenberg, Stravinsky, Bartók, and others were seen to be creating a radically new twentieth-century harmonic, formal, tonal, and instrumental language, Gershwin was writing tonal, triadic music and shaping his pieces according to nineteenth-century formal structures. Accordingly, his Concerto in F (1925) was judged to be "conventional and dull" by such critics as Lawrence Gilman, and even sympathetic reviewers pointed out that since the piece was a "classic piano concerto in three movements," it should be discussed according to critical standards already established for such pieces. Likewise with his songs: Alec Wilder expressed surprise that "a man so concerned with the wide scope of larger forms of music" would not "have experimented more with the popular song form," finding that "the bulk of his songs are in the conventional A-A-B-A pattern."[7]

Thus, Gershwin's compositions fit uneasily into the conceptual framework adopted by so many Western music historians and critics. Since all empirical evidence suggests that his music has been more central to the cultural life of the twentieth century than is revealed by this sort of analysis, one is forced to question this way of thinking about music history, in connection with Gershwin and also in general.

Until quite recently, the vast majority of descriptive and critical writing on Gershwin centered around his putative relationship to jazz. In order to deal with this issue, one must first understand that three quite different bodies of music were labeled "jazz" in the 1920s:

1. Jazz (and blues) performed by black musicians for black audiences within the social context of black American culture. Phonograph discs of this music were marketed as "race records" by small independent record companies, or by subsidiaries of major companies. This music was rarely heard on commercial radio, and then only locally. Given the social struc-

tures of American life at this time, few whites (including Europeans) heard this music, which is now regarded by jazz historians as the most authentic and important type of jazz.

2. Jazz (and blues) performed by black musicians for white audiences within the social context of white American culture. By the late 1920s, and throughout the 1930s, major record companies were distributing such music nationally, and some of it could be heard on network radio. Decisions of repertory and even musical style were usually made by white entrepreneurs and producers.

3. So-called jazz performed by white musicians for white audiences within the social context of white American culture. This repertory made up the major share of all commercially recorded popular music in the 1920s and was widely broadcast both locally and nationally.

Virtually all writing on "jazz" during Gershwin's lifetime was concerned with category 3. Henry O. Osgood's *So This Is Jazz*,[8] the first book on this topic, devotes entire chapters to Irving Berlin, Paul Whiteman, and Gershwin, and only a single footnote to jazz by black musicians. Paul Whiteman's *Jazz*[9] also concentrates on white musicians. Isaac Goldberg's biography of Gershwin mentions "jazz" repeatedly in connection with his music and concludes with essays on "Jazz-Analysis" and "Jazz and the Machine Age"; he insists that even though jazz is "traceable, in part, to the Negro, it is developed, commercially and artistically, by the Jew," and he traces its history through successive stages of "Tin Pan Alley . . . The Musical Show Racket . . . Operetta . . . Lady Jazz in the Concert Hall . . . The Wedding of Jazz to Symphonic Art."[10]

The decade of the 1920s has been labeled "the Jazz Age" by cultural historians: its central characters are taken to be such men as F. Scott Fitzgerald, Babe Ruth, Gershwin, Al Capone—not black jazz musicians in the South, Chicago, and the Midwest. Irving Berlin's songs of the early 1920s were labeled "jazz songs," and his first biographer insisted that "[Berlin] must be regarded as a pioneer in jazz."[11] Al Jolson was known as a "jazz singer," performing such songs as Berlin's "Blue Skies" in the landmark film *The Jazz Singer* of 1927. Paul Whiteman, the "King of Jazz," was one of hundreds of white musicians leading white "jazz" bands; among others were Roger Wolfe Kahn, Ben Selvin, Ben Pollack, Ted Lewis, Sam Lanin, Vincent Lopez, even Jimmy Durante.

This conceptual confusion between "jazzed" popular songs in Tin Pan Alley style and authentic black jazz was widespread in both America and Europe in the 1920s. Even the French, with their great enthusiasm for jazz, had virtually no contact with "authentic" black jazz at this time; they were exposed instead to performers like Josephine Baker, whose music was mediated for consumption by white European audiences.

Here again a questionable theoretical assumption—that "jazz" was a product of white American culture in the 1920s and that it grew out of the New York–based Tin Pan Alley style of songwriting—has shaped and informed discourse on Gershwin. But it should be noted that none of Gershwin's compositions uses the word "jazz" in its title or subtitle. *Rhapsody in Blue* was written for "Jazz Band and Piano," true enough, but merely because Paul Whiteman, who commissioned the piece, called his orchestra a "jazz band." And even though Gershwin did write a brief article entitled "Jazz Is the Voice of the American Soul"[12] during the height of the initial excitement over his *Rhapsody*, he otherwise avoided the word in connection with his own music. "Jazz is a word which has been used for at least five or six different types of music," he wrote near the end of his life. "It is really a conglomeration of many things . . . ragtime, the blues, classicism and spirituals. . . . An entire composition written in jazz could not live."[13]

It should also be noted that Gershwin, more than any other composer (or critic, or historian) of his time, constantly sought out black musicians and listened to the widest possible range of black music. He knew Will Vodery, Lucky Roberts, Duke Ellington; he heard New York "stride" pianists play downtown and often visited the Cotton Club and other spots in Harlem to hear the bands of Ellington and Cab Calloway; through his friendship with Carl Van Vechten, he heard Bessie Smith and other black singers perform at social gatherings; and while in South Carolina to work on *Porgy and Bess*, he heard and even participated in rural black church singing. Gershwin's reluctance to use the term "jazz" in connection with his own music was a result of his knowing enough about black music to understand, more clearly than his critics, that jazz was essentially a form of African American music, not a product of New York's Tin Pan Alley.

Why, then, have so many writers concentrated on the "jazz connection" in Gershwin's music? For the same reason they have discussed his compositions in the context of historical style periods: it is easier to measure any music against preexistent theory than to search for a new context. Also, discussions of "jazz" elements and influences in Gershwin's concert pieces were useful to critics in explaining the favorable reception of this music in the 1920s and 1930s. Classical music was not supposed to be taken seriously unless it was "progressive" in some way. It was difficult for critics to discover anything "new" in Gershwin's harmonic, melodic, or structural techniques. But by calling attention to his use of "jazz" rhythms, tricks of instrumentation, and "blue" notes, these writers were able to suggest that his music was "progressive" in the sense that it introduced such elements to classical music and thus reconcile popular reception of his music with their own critical ideology.

A clearer understanding of Gershwin's music has also been hindered by family intervention, following his death.

When Gershwin died in 1937, at the age of thirty-eight, he was survived by his older brother, Ira, who had written lyrics for most of his songs; Ira's wife, Leonore; his younger brother, Arthur; his sister, Frances; and her husband, Leopold Godowsky II, son of the well-known pianist and composer. This group, headed by Ira, inherited Gershwin's physical possessions, including his musical manuscripts and personal papers, and also took control of copyrights, permissions, and performance rights to his music. Over the years most (but not all) of Gershwin's manuscripts, and a selection of his correspondence, have been given to the Library of Congress in Washington, D.C., where they can be studied; but other materials remain unavailable, in the private Gershwin Archives.

With a single exception, biographers of Gershwin have had close ties to one or another member of the family. Isaac Goldberg's early biography, mentioned earlier, appeared while Gershwin was still alive and was based on information and material supplied by Gershwin himself. The most recent biography is by Edward Jablonski,[14] who was for many years a friend and confidant of Ira Gershwin; he had access to Ira's diaries, and he quotes selectively from them, but no other scholar has been able to see this material. As a result of this situation, most writing about Gershwin has reflected the attitudes and wishes of his immediate family.

Family control over personal information about famous people after their death is common, of course. The Gershwin family was close-knit and proud of George's fame, and it is understandable that they would want a favorable and positive image projected to the world. As Jablonski sketches this image, "The young composer typified eternal youth in a vibrant, strident America wakening to its potential and power in the arts, business, industry, finance, sports, in a world only recently shocked into the twentieth century. . . . Besides his musical gifts, [he had] other attractive attributes: youth, fame, success in an era that venerated success."[15] He made a great deal of money, he became a media "personality," he consorted with a succession of attractive and talented women. He appeared to epitomize the American Dream, and his success was cherished and cultivated by a family headed by a father who had been a worker in a shoe factory in Russia before emigrating to New York.

It is not of much importance to scholars that this mediated image of Gershwin ignores or marginalizes some details of his personal life. Even if it were true that he frequented brothels, or fathered an illegitimate child, or was a "sleazy opportunist," as the one dissident biography insinuates,[16] these things would have little effect on our understanding of his music and its relations to his contemporary world. What might help, however, would be a clearer understanding of what sort of person he was, intellectually. The family-approved image is of a cheerful, apolitical, nonintellectual extrovert, too absorbed in his music and his career to give much thought to such issues as the place of music in America's evolving democratic, capitalistic society. If one searches, though, there are many hints that Gershwin was a more complex and thoughtful person than this.

As a member of the artistic and intellectual Jewish community of New York, he must have known of the involvement of members of this community in radical politics in the early 1930s. There was, for instance, the Composers Collective of New York, affiliated with the Workers' Music League (WML), an arm of the American Communist Party, which "sought to make an American contribution to the international working-class music movement then flourishing in Europe under writers such as Bertolt Brecht and composers such as Hanns Eisler."[17] Members of this group wrote most of the pieces in the *Workers' Songbook* published by the WML in 1934–35.

While there is no evidence whatsoever that Gershwin was connected with this group, whose membership included Marc Blitzstein, Aaron Copland, and Elie Siegmeister, one can see a clear change in Gershwin's own rhetoric at this time, in his interviews with the press and in the few surviving bits of his writing. For instance, the concept of "folk music" seems not to have interested him before, but this term begins to creep into his vocabulary in the early 1930s, sometimes in connection with his own music, at just the time folk music was becoming an issue in American radical circles. In the aforementioned "The Composer in the Mechanical Age" (1930), he wrote that "the only kinds of music which endure are those which possess form in the universal sense and folk music. All else dies. Folk songs are being written and have been written which contain enduring elements of jazz." He insisted that *Porgy and Bess* (1935) was a "folk opera," because the story was a "folk tale" and "its people would naturally sing folk music." Gershwin was both praised and criticized for the opera's portrayal of blacks; but he insisted in a press interview that such criticism was beside the point, since he intended *Porgy and Bess* to be understood in a more general context, as "exemplifying the typical American proletariat point of view in its fundamentals, regardless of race or color."[18] There is none of this sort of rhetoric from him in the 1920s, and it should also be noted that his works for the musical stage progress (though not always in a straight line) from early topical, entertaining shows such as *Lady, Be Good!* (1924), *Oh, Kay!* (1926), and *Girl Crazy* (1930) through the political satire of *Strike Up the Band* (1927, 1930), *Of Thee I Sing* (1931), and *Let 'Em Eat Cake* (1933) to the celebration of the "typical American proletariat" in *Porgy and Bess* in 1935.

According to Gershwin's aesthetic, as well as it can be pieced together from scattered sources, he believed that popular songs "die at an early age and are soon completely forgotten," as a result of being "sung and played too much when they are alive, especially since the invention of the phonograph and more so since the widespread conquest of the radio." Because of their nature, they "cannot stand the strain of their very popularity."[19] Music can endure over a period of time only if it possesses "form in the universal sense," or is written "in serious form. When I wrote the *Rhapsody in Blue* I took 'blues' and put them in a larger and more serious form. That was twelve years ago and the *Rhapsody in Blue* is still very much alive, whereas if I had taken the same themes and put them in songs they would have been gone years ago."[20]

Piecing these two attitudes together, one can see that Gershwin's ideological position and strategies resemble those of many politically aware European and American musicians of the 1930s. If Gershwin did indeed set out to "exemplify the American proletariat" in *Porgy and Bess*, he did so by using his skill and training as a composer to create a stage work representing their relations to the power structure of contemporary American society, not by drawing on proletariat music itself; but at the same time, this music was written in a style accessible to the proletariat as well as to theater audiences. He pointedly refused to use "authentic" musical materials in *Porgy and Bess*; but he insisted that the composed spirituals and songs were indeed "folk" music, since they were part of a "folk opera." And though there was some black criticism of the opera, J. Rosamund Johnson called Gershwin "a musical Abe Lincoln," Warren Coleman (who created the role of Crown) felt that the composer had a "serious and dignified" approach to his black characters, and Todd Duncan, the first Porgy, remembered that Gershwin "loved what the unspoiled South Carolina Negro stood for" and told the cast: "They're beautiful. They're not educated, but they have such virtues."[21] It should be noted in this connection that one of the earliest performances of *Porgy and Bess* was an amateur production by the "maids and porters"—all black, of course—at Bryn Mawr College in Pennsylvania, 15–16 March 1940.

Nothing more than these tantalizing scraps of information are available to help us reconstruct Gershwin's ideology, and if more documentation exists, in the form of letters or diaries, it remains under family control. There may not be enough to build a case that Gershwin underwent political transformation in the last years of his life, but there is enough to suggest that he was more intellectually and politically alert than the family-approved portrait would have us believe.

Family intervention of another sort is easier to document. Gershwin died at the height of his career, at a time when some of his compositions had been assimilated into the standard performance repertory but others were still rarely performed. He had performed much of his concert music himself, as pianist or conductor, and also insisted on certain controls over other performers who wanted to play his music. After his death, his family tended to authorize performances that gave the most promise of financial return or favorable publicity, with less regard for quality or integrity. Some pieces not available in commercial editions before his death—Concerto in F, *An American in Paris, Variations on "I Got Rhythm,"* and Second Rhapsody—were published in editions, prepared from Gershwin's manuscripts, that often violated the composer's intentions in small and even large details. The original version of *Rhapsody in Blue*, as orchestrated for Paul Whiteman's "jazz band" by Ferde Grofé, was never published; instead, the piece was available only as scored for full symphony orchestra by Grofé in 1926. Gershwin's songs became known to later generations through such commercially successful but artistically questionable recordings as *Ella Fitzgerald Sings the George and Ira Gershwin Song Books* (Verve, V-29-5), in which Nelson Riddle's arrangements and conducting style impose a neoromantic, 1950s ethic on the music, robbing it of all vitality and rhythmic life.

Most revealing has been the fate of *Porgy and Bess*. Gershwin was intimately involved in the first production of his opera, by the Theatre Guild, which opened at the Alvin Theatre in New York on 10 October 1935. In the course of rehearsals and a tryout performance in Boston, Gershwin (working closely with the stage director, Rouben Mamoulian, and the musical director, Alexander Smallens) made extensive revisions in his score: tightening dramatic action, shortening or eliminating musical numbers that proved to be less effective on stage than he had hoped, interpolating new material. *Porgy and Bess* as it took the stage in New York in 1935 was some forty-five minutes shorter, and in the opinion of Gershwin and Mamoulian a tighter and more effective show, than when it first went into rehearsal. But Gershwin had died before Cheryl Crawford mounted her radically revised production in 1941, with most of the recitative eliminated and the cast and orchestra reduced by half; one cannot imagine that the composer would have allowed such violations of his score had he been alive. And even though the Everyman Opera production of 1952–58, directed by Blevins Davis and Robert Breen, which took Gershwin's opera all over the United States and also to Eastern and Western Europe, North Africa, and Latin America, was more faithful to Gershwin's intentions, it too had its idiosyncrasies and distortions.

Equally problematic have been recent performances of *Porgy and Bess* by the Cleveland Orchestra, the Houston Grand Opera Company, and the Metropolitan Opera. These purport to be musicologically correct, "complete" performances, the opera "as Gershwin intended it to be played," based on the published piano-vocal score. But this score was completed and in the hands of the publisher some six months before the first performance, in order for it to be commercially available when the opera was premiered, and has never been revised. Thus, the extensive revisions made and approved by Gershwin himself have never been incorporated into the score, and these recent pseudo-musicological "complete" performances are in fact serious misrepresentations of *Porgy and Bess*.[22]

My argument here is simply that Gershwin's premature death shifted artistic control of his music from himself to his family, with the unfortunate result that most of his pieces are now known through performances that violate both the letter and the spirit of his music. Journalistic and scholarly discourse has been based to a large extent on these faulty scores and performances of Gershwin's music.

For more than a century, historical musicology has been concerned with the recovery of musical compositions from the past and the preparation of scholarly editions of these pieces, to make it possible for this music to be heard as the composer intended. An important secondary and complementary concern has been the study of performance practice in earlier times: since "the history of music . . . cannot be grasped except by first-hand knowledge of the music itself,"[23] it is not enough to hear the correct notes; they must also be performed with proper phrasing, tempi, dynamics, articulation, and instrumentation. According to the historical musicologist, we must have any piece of music in "accurate" form before we can move on to theoretical and contextual studies of it, hence the ideology of studying a piece of music as an autonomous object.

As I suggested earlier, there are problems with Gershwin's music at this level. We "know" his music mostly from corrupt texts and from performances having little to do with the easily documented performance style of the 1920s. Gershwin's own recordings as pianist, accompanist, and conductor inform us of the intensely rhythmic, brisk, brittle nature of the sound and style he favored. But if one depends on more recent interpretations, by Leonard Bernstein or Michael Tilson Thomas, for instance, one hears Gershwin's music as lush, rhythmically insipid and erratic, neoromantic.

Thus, we would be able to "know" Gershwin's music better if musicologists were to recover the authentic texts of his compositions, as they have for Haydn, Handel, and Palestrina, and if musicians were to study performance style of the 1920s, rather than playing and singing his music as though it were from another era. It would also help if critics were to inform themselves on these issues, in order to comment with more perception on performances of Gershwin's music.

But even if historical musicologists were to furnish us with accurate texts of Gershwin's compositions, and his music were to be performed in a more accurate and responsible manner, larger conceptual problems would remain. How are we to understand Gershwin's music, if we are not to measure it against a sliding scale of historical style periods, or mindlessly chatter about its relationship to jazz?

The more general question, of course, is how *any* work of art can best be understood. Literary criticism is an instructive battleground to examine in connection with this issue. In reaction to the nineteenth century's fascination with empiricism (the collection and organization of historical "fact" with no apparent theoretical basis), on the one hand, and the twin specters of Marxist scholarship and the social sciences, on the other, academically based literary scholars developed what was called the New Criticism, and then structuralism, "formal, structural and text-centered literary studies" taking as a point of departure the conviction that whatever was important in literature could be found in the "texts" themselves, which were to be studied as "self-enclosed verbal constructs, or looped intertextual fields of autonomous signifiers and signifieds." The deconstructionist school, led by Jacques Derrida, represented a first influential rejection of the theoretical assumptions underlying the New Criticism, and in the 1980s various scholars have "[shared] a commitment to explore the social and historical dimensions of literary works [and to] reconstruct sociohistorical methods and interests as the heart of literary studies."[24]

One can see, from this brief summary, obvious parallels between the recent histories of literary criticism and historical musicology. Both embraced the notion of "autonomous art" for a good part of the twentieth century; and just as recent literary criticism has forcefully challenged the New Criticism and its assumptions, some music historians are now beginning to question the long-held tenets of their discipline, proposing a shift to sociohistorical methodologies. The recent literature suggesting that music is best understood as a product of social and economic forces, not as an autonomous object, is too numerous to be listed here. I will merely state the obvious: most of this writing derives from Marxist and neo-Marxist theory, often by way of the Frankfurt School; and American musicologists have lagged far behind Europeans in exploring alternative ways of understanding the history of music. Janet Wolff, in a recent essay challenging the notion that "art . . . transcends the social, the political and the everyday," gives a useful summary:

> The social and economic factors relevant to the understanding of an art include: contemporary forms of patronage; dominant institutions of cultural production and distribution (workshops, academies, art schools, publishers, galleries, concerts, music publishers, broadcasting companies, and so on— each of which has its own social history and specific social relations); the relationship of the State to cultural production (censorship, control of certain institutions, funding); the sociology of cultural producers (background, class, gender); and the nature and constitution of consumers. The history of any art is a history of the interplay of these many factors.[25]

Despite the variety of approaches suggested by different writers, there is virtual consensus on two points: sociohistorical analysis must replace historical positivism; and works of art are "modeling rather than mirroring forms."[26] That is, works of literature (or music) do not "point to a prior, authorizing reality, they themselves constitute—in both the active and passive senses—what must be taken as reality."[27] Or, as Jacques Attali puts it in a slightly different way, music is a "prophetic" art, on the cutting edge of the onward march of human affairs and relations.[28]

The task, then, if we are to apply any of this to the understanding of Gershwin's music, is to identify critical sociohistorical issues in which American music of the 1920s and 1930s was embedded, and to measure Gershwin's role in "modeling" these. I'll suggest three large areas that might reward closer attention.

1. Some scholars are now suggesting alternative periodizations of the history of music, based on economic and social relations rather than musical style. For instance, a team of European musicologists,[29] in preparation for the writing of volume 7 of *Music in the Life of Man: A World History*, a multivolume global history sponsored by UNESCO, has proposed the following overview of Western music history:

A. From Prehistory to the Birth of Europe (until ca. 500)
B. Church (from ca. 500 to ca. 1520)
C. Court and Town (from ca. 1520 to ca. 1740)
D. Concert Life (from ca. 1740 to World War I)
E. Mass Media (from World War I to the present)

And Jacques Attali has suggested a more abstract fourfold periodization of music (sacrificial ritual, representation, repetition, and composition), agreeing in broad outline with the UNESCO scheme.[30]

Gershwin's music comes into different focus when measured against these new frameworks. His first compositions appear at the very beginning of an era of "Mass Media" or "repetition," rather than several decades into a "Modern" or "Twentieth-century" style period. The critical issues of his time become the impact of the electronic mass media on the invention, production, and consumption of music—not experiments in abstract manipulation of tones. The following should be noted about Gershwin:

- He enthusiastically embraced the mechanical player piano and produced more than a hundred commercial piano rolls, beginning in 1916.
- He was the first American composer whose early career was built largely on the success of sales of phonograph records of his songs. For instance, his first hugely popular song, "Swanee," as recorded by Al Jolson (Columbia 2884), was the best-selling record in America for nine weeks in 1920.[31]
- "It should be kept in mind [in connection with his extraordinary popularity] that the advent of radio occurred just as his career was getting under way. The enormous exposure provided by this medium had much to do with the public's enthusiasm for his songs."[32]
- Gershwin's only extended essay, "The Composer in the Machine Age," develops the argument that "the composer, in my estimation, has been helped a great deal by the mechanical reproduction of music."[33]
- Gershwin not only wrote songs for a number of films, beginning with *Delicious* in 1931, but his *Second Rhapsody* (for piano and orchestra) was written for that film as well, for a ballet sequence, though only a section of the concerto was used in the film.
- In 1934, Gershwin began hosting a twice-weekly radio show for CBS, *Music by Gershwin*, on which he chatted about his music, talked with guests, played the piano, and introduced pieces by himself and other composers, later played by a studio orchestra. The program was carried by stations all across the country, making Gershwin and his music accessible to millions of people who had never been able to hear live performances of his music.
- The first production of *Porgy and Bess*, by the Theatre Guild in 1935, had only a moderate run, but a later production by Cheryl Crawford ran for almost four years, in New York and on the road. Many observers, including the librettist, DuBose Heyward, insisted that the second production was much more successful than the first because so many people had become familiar with "Summertime," "I Got Plenty o' Nuttin'," and "It Ain't Necessarily So" in the meanwhile, from hearing this music on the radio and phonograph.

From these and other facts of his career, it emerges that Gershwin was not a mere passive observer of the new technology of his age; on the contrary, he enthusiastically explored and exploited ways of utilizing the new electronic mass media for the production and dissemination of his music. By contrast, Charles Ives despised and shunned all mass communications: radio, phonograph, telephone. Thus, by a shift of conceptual framework, away from privileging the moment of creation of a piece of music (and thus forcing one to study it as an autonomous object) toward considering the issues of production and reception, Gershwin can be seen as progressive and

Ives as reactionary—a reversal of the judgment handed down by mainstream historical musicology.

2. During Gershwin's lifetime, the United States was struggling to absorb many millions of new immigrants. The older "mainstream" American population was mostly Protestant, tracing back to the British Isles, Western Europe, and Scandinavia; the new immigrants were overwhelmingly Catholic (Roman or Orthodox) or Jewish, from the Mediterranean or from Central and Eastern Europe. Relations between the two groups became highly problematic in the first decades of the twentieth century. "Older" Americans, fearing the possible economic consequences of the presence of millions of new workers in the country (many of them highly skilled and most of them willing to work for low wages in order to establish themselves in an alien land), resorted to attacks on the new population on ethnic grounds. A congressional committee issued a "scientific" report in 1911 detailing the problems stemming from the presence of so much "inferior ethnic stock." New laws were passed putting an end to further immigration from Mediterranean, Eastern European, and Third World countries. The revived Ku Klux Klan spread from the South to all regions of the United States, and social and economic discrimination became even more entrenched at various levels of American life.

Faced with such a hostile climate, many minority ethnic groups, including America's Jews, adopted a twofold strategy: (1) trying to become "invisible," by modifying all obvious signs of ethnic origin (dress, language, sometimes their names and even physical appearance) in an attempt to be indistinguishable from "mainstream" Americans; and (2) trying to make positive and visible contributions to American life and culture.[34] In no area were they more successful than in entertainment. The contributions of American Jews to music (as Tin Pan Alley songwriters and singers), stage, comedy, and film in the 1910s, 1920s, and 1930s put them in the absolute center of American popular culture[35] and played a major role both in improving their social relations with other Americans and in setting the stage for the next generation's contributions to education, law, and other fields they now could enter.

In this context, Gershwin was clearly a "modeler." The popular success of his songs, musical comedies, concert pieces, and films represented an important contribution to American culture by a Jew; and his public image as a "celebrity" and a member of the social, artistic, and intellectual "scene" of New York and Hollywood helped establish those positive social relations between Jews and non-Jews that were becoming such a positive factor in American society.

Here, too, Ives pursued a conservative course, retreating from New York City and its burgeoning new popular arts to the cultural isolation of a small New England town. He quoted, with approval, Daniel Gregory Mason's sour dismissal of the contemporary world: "If indeed the land of Lincoln and Emerson has degenerated until nothing remains of it but a 'jerk and a rattle,' then we at least are free to repudiate the false patriotism of 'My country, right or wrong,' to insist that better than bad music is no music, and to let our beloved art subside finally under the clangor of the subway gongs and the automobile horns, dead but not dishonored." Ives then added, "And so may we ask: Is it better to sing inadequately of the 'leaf on Walden floating,' and die 'dead but not dishonored,' or to sing adequately of the 'cherry on the cocktail,' and live forever?"[36]

3. In America, as elsewhere, classical music had first been associated with the most privileged layers of society. As a distinctively American form of democracy emerged in the nineteenth century, populist criticism of classical music mounted, and by the end of the century it appeared that classical music would become even more marginal to American life and might disappear altogether.

This did not happen, of course. By the late twentieth century, the number of symphony orchestras, opera companies, choral groups, community concert series, schools of music, new compositions, attendance at concerts and recitals, sales of phonograph discs, and radio programs of classical music have all proliferated far beyond what the nineteenth century could have imagined. All this has come about as a result of a sweeping democratization of every aspect of classical music in the first half of the century: repertory (programming based largely on a "standard" repertory); the education of musicians and composers; social relations, with the gradual shift of patronage from the most privileged classes to public, municipal, and state support corresponding to a similar change in the constitution of the audience itself; and the education of potential listeners.

If the issue is defined as the gradual demystification of classical music and the severing of its exclusive ties to the moneyed classes, there can be no mistaking Gershwin's role in this revolution. Simply put, he was the first American composer to write concert pieces accessible to those people who already enjoyed the now-standard classical repertory, and also to many people whose listening tastes had not included classical music. Contrary to common belief, the proliferation in classical music in the critical era of the 1920s, 1930s, and 1940s in the United States was accompanied by, and to some extent the result of, the growth of a popular repertory by contemporary American composers. Gershwin played and conducted his own compositions for large crowds in Lewisohn Stadium and elsewhere; orchestras could be sure of attracting good audiences if they programmed his music. Soon other composers as well—Ferde Grofé, Morton Gould, Aaron Copland, Virgil Thomson, Roy Harris, and then Leonard Bernstein—began to write concert works similar to those of Gershwin in that they made use of the basic harmonic, tonal, and structural vocabulary of the standard symphonic repertory, with references to contemporary popular and ethnic styles.

Charles Ives, on the other hand, had become the epitome of the romantic, misunderstood genius, the artist as neglected visionary. After failing to find an audience for his early compositions, he withdrew into a contemptuous isolation, scornful of performers and audiences who seemed unable to comprehend his music.

Tin Pan Alley, as a musical style and as an industry for producing and disseminating popular music, was well established when Gershwin began writing his songs and musical comedies. He worked within already established boundaries, both musically and socially, and even though many of his songs have become "classics" of the Tin Pan Alley repertory in the sense of being "of the first or highest class or rank," he was in no sense an innovator, and his popular songs are no more "classical," in the sense of using techniques of classical music, than those of his peers.

But his "classical" pieces did become widely popular. There were no important precedents for them, and sociohistorical analysis enables us to see them as important "modeling" and "prophetic" works, much more so than his popular songs. This merely confirms Gershwin's own judgment on these matters.

Notes

1. Donald J. Grout, *A History of Western Music* (New York: W. W. Norton, 1960), xiii.

2. Rey M. Longyear, *Nineteenth-Century Romanticism in Music* (Englewood Cliffs, N.J.: Prentice Hall, 1988), vii.

3. Stanley Sadie, ed., *New Grove Dictionary of Music and Musicians* (London: Macmillan, 1980), 18:11.

4. Longyear, *Nineteenth-Century Romanticism in Music*, 63.

5. H. Wiley Hitchcock and Stanley Sadie, eds., *The New Grove Dictionary of American Music* (London: Macmillan, 1986), 2:503.

6. Sadie, *New Grove Dictionary of Music and Musicians*, 15:550.

7. Alec Wilder, *American Popular Song: The Great Innovators, 1900–1950* (New York: Oxford University Press, 1972), 122.

8. Henry O. Osgood, *So This Is Jazz* (Boston: Little, Brown, 1926).

9. Paul Whiteman and Mary Margaret McBride, *Jazz* (New York: J. H. Sears, 1926).

10. Isaac Goldberg, *George Gershwin: A Study in American Music* (New York: Simon & Schuster, 1931), 278, 292.

11. Alexander Woollcott, *The Story of Irving Berlin* (New York: G. P. Putnam's Sons, 1925), 212.

12. George Gershwin, "Jazz Is the Voice of the American Soul," *Theatre Magazine* (June 1926).

13. George Gershwin, "The Composer in the Machine Age," in *Revolt in the Arts*, ed. Oliver M. Saylor (New York: Brentano's, 1930), 266, 267. Duke Ellington, in his book *Music Is My Mistress* (Garden City, N.Y.: Doubleday, 1973), insisted that "*jazz is only a word and really has no meaning. We stopped using it*" (471).

14. Edward Jablonski, *Gershwin: A Biography* (New York: Doubleday, 1987).

15. Ibid., ix–x.

16. Charles Schwartz, *Gershwin: His Life and Music* (Indianapolis: Bobbs-Merrill, 1973).

17. Hitchcock and Sadie, *New Grove Dictionary of American Music* 1:479.

18. George Gershwin, "Rhapsody in Catfish Row: Mr. Gershwin Tells the Origin and Scheme for His Music in That New Folk Opera Called 'Porgy and Bess,'" *New York Times*, 20 October 1935, sec. 10, pp. 1–2.

19. George Gershwin, *George Gershwin's Song-Book* (New York: Simon & Schuster, 1932), ix.

20. Gershwin, "Rhapsody in Catfish Row."

21. Sheryl Flatow, "Premiere Porgy: The Venerable Todd Duncan Recalls the Creation of Gershwin's Opera," *Opera News* 49 (16 March 1985): 35.

22. These matters are discussed in detail in Charles Hamm, "The Theatre Guild Production of *Porgy and Bess*," *Journal of the American Musicological Society* 40 (Fall 1987): 495–532.

23. Grout, *A History of Western Music*, xiii.

24. All paragraph quotes are from Jerome J. McGann, "A Point of Reference," in *Historical Studies and Literary Criticism* (Madison: University of Wisconsin Press, 1985), 3–21. This essay is a useful summary of recent literary criticism.

25. Janet Wolff, "The Ideology of Autonomous Art," in *Music and Society: The Politics of Composition, Performance and Reception*, ed. Richard Leppert and Susan McClary (Cambridge: Cambridge University Press, 1987), 5. Cf. also Rose Subotnik, "The Role of Ideology in the Study of Western Music," *Journal of Musicology* 2, no. 1 (1983): 1–12.

26. McGann, "A Point of Reference," 4.

27. Ibid.

28. Jacques Attali, *Bruits: Essai sur l'economie politique de la musique* (Paris: Presses Universitaires de France, 1977).

29. Janos Karpati, Budapest; Jens Brincker, Finn Gravesen, Carsten E. Hatting, and Niels Krabbe, Copenhagen.

30. Attali, *Bruits*.

31. Joel Whitburn, *Pop Memories, 1890–1954* (Menomonee Falls, Wis.: Record Research, 1986), 233.

32. Wilder, *American Popular Song*, 122–23.

33. Gershwin, "The Composer in the Machine Age."

34. For an excellent discussion of these issues, see Irving Howe, *World of Our Fathers* (New York: Harcourt, Brace, Jovanovich, 1976).

35. Charles Hamm, *Yesterdays: Popular Song in America* (New York: W. W. Norton, 1979), 326–57.

36. Charles Ives, *Essays before a Sonata, and Other Writings* (New York: W. W. Norton, 1962), 94–95.

Analysis and Manuscript Studies

2 : "*Rotating*" Porgy and Bess

WAYNE D. SHIRLEY

Since 1969 the George and Ira Gershwin Collection in the Music Division of the Library of Congress has contained, among its sketches for *Porgy and Bess*, a set of four leaves, in Gershwin's hand,[1] which show the Porgy motive in four distinct forms.[2] The leaves, each written on one side only, are labeled A, B, C, and D. (These leaves, and the music on them, will be referred to in italics— *A, B, C, D*—to differentiate them from other As, Bs, Cs, and Ds in this essay.) Leaf *D* contains, besides its version of the motive, the cabalistic symbol

a	b
d	c

Leaf *A* contains the full Porgy motive in the following form.[3] (See example 2.1.) Those who know the score of *Porgy and Bess* will find this version of the Porgy motive familiar in its general outlines. It is in the key of the motive's first appearance (act 1, scene 1, cue 70), and the harmonization is similar to that of the first extended statement of the motive, starting at the fifth measure of cue 71. Even the final five measures, less familiar to the casual listener than the opening, occur often in the score, always as a continuation of the Porgy motive.[4] (These five measures will be called the "tail" of the Porgy motive. The opening three measures will be called "the Porgy motive proper." The combination of the two will be called "the full Porgy motive.")

EXAMPLE 2.1

Yet what leaf *A* shows is not the full Porgy motive as one might print in a *Motiventafel* for *Porgy and Bess*. No appearance of the Porgy motive in the score[5] has a separate eighth note on the final half beat of the first measure. No appearance of the Porgy motive makes leaf *A*'s odd, hiccuplike repeat of measures 2 and 3 before continuing to the "tail."

Leaves *B*, *C*, and *D* present the Porgy motive in considerably less familiar forms. Leaf *B* consists of the music of *A* written out backward—literally and mechanically, save for an occasional enharmonic adjustment and for the fact that grace notes still precede the notes they grace. Leaf *D* consists of the music of *A* in inversion; the axis of inversion is E (bottom line of the treble clef). Some liberty is taken with grace notes; otherwise the inversion is literal, semitone-equals-semitone, rather than tonal. Leaf *C*, as the reader will probably have intuited, is *D* backward (*A* in retrograde inversion). Here is how the first measure of *A* appears in the three other versions (note that the left hand of *B* ends on G♯ and B rather than on E and G♯ and that *C* fudges grace notes and rhythm a bit). (See examples 2.2–2.4.)

These thematic manipulations are clearly inspired by Gershwin's studies with Joseph Schillinger. Schillinger had shown these techniques to Gershwin as early as June 1932; "Notebook B" of the notebooks that document Gershwin's studies with Schillinger contains a demonstration of this

EXAMPLE 2.2 (*B*)   EXAMPLE 2.3 (*C*)   EXAMPLE 2.4 (*D*)

technique applied to a single (rather nondescript) melodic line, accompanied by the cabalistic symbol shown earlier.[6]

In *The Schillinger System of Musical Composition*, book 3, part I ("Variations of Music by Means of Geometrical Projection. Chapter 1. Geometrical inversions"), Schillinger deals with the same process to which Gershwin has subjected the Porgy motive in these sketches, and he deals with it using the same letter symbols—b for retrograde, c for retrograde inversion, d for inversion. Schillinger, who calls all three of the generated forms of a theme "geometrical inversions," refers to the process of generating these forms as the "rotation" of the theme. This essay will call the generated forms "rotated versions of the theme," since it is difficult for most musicians to think of a retrograde as an "inversion." Occasionally, when a particular form is being referred to, "rotation (retrograde)" or "rotation (inversion)" will be used. In the context of Schillingerian "rotation," however, inversion equals strict interval-for-interval inversion, with minor second answering minor second and major second answering major second, not the tonal inversion familiar from earlier music.[7]

On first glance these four leaves seem primarily a demonstration of Gershwin's interest in Schillinger's methods, rather than building blocks for the final score of *Porgy and Bess*. The "tail" of the Porgy motive is typically Schillingeresque, neutral music capable of being "rotated" with no particular harm or gain; but the Porgy motive proper is a *donnée*, an inspiration that dictates its own shape. Retrograding it destroys its rhythmic drive; inverting it destroys its bluesy inflection—such compositional manipulations trade in one of the great propulsive forces in the *Porgy* score for another bit of neutral music, mainly interesting for its off-kilter grace notes. Surely Gershwin would have seen that *B*, *C*, and *D* were unusable.

Yet *B* and *D are* used in the final scene of *Porgy and Bess*. They appear between cues 131 and 134, when Porgy is describing his experiences in jail. They are duly prepared by a statement of the full Porgy motive (without the "hiccup") in C major/minor, which is the "real" key of *D*.[8]

Version *D* (inversion) appears in full, though without the "hiccup." The key signature is C major/A minor rather than the four sharps of the sketch; the G♯ grace notes have been replaced by b♭s ("bluer" in C major); there is much enharmonic respelling; yet the version is clearly that of version *D*. Indeed, one suspects that leaf *D* was at hand as Gershwin prepared the sketch-score.

EXAMPLE 2.5

B is used only in part, but the part used is the Porgy motive proper, in the C minor/major that follows logically from the use of *D* in its proper key. This time the "hiccup" is included. (See example 2.5.)

Thus, Schillingeresque "rotation" has its place in *Porgy and Bess*. The place of this particular example of "rotation" is minor: it occurs late in the opera; it occurs early in a long monologue for Porgy that should not blossom into new, impassioned lyricism until "Bess, Oh Where's My Bess?"; it is left behind well before all four versions of the motive are used.[9] Indeed, it can be heard as consciously neutral music, calming the texture down from the exuberance of the welcome to Porgy, preparing for the climb to the emotional climax of the trio. The music works well with the scene: the grace notes, robbed of any bluesy significance, give a Falstaffian jocosity to Porgy's description of his experiences in jail. But this example does not suggest that the "rotation" of significant sections of music is an important device in *Porgy and Bess* (as it is, for example, in *Lulu*, another opera of 1935).[10] Rather, the device seems to be used once—just as "geometric expansion," the other technique described in book 3 of *The Schillinger System,* is used only once.[11]

Schillinger himself claimed that "rotation" played an important role at one (unidentified) spot in *Porgy and Bess.*[12] In the only passage in *The Schillinger System* to mention *Porgy and Bess,* he says:

> When a composer feels dissatisfied with his theme, he may try out some of the inversions [that is, some of the "rotations" of the theme]—and he may possibly find them more suitable for his purpose, discarding the original. Such was the case when George Gershwin wrote a theme for his opera *Porgy*

and Bess, where position C [that is, the upside-down-and-backward version] was used instead of the original which was not as expressive and lacked the character of the latter version.[13]

What "theme" could this be? If one takes Schillinger's phrase "discarding the original" literally, the theme appears in the opera only in "position C": one cannot, therefore, discover it by examining the score. Unless a sketch comes to light documenting Schillinger's claim, one could identify the spot only through intuition.[14] More likely, the statement quoted here represents Schillinger's wishful misremembering of the session that created leaves *A*, *B*, *C*, and *D*—perhaps Gershwin said, when he played *C*, "That's nice. I'll have to use it" or some other encouraging phrase.[15]

Small-scale "rotation" of single melodic lines does occur elsewhere in *Porgy and Bess*. An example of inversion preserving the precise interval structure of the original version occurs in the introduction to the final scene, at cues 104–8. A good example of the melodic retrograding of a single phrase occurs in the crap-game music first heard at cue 91 of act 1. In its initial appearance the crap-game music runs as follows (vocal lines omitted; analysis added). (See example 2.6.) The analysis shows two Schillingerian techniques at work: each version of X contains the three cells a, b, and c in a different order (b, for good measure, is "rotated" in X"), while the second statement of Y is "rotated"—in retrograde.[16] This music plays an important role in the second half of this essay.

A set of sketches newly acquired by the Gershwin Collection[17] suggests that Schillingeresque "rotation" may play a more important role in the creation of Porgy and Bess than previously assumed. These new materials also suggest another source for Gershwin's interest in this technique. The sketches consist of two single leaves, each written on one side only, labeled A and B.[18] (These leaves and the music on them shall be referred to in boldface, as A and B.) Leaf A contains the music that is to be the orchestra parts of act 1, scene 1, cues 99–100—immediately after Porgy's brief reprise of "A Woman Is a Sometime Thing."[19] (This music recurs, slightly altered and expanded, between cues 108 and 111.)

The top line of A contains music not heard in *Porgy and Bess* before cue 99. The other two lines, however, consist of music presented earlier in the opera. The central line—central in importance as well as in position—is a restatement in G minor of example 2.6. The bottom line of A presents, in G minor, the bass line added to example 2.6 on its restatement (starting one measure before cue 93).

Leaf B, as the reader may have guessed, contains the music of A backward.[20] Since the middle line of A is based on example 2.6, which contains sections that retrograde other sections of the line, there are spots in the middle line of B that are identical to spots in the middle line of A—a nice bit of invariance between the two.

The music of B does occur in act 1, scene 1, of *Porgy and Bess*, though not nearly so literally transferred from sketch to score as A. B occurs, without its

EXAMPLE 2.6

EXAMPLE 2.7

[*eighth rest in ms]

first two and last two measures, around cue 104.[21] Since the published vocal score simplifies this spot by leaving out the middle line (the top line of **B**), several measures of **B** and their corresponding measures in the sketch-score are reproduced here as a help to the reader. (See examples 2.7, 2.8.)

As can be seen from these examples, the score exchanges the octaves of the top two lines of **B**, bringing the middle line (which contains the principal material) clearly to the top. Such changes are anticipated in the sketch for **B**, which contains arrows at the start of the top and middle lines suggesting this exchange of registers.

B contains no verbal notations. **A** contains the mantra

$$
\begin{array}{c|c}
a & b \\
\hline
d & c
\end{array}
$$

and also the notes: "B—backwards[;] C—backwards/upside down[;] Bass on top/sop[rano] in bass[;] D is A upside down" and "revolving around G"; this second note is useful for constructing the missing **C** and **D**. All writing on both leaves is in Gershwin's hand.[22]

EXAMPLE 2.8

[*eighth rest in ms]

TABLE 2.1

91–one before 93	Subject (E♭);countersubject suggested in percussion
one before 93–one before 95	Subject and countersubject (E♭)
one before 95–99	Interlude
99–101	**A** (in B♭: = answer?)
101–two before 104	Episode
two before 104–two before 105	**B** (in B♭)
two before 105–three before 109	Episode/interlude
three before 109–111	**A** (in B♭)

If **A** is indeed "revolved around G"—specifically, around the G on the top space of the bass clef—then D would read as follows (remember: D is inversion, and C is upside-down *and* backward). (See example 2.9.)

Did Gershwin actually write out a **D** and a **C**? Probably not. The score certainly shows no sign of material derived from example 2.9—at any pitch level, forward or retrograde. At the place in the scene where music from the presumptive **C** or **D** might well have been used—between cues 108 and 111—Gershwin prefers to reuse version **A**.[23] (Here, in fact, is one case where retrograde is less destructive to the material being "rotated" than inversion. Retrograding this middle line of **A**—its most important strand—displaces the minor-second clashes to the off-sixteenths of the measure but leaves their "blue" feeling intact; inverting this line wipes out the seconds' bluesy character [save for the B♭/A clash] and makes the line sound like a mere exercise in wrong-note music.)[24]

These sketches do more than provide another example of Schillingeresque "rotation." They also help explain the references in the early literature on *Porgy and Bess* to "the crap-game fugue."[25] Previously these references have seemed merely muddled: the fugue in *Porgy and Bess* starts at cue 127, when the crap game is broken up by Crown and Robbins's fight.[26] But if **B** is seen as a straightforward manipulation of **A**, then the possibility arises of seeing the central section of the crap game, after the assembly of all the players, if not quite as "a fugue," then as using "fugal sections" to weld together its heterogeneous material. In these fugal sections the subject is example 2.6, while the countersubject is the music that becomes the bottom line of **A**. A rough analysis of the fugal aspects of this section, starting with cue 91, is given in table 2.1.[27] From cue 111 on there is no suggestion of the continuation of this design, though at cue 122, as Robbins picks up the fatal dice, the opening of the fugue subject makes one final appearance.

In the 105 measures between cue 111 and cue 127, Gershwin certainly would have had plenty of opportunity to use the conjectural versions **C** and **D** of the "rotation" had he wished. Few listeners will regret that he chose instead to write music that reflects each of the players in turn, as each takes up the dice, through the use of his motive.[28] The choice of motives allows the music to match the action more clearly—an operatic crap-game, like

EXAMPLE 2.9

EXAMPLE 2.10

any game in opera, needs careful differentiation if it is to be followed at all—and allows the game to flower into Porgy's dice-conjuring song over the harmonies of "I Got Plenty o' Nuttin'." Such a lyrical flowering provides necessary relief before the fast and intense music of the remainder of the scene.

Seeing the section from cue 91 to cue 111 as a sort of proto-fugue also casts the fight fugue itself and its subject in a new light. (See example 2.10.) Previously, example 2.6 and its later recurrences have been considered a kind of preluding, with example 2.10 as that material's final crystallization into a fugue subject. But if example 2.6 is itself a fugue subject, then example 2.10, with its frantic recasting of example 2.6 "contaminated" with the Crown motive, is a wrenching transformation of the material of the previous fugue—the fight fugue becomes not merely a fugue but a fugue run mad.

Up to now sketches **A** and **B** have been considered purely as examples of Schillingerian "rotation." While such "rotation" is certainly the main impetus for Gershwin's use of this technique, another source might have made Gershwin interested in trying out a procedure this *recherché*.

In the Gershwin Collection of the Music Division of the Library of Congress there is a photograph of Alban Berg, inscribed in Berg's hand, "Mr. George Gershwin zur freundlichen Erinnerung an [opening measures of the second movement of the *Lyric Suite*]." Gershwin, in the company of Berg, heard a private performance of the *Lyric Suite* in Rudolf Kolisch's house in 1928 and subsequently brought a score of the newly published work home with him from Europe.[29] If Berg showed Gershwin some of the structural tricks of the *Lyric Suite*, he would have certainly shown him the outer sections of the third movement, where the music of the opening—contrapuntal wisps of sound not astronomically removed in style from those forming the bottom line of **A** and **B**[30]—runs backward to form the close. Perhaps Gershwin hoped to produce something of the same effect in his new work? At any rate, it's pleasant to think that the score of *Porgy and Bess*, like that of another great opera being written in 1935, does have at least one section that runs backward.

How important, finally, is Schillingerian "rotation" to *Porgy and Bess*? A look at Charles Hamm's study of the first production[31] shows that all of the "rotations" save for the **B** version of the Porgy motive—example 2.5—are among the portions of the score cut during the first run of *Porgy and Bess*.[32] If, like Hamm, we consider the definitive text of *Porgy and Bess* to be the version established during the run of the first production, then all of the "rotations" must be considered material tried and discarded—no more a part of the final *Porgy* than the never-used C version of the Porgy motive.[33]

But are these all the "rotations" in *Porgy and Bess*? In the formulaic sequencing that forms much of the "neutral" and transitional material of the score—a sequencing that is itself a Schillingerism—there may well be other systematic Bs and Ds—and perhaps even a full-fledged C, the upside-down-and-backward form that Gershwin does not attempt in either of the sections examined here. The careful scrutiny that the *Porgy* score is now undergoing by a new generation of Gershwin scholars will certainly help us to find out.[34]

Notes

The principal composition draft for *Porgy and Bess*, referred to as "the sketch-score" throughout this article, was used as the basis for the published vocal score. (This relationship is described in detail in my article "Reconciliation on Catfish Row," *Library of Congress Quarterly Journal* 38 [Summer 1981]: 144–65. The currently purchasable vocal score corresponds to the score as published in 1935 save for the introductory matter and for some minor verbal changes made in the 1950s.) While that score was prepared for printing, Gershwin created the opera's full score. Thus, the published vocal score represents a stage of *Porgy and Bess* previous to the scoring of the work rather than a condensation from the full score. In this essay the published vocal score may be assumed to reproduce the reading of the sketch-score—and thus to represent the stage in the evolution of *Porgy and Bess* immediately following the sketches being discussed—unless noted otherwise.

1. One and perhaps two other hands are present in this manuscript. One hand is Ira Gershwin's; he notes "Porgy's Theme. A, B, C, D" at the top of leaf *A*, and, lower on the same leaf, "Porgy entrance." The "cabalistic symbol" described later in this essay may be in the hand of Joseph Schillinger. The music itself, however, is in the hand of George Gershwin.

The four leaves are written in a hand somewhat more constricted than Gershwin's usual hand of the 1930s: it resembles the "respectable" hand of Gershwin's mid-1920s works. (An occasional burst of the full, free mid-1930s hand—particularly at measure 8 of leaf *B*—reassures the researcher.) Gershwin seems to have put himself on his best handwriting behavior when working with Schillinger—the "Schillinger notebooks" in the Music Division of the Library of Congress show him writing his counterpoint exercises in a more restrained hand than he used for his compositions of the 1930s. Gershwin probably wrote out the four leaves as an exercise for Schillinger. (The handwriting of the four leaves, save perhaps for the "cabalistic symbol," is definitely *not* the hand of Joseph Schillinger.)

2. The sketches are among the material in box 7, item 6 of the Gershwin Collection.

3. The version of leaf *A* given in example 2.1 omits the small notes that add a lower line to the parallel dyads in the bass clef. These notes seem to have been added later and

do not affect the *B*, *C*, and *D* versions of the sketch. (They are present in the Porgy motive as it appears at cue 71 of act 1.)

4. They occur, slightly altered to give Porgy silence against which to declaim his spoken line, between cue 71 and cue 73 of act 1. They occur in straightforward fashion, transposed to C major, at cue 59 of act 2, when Porgy pays Lawyer Frazier for the divorce.

5. Save for the appearances of versions *B* and *D* described later. But these are not the straightforward Porgy motive.

6. Gershwin Collection, Music Division, Library of Congress, box 1, folder 2. The demonstration, labeled "Variation thru rotation around horizontal and vertical axes," is on page 11; page 41 is dated "June 3, 1932." The "cabalistic sign" is somewhat marred by the fact that Schillinger's script "b" here looks like his script "a."

7. Joseph Schillinger, *The Schillinger System of Musical Composition* (New York: Carl Fischer, 1941), 1: 185–201. Schillinger's idea of this process as "rotation" explains why he labels retrograde inversion c and inversion d: each new letter represents one further stage in the 360-degree rotation of the theme.

Schillinger actually thought of tonal inversion as a mistake—or, rather, as a "misinterpretation": "As [earlier composers] did not do it [that is, invert musical material] geometrically but tonally, they often *misinterpreted* the tonal structure of a theme appearing in an upside-down position. They tried to preserve the tonal unity instead of preserving the original pattern" (*The Schillinger System*, 198; emphasis in the original). Schillinger, who provides "geometrical" inversions of several Bach fugue subjects, does not mention Bach's own stunning use of strict, interval-for-interval inversion in the Duet, BWV 803.

8. The key signature of the sketch is dictated by the key signature of version A. Invert a melody in E major semitone-for-semitone with the tonic as an axis and the melody ends up in A Phrygian.

9. Certainly one would not want it to continue under the next part of the scene: Porgy's gift to Scipio of a harmonica with "a picture of a brass band on it" calls out for the harmonica imitation it receives.

10. I do not wish to suggest that Schillinger is the source of Berg's use of what Schillinger would call "rotation."

11. Such a technique is used in the introduction to act 2, scene 2. Here, "geometric expansion" of the Catfish Row motive can be heard as suggesting Bess's fever-ridden perception of her surroundings. Probably no such intellectualization is helpful in understanding the use of "rotation" in the final scene ("dissolution of the Porgy motive" might be one possibility).

12. This passage was first pointed out in Paul Nauert's article "Theory and Practice in *Porgy and Bess*: The Gershwin-Schillinger Connection," *Musical Quarterly* 78 (Spring 1994): 9–33. Nauert wisely refuses to rise to the bait and suggest any specific spot Schillinger may be talking about.

13. Schillinger, *The Schillinger System*, 195. The C of "position C" is in a circle in the original.

14. The songs written to lyrics by DuBose Heyward may be dismissed from consideration immediately—they are wedded to the rhythm of their texts, a rhythm that is destroyed in retrograding. (Text-setting receives no consideration in *The Schillinger System*.) The songs with lyrics by Ira Gershwin might seem a more likely place to look—in them the music came before the words. But a tune in the major becomes a tune in the Phrygian mode in Schillingerian, interval-for-interval inversion, and Gershwin is not likely to have written a tune in Phrygian for *Porgy and Bess*. So for vocal numbers, one is left with the tune in the minor (inverts to Dorian, close enough to minor for a bluesy

opera) with a text by Ira Gershwin. That tune is "It Ain't Necessarily So." Anyone interested can try to generate the retrograde inversion of the opening of this song and consider whether it could possibly have been the original.

There remain the purely instrumental themes and motives of the opera. Yet when one tries them out in retrograde-inverse form they seem to violate musical gravity (which asks that larger intervals be lower in the line, and that the general trend of a line, after an initial surge up, be downward), or musical inertia (which asks more rapid movement later in the phrase, and expects that dotted notes will most often come before, not after, the shorter notes which complement them), or both: the result is sometimes interesting and sometimes even usable, but it never suggests a first inspiration.

15. This suggestion implies that Schillinger did not know *Porgy and Bess* very well: anyone with a modest knowledge of the score knows the Porgy motive in its standard version as one of the principal themes of the piece. But Schillinger apparently did not know *Porgy and Bess* well enough to cite "Gone, Gone, Gone," the classic use of Schillingerian "chords in four tonics," when he discusses this technique on page 399 of *The Schillinger System*. (On "Gone, Gone, Gone" as Schillingerian, see Nauert, "Theory and Practice," 14–18.)

16. The opening five measures of example 2.6 are sketched at the top of page 18 of the Gershwin sketchbook usually referred to as the "Tune Book" (Library of Congress, Music Division, Gershwin Collection, box 2, item 1), a sketchbook that contains some material documenting Gershwin's lessons with Schillinger along with sketches for *Let 'Em Eat Cake*, *Porgy and Bess*, and the late Hollywood musicals. The five measures are in Gershwin's hand; the elements called cells a, b, and c in the preceding analysis have been labeled A, B, and C by Schillinger. (I assign these letters to Schillinger's hand because the A is the flat-topped capital A that Schillinger occasionally uses.) Beside the sketch, in two columns, Schillinger has written out the six possible orders of the three elements:

    abc bac
    acb bca
    cab cba

There is no suggestion in this sketch for the retrograding of element b or of phrase Y.

17. The sketches were purchased in April 1994 from Lion Heart Autographs. They were at one time owned by Kay Swift.

18. A "2" in a circle appears under the A. I have no explanation for this marking.

19. The music extends to the downbeat of the measure before cue 101. The sketch does not contain the voice parts; the top and bottom lines are not in octaves (there are indications in both lines for doubling); tempo, dynamics, and accents are missing. Otherwise the sketch corresponds closely to the published vocal score.

20. B also contains, wedged into unused space, sketches for a sequenced version of the final four sixteenth notes from the top line of A—material apparently not used in the final score of *Porgy and Bess*.

21. From two measures before cue 104 to just before the downbeat of two measures before cue 105. The first two and last two measures of B do not appear in the final score.

22. The clear, confident hand that is Gershwin's regular mid-1930s hand, not the best-behavior hand of leaves A–D.

23. At cue 127, the start of the fight between Crown and Robbins, the possibility of using the material generated from A—straight crap-game music—ends.

24. I admit to enjoying the inverted line A as sound.

25. For example, "the ingenious 'crap game' fugue from *Porgy*" (Vernon Duke, "Gershwin, Schillinger, and Dukelsky: Some Reminiscences," *Musical Quarterly* 33 [Jan-

uary 1947]: 109). The name "crap-game fugue" is still routinely applied to the music of the Crown-Robbins fight fugue (see Nauert, "Theory and Practice," 21–26).

26. This identification of the fugue is strengthened by the sketch-score, which contains two versions of the music from cue 127 to the downbeat of cue 138. The earlier version (bound second in the manuscript as it now exists) is labeled "Fugue"; it is in Gershwin's pencil hand and contains the four voices of the orchestral fugue fully worked out on four separate lines, but only a small part of the vocal overlay. The second version (bound first in the manuscript as it now exists) contains the instrumental fugue in ink in a copyist's hand (still on four separate lines), with vocal parts in Gershwin's pencil hand above them. Blank lines of score from cue 130 to the downbeat of cue 136 show that Gershwin intended to continue the vocal overlay throughout the fugue (compare *Die Meistersinger*, act 2, the fight fugue near the end) but ran out of words—and, later, of time. (There are no such blank lines—or, rather, there are not sufficient blank lines to give each soloist an independent line to sing—in the manuscript full score.)

27. A flick of subject-and-countersubject occurs between 95 and 96.

28. Sporting Life is represented here not by his characteristic "It Ain't Necessarily So" but rather by a version of Mingo's dice-conjuring tune of cue 105. Perhaps "It Ain't Necessarily So" had not been written when this scene was sketched; perhaps Gershwin felt that it was too idiosyncratic to work in this context. Whichever is true, the motive is not missed here, where Sporting Life must not be too sharply differentiated from the other crap-shooters.

29. Joan Peyser, *The Memory of All That: The Life of George Gershwin* (New York: Simon & Schuster, 1993), 161.

30. In fact, when I first saw sketch **B** I immediately thought of this section of the *Lyric Suite*.

31. Charles Hamm, "The Theatre Guild Production of *Porgy and Bess*," *Journal of the American Musicological Society* 40 (Fall 1987): 495–532. The list of cuts is on pp. 526–31.

32. These cuts do *not* include, of course, the "unrotated" Porgy motive (leaf *A*). They do, however, include version **A** of the crap-game music.

33. Probably not all of the cuts made by the Theatre Guild should be accepted unquestioningly. Some, it seems clear, were made because of the inability of the performer playing Maria, who had been taken over from the cast of the play *Porgy*, to deal with the music; others (notably the six simultaneous prayers that open act 2, scene 4) remove music that it would be sad to omit. But Hamm (see n. 31) is correct that the majority of the cuts do benefit the opera. Looking dispassionately at the cuts involving "rotated" material, I admit that the opera plays better if these cuts are made.

34. Paul Nauert's article in *Musical Quarterly* (see n. 12) is an excellent example of such work. Nauert's article appeared after mine had been written; since the articles differ in focus it seemed unnecessary to rewrite this article even though, as in the material on the various fugues in act 1, scene 1, the two essays share examples.

Gershwin's Operetta Overtures: Medley or Composition?

WAYNE SCHNEIDER

Leonard Bernstein, in his essay "Why Don't You Run Upstairs and Write a Nice Gershwin Tune?," praised Gershwin's gifts as a songwriter—"[Gershwin] had the magic touch. Gershwin made hits, I don't know how. . . . He wrote tunes, dozens of them, simple tunes that the world could sing and remember and want to sing again. He wrote for people, not for critics. . . . Gershwin was a songwriter who grew into a serious composer . . . starting with small forms and blossoming out from there"[1]—but seriously questioned his prowess as a composer. He pointed out that *Rhapsody in Blue*, Concerto in F, *Cuban Overture*, and the other instrumental works feature, even depend on, the captivating melodies that are the genius of Gershwin. But he added that a string of such tunes in the guise of concerto, rhapsody, or variation set does not necessarily equal a composition:

> The *Rhapsody* is not a composition at all. It's a string of separate paragraphs stuck together—with a thin paste of flour and water. Composing is a very different thing from writing tunes, after all. I find that the themes, or tunes, or whatever you want to call them, in the *Rhapsody* are terrific—inspired, God-given . . . perfectly harmonized, ideally proportioned, songful, clear, rich, moving. The rhythms are always right. The "quality" is always there. . . . But you can't just put four tunes together . . . and call them a composition. Composition means a putting together, yes, but a putting together of elements so that they add up to an organic whole. *Compono, componere*—
> And the trouble is that a composition lives in its development. . . . *Rhap-*

35

sody in Blue is not a real composition in the sense that whatever happens in it must seem inevitable, or even pretty inevitable.[2]

Many of the essays in this book discuss the compositional nature of Gershwin's instrumental works and songs. This essay confronts the problem raised by Bernstein of Gershwin as *composer* in his music that combines the genres of songs and instrumental pieces: his overtures to works for the musical stage. Bernstein centers the problem on definition. The Latin verb *compono* does indeed mean "to put together," especially unlike things. However, the ideas of composing's organic nature, its dependence on development, and its inevitable logic are Bernstein's own thoughts, although they reflect a good deal of musical thinking about Western music from, say, Bach to Schoenberg. But Gershwin and many others (including composers of most music written before 1600 and much music written since World War II) did not create his musical edifices on a germinal idea that was subjected to *Fortspinnung* or developed motivically. Gershwin's unit of composition was the *tune*. (That the tune itself, the result of happy inspiration, is subjected to the processes of composition is demonstrated again and again in the essays in this book.) Moreover, in his instrumental music, the way in which Gershwin calculatingly surrounded his tunes with music that dramatically *reveals* and *recollects* is a hallmark of his singular gift as a composer and represents one of the chief stylistic characteristics of his music.

Bernstein, too, recognizes the importance of Gershwin's connecting music:

Each work got better as he went on. . . . He had by that time [late 1920s] discovered certain tricks of composition, ways of linking themes up, of combining and developing motives, of making an orchestral fabric. But even here they still remain tricks, mechanisms borrowed from Strauss and Ravel and who knows where else. And when you add it all up together it is still a weak work because none of these tricks is his own. They don't arise from the nature of the material; they are borrowed and applied to the material. Or rather *appliquéed* to it, like beads on a dress.[3]

To say that the tools, or "tricks," of making music in the connecting passages of his instrumental works are not original to Gershwin is certainly no ringing condemnation: Strauss and Ravel, too, borrowed and absorbed from heritages past. Very little musical stuff is new under the sun. But something in Gershwin's instrumental music and music for the stage makes them work, and an important ingredient of that something is the close and subtle relationship that exists between tune and non-tune music. Indeed, the gradual sophistication of the connecting tissue in these works, on which Bernstein comments several times in his essay, traces perhaps the most important "historical" feature in Gershwin's music—for which the tunes are a brilliant constant.

In short, Gershwin's musical building blocks are not those of Bach or Beethoven or Brahms, but the ways in which he fashions music by carefully foreshadowing and lovingly remembering his million-dollar tunes should not be denied their aesthetic right: Gershwin's instrumental works, his overtures, his songs and other music for the theater are *composed*.

Gershwin's overtures, like all show overtures, are built around songs from their respective productions. Gershwin composed his overtures (and all his instrumental music, according to Bernstein) as if they were scenes in his musical comedies or operettas. There exists a carefully planned key scheme. The tunes are judiciously selected and attractively placed; the overture is, after all, the preview, or first "plug," for the several songs destined, their creators hoped, for stardom. A pleasant, effective setting in flattering harmonic surroundings, in this first hearing, could make the difference between a song's success or failure.

Gershwin probably composed the overtures of his shows last. In a typical Tin Pan Alley popular song, the introduction and verse often foreshadow the music of the refrain; the most efficient way of composing such prescient music is to write the refrain first and then write the verse and introduction. Similarly, large scenes in musical comedies and especially operettas are often held together by reprised connective music that acts as a structural glue and often presages music that occurs later on in the number; such music was probably composed after the other tunes had been written and inserted into their appropriate slots. And such efficient methods of composing were probably followed in the overture: Gershwin wrote the songs first, then wrote the overture around them.[4] A provisional overture was probably used in out-of-town tryouts—it spotlighted aspiring song hits from the show. When the roster of songs was firmly established in the tryouts, the final overture was constructed for the New York opening. A Gershwin overture, then, is a musical "opening night," wherein hopeful songs receive their chance finally to make good.

The exact relation of Gershwin's overtures to his musical comedies and revues of the 1920s is not easily determined. Overtures were not published unless part of a piano-vocal score, and precious few manuscripts of overtures from this period are known to have survived. Those few show overtures from the 1920s that do survive are a string of wonderful song refrains, usually minus the last bar or so, and often separated by little modulating interludes that foreshadow and recall music just forthcoming and music just heard. The introductions of the overtures, especially their opening bars, are usually the most imaginative and adventuresome music, featuring fanfares or other assertive musical announcements based on a tune or two, clever combinations of tunes, sequences and compressions of a tune's most memorable phrase, and the like. The endings usually repeat a portion of the last tune to be plugged, played in grandiose fashion. The overtures spotlight most of the songs seeking fame from their shows, and the song-most-likely-to-succeed is kept for the last song slot. The songs are in different keys, not always nearly related, and the overtures' overall harmonic schemes may ramble.

Although a survey of Gershwin overtures from the 1920s is impossible

EXAMPLE 3.1

EXAMPLE 3.1

due to lack of sources, a convenient glimpse is afforded by examining the only published overture from that decade: the overture to *Girl Crazy*.[5]

The overture to *Girl Crazy* (1930) consists of an introduction; a grandiose ending; and refrains of the songs "Embraceable You," "I Got Rhythm," "Land of the Gay Caballero," "But Not for Me," and "Broncho Busters," usually separated by short interludes.

The introduction begins with twenty-three bars of music in octaves, the melodic and rhythmic patterns (pairs of eighth notes and bunches of quarter notes) of which are very similar but never repeat bar to bar. (Indeed, this odd, nonrepetitive music occurs only in the overture to *Girl Crazy*, not in the show.) (See example 3.1.) The first four bars are in B♭ major, the next ten in G major, the last nine in A♭ major. The first three phrases of "I Got Rhythm" are heard in combination with the nonrepeating octaves in the middle ten bars. The first two phrases of "I Got Rhythm" sound again at rehearsal 2 of the introduction, directly after the octaves, in sharply accented and separated block chords, 4 + 4 bars, in A♭ major and then B♭ major. Compression of the song's opening phrase follows, 2 + 1 + ½ + ½, in C major. A sudden fortissimo A♭$_9$ chord halts the compression and effectively breaks the music's stride: introductory music to the first song refrain, two bars in A♭ major, repeated in D major (G: ♭II$_9$–V$_7$), pours the music and listener into "Embraceable You." (See analysis 3.1.)

ANALYSIS 3.1

	4	non-repeating octave patterns	Bb
"1"	10	non-repeating octave patterns (with "I Got R")	G
	9	non-repeating octave patterns	Ab
"2"	4	"I Got R" block chords	Ab
	4	"I Got R" block chords	Bb
2 + 1 + 1/2 + 1/2		"I Got R" compression	C
2 + 2		introduction to "Embraceable You"	G: bII$_9$—V$_7$

ANALYSIS 3.2

$$(\mathrm{C}^{(6)}) \qquad \mathrm{A}_7 - \mathrm{D}^{(6)} - \mathrm{B}_7 - \mathrm{E}^{(6)} - \mathrm{C}°{}^{9}_{7} - \mathrm{A}_7$$
$$\text{D: } \mathrm{ii}_{\flat}{}^{7}_{5} - \mathrm{V}_7$$

The refrain of "Embraceable You," in G major, is incomplete: Gershwin gives thirty of its thirty-two bars.

The first interlude, at rehearsal 4, *Poco maestoso*, remembers the melody and rhythm of "Embraceable" for seven bars, a chord change each bar: G, C_7, E_7, A_7, D_7, $\mathrm{F}\sharp_7$, B_7. The following two bars, *Allegro subito*, C_7 (V_7 in F major, the subsequent key), foreshadow the famous rhythmic figures of the next song refrain, "I Got Rhythm."

The refrain of "I Got Rhythm," in F major, is incomplete by one bar (thirty-three of its thirty-four bars are given). In fact, the music simply breaks off suddenly, followed by a pause.

Without interlude, the overture plunges headlong into a lusty four-bar (1 + 1 + 2) introduction-vamp to "Land of the Gay Caballero," the next song refrain. F major, the key of "I Got Rhythm," now falls through chords $\mathrm{E}\flat$, $\mathrm{D}\flat_9$, and G_7, the latter two a $\flat\mathrm{II}_9-\mathrm{V}_7$ cadential figure similar to that at the close of the overture's introduction.

All thirty-two bars of the refrain of "Land of the Gay Caballero," rehearsal 7, are heard, but the music of the last bar of the song repeats in modulating sequence as a brief interlude. (See analysis 3.2.) Again, a pause.

An abrupt change of mood occurs when the beautifully lyrical song refrain "But Not for Me" follows at rehearsal 8. This refrain is complete, thirty-two bars with a one-bar pickup, in D major. The song gives the overture a quiet moment in the middle and, moreover, ends peacefully without interruption.

Rehearsal 9, the following interlude, marked *Vivamente*, effectively cranks up the tempo and excitement of the overture in its eight bars (4 + 4) of newly composed music (which, like the nonrepeating octaves of the introduction, are never heard again in *Girl Crazy*): the harmony moves rapidly—from the D major of "But Not for Me" to chords $\mathrm{E}\flat$, D_7, C, and B in abrupt, eyebrow-raising progressions.

"Broncho Busters" follows. It is the last song refrain of the overture and is heard twice. Its first hearing is in E major/minor, complete in thirty-two bars. The last bars of the refrain are repeated, in C major, dominant of F major/minor, the key of the second hearing of this rollicking song. The sec-

ANALYSIS 3.3

$$
\begin{array}{ccccccc}
4 & + & 4 & + & 4 \\
(2 & + & 2) & & \\
\text{F–Bb}_7 \ \ \text{F–Bb}_7 & & \text{Eb}_7^9\text{–Db}_7^9 & & \text{F}
\end{array}
$$

ond hearing, also complete, presents the last two bars of the refrain now in augmentation, two bars stretched to four, sporting a brash progression of parallel harmonies: Db–Eb–F–G.

The ending of the overture is in F major, an awkward surprise after the concluding G-major chord of the series of parallel harmonies at the end of the preceding refrains. The athletic rhythm and tune of the first phrase of "I Got Rhythm" rumbles in reminiscence through these last twelve bars as the overture rushes to a *Vivo* close. (See analysis 3.3.)

The overture to *Girl Crazy* does seem to have an overall harmonic outline, for all its occasional audacities, marked by the keys of the song refrains, introduction, and ending. (See analysis 3.4.) Centered in F major, the overture's foundational keys sound subdominant, supertonic, and dominant, and a string of harmonies moves upward by step. Harmonic transitions in some of the interludes jar and jolt, but overall the direction seems sure.

The overture to *Girl Crazy*, in sum, is a potpourri or medley of splendid songs, usually separated by little interludes that change key and recall or introduce the songs of the show. Gershwin's choice for the last song is unusual, for "Broncho Busters" is not one of the show's roster earmarked for stardom, nor was it published separately. Finally, the overture seems to be endowed with a large harmonic plan, but harmonic details of the progressions in the interludes occasionally reveal some awkward seams.

By contrast, the overtures to Gershwin operettas from the 1930s are not medleys or potpourris of their shows' pretty, melodious gems strung to-

ANALYSIS 3.4

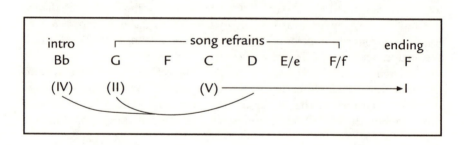

gether in logical musical order. Again, Gershwin's musical thinking in the early 1930s reveals a new compositional direction. Gershwin now controls the medley through the processes of selection and pacing. First, many—in fact, most—of the songs from the operettas are not included in their overtures. For example, in the overture to *Of Thee I Sing*, hints of "Wintergreen for President" and "Because, Because," two refrains of "Who Cares?," a bit of Diana Devereaux's sultry arioso ("I was the most beautiful blossom"), and the title song are included. "Love Is Sweeping the Country," "The Illegitimate Daughter," "Posterity Is Just around the Corner," "Jilted," "Trumpeter Blow Your Golden Horn," and lesser tunes are not. Second, the tunes are revealed and recollected to the listener in a musically *dramatic* way: the connecting music preceding any tune hints at that tune, teases the listener, builds excitement with passages of extended harmonic sequences and repeated melodic snatches from the tune, finds an appropriate dominant, and only then opens the curtain on the tune; music following a tune does so with lingering references to it—melodic and harmonic—before moving on to the next. Each tune, in turn, is placed in an overall dramatic hierarchy of importance in the overture: generally, the opening, middle, and, of course, concluding slots are the most "desirable" and prestigious. The final slot is usually reserved for the Big Tune or the title song (they may be the same). "Of Thee I Sing" and "Let 'Em Eat Cake," for example, are revealed at the ends of the overtures to *Of Thee I Sing* and *Let 'Em Eat Cake*. Gershwin controls the arrival of this moment through a carefully paced buildup of musical thrills and tension, so that when the overture's footlights come up on the final song refrain, the Big Tune, that moment is climactic indeed.

The two operettas, *Of Thee I Sing* and *Let 'Em Eat Cake*, serve as test cases to demonstrate Gershwin's new dramatic overture. The overture to *Of Thee I Sing* is published with that show's piano-vocal score; no manuscript sources survive. The overture to *Let 'Em Eat Cake* survives only in manuscript: a short score and a sheaf of working sketches.

The overture to *Of Thee I Sing* (1931) opens in dramatic turmoil. Four bold octave statements, *Vigoroso*, of the first phrase of "Wintergreen for President" sound in C minor. Each is followed by single-bar punctuating flourishes (the "Ah!" responses from the song), also in C minor, their melodic motion inching sequentially upward (g–$a\flat$–g, $a\flat$–$a\natural$–$a\flat$, a–$b\flat$–a, $b\flat$–$c\flat$–$b\flat$) over decorative, chromatic harmonies. The meter in this passage underlines the turmoil, alternating between $\frac{3}{4}$ ("Wintergreen") and $\frac{2}{4}$ ("Ah!"). A new tempo follows, *Allegro giocoso*, in which soaring sixteenth-note filigree, supported by chromatically descending harmonies c_7–$D\flat_7$–c_{dim7}–b_{dim7}–$A\flat_7$–G_7 (c: V_7)—leads to two further two-bar statements of the "Wintergreen" phrase, the first cadencing in C minor, the second in C major, the new key. (See analysis 3.5.)

The music quiets, but tension remains. The following long passage, in C major, that precedes the song refrain "Who Cares?," in G major, alludes to,

ANALYSIS 3.5

$$\text{i} \quad - \quad V_7/IV \quad - \quad V_7 \quad \begin{array}{c} \text{i} \\ \diagdown \\ \text{I} \end{array}$$

(with "(2" and "+" and "2)" above)

but never completely states, "Because, Because," from act 1. Dotted-rhythm noodling back and forth on various whole steps previews only the opening melodic idea of that song's refrain. The underlying harmonic stuff in these bars of the overture moves in typical Tin Pan Alley fashion by thirds and fifths; the chromatic brocade that gives this section its "modernist" sound is not functional but decorative—it colors and blurs, but does not supplant, basic harmonic progressions. Similarly, while the dotted-melodic noodling may pursue fanciful flights of bitonality, it is enjoined to those functional harmonies at key moments in the music—as an exotic embroidery, in short, that helps stitch the musical fabric. This transitional passage to "Who Cares?" climaxes on a dramatic D pedal and is made up of the following details:

1. Four bars of dotted d–c, unaccompanied, introduce the "Because" patterns; I in C major is implied.
2. Four bars of "Because" patterns, d–c, are accompanied by a harmonic palindrome, ii <————————> ii in C major.
3. Two bars of "Because" patterns, unaccompanied; d–c is joined by g–f (an aural effect similar to a mutation stop on an organ).
4. Six bars of solid ii–V_7 progressions in C major; "Because" patterns invade the harmonic fabric.
5. Two bars of an E♭ chord and its dominant (Ger$_6$ in the new key, G major; the key signature remains no flats or sharps, however); "Because" patterns.
6. Eight bars of solid ii–V_7 progressions in G major (with an occasional fleeting V_7/V in the new key); "Because" patterns.
7. Eight bars of dramatic D pedal; the opening phrase of "Of Thee I Sing" in the rhythmic patterns of "Because" is repeated and compressed in a harmonic sequence of chromatic chords.

Incidentally, the harmonies over pedal D in passage 7 were probably composed "backward." First, Gershwin determined the harmonic end-point of the passage (D major), then the number and spacing of sequential patterns, and the interval between patterns (whole steps); finally, since all the chords were more or less decorative chords firmly anchored on the pedal, Gershwin merely had to work the patterns in reverse order to find the opening triad. (See example 3.2.)

8. Two bars of dotted d–c again, unaccompanied; but now $\hat{5}-\hat{4}$ in G major is implied.

EXAMPLE 3.2

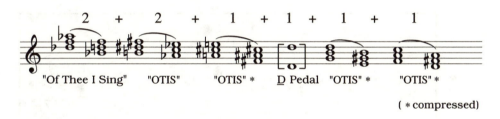

(* compressed)

9. Four bars of V_7 in G major in various spacings and registers; "Because" patterns.

The first setting of the refrain of "Who Cares?"—the first complete hearing of a song in the overture—is subdued and lyrical. (Perhaps Gershwin had in mind the effective, quiet reprise of the song in the second act.) Decorative melodic "Because" patterns continue to swirl through the texture, darting in and about the refrain.

A four-bar modulating interlude separates the two settings of "Who Cares?" The G major of the first refrain is undermined by F♮s and harmonies in parallel motion to F-major triads; weakened G major falls to E minor, and, supported by an appoggiatura C# in the bass (that hints at V/V), dons its new guise as G_7, or V_7, in the new key of C major. "Because" patterns, in parallel fourths (another organ mutation stop effect), still sound relentlessly.

The second setting of the refrain of "Who Cares?," in C major, *Moderato*, $\frac{2}{2}$ time, is exactly that of its first hearing in the second act, and that of the sheet music. The "Because" patterns cease.

An eight-bar interlude in C minor follows, *Slowly*, in $\frac{2}{4}$ time. Four statements of the opening phrase of "Wintergreen" are set over a seven-bar harmonic palindrome, i <————————> i, the concluding chord of which moves to V^7_{+5} in the final bar of the interlude.

A graceful violin cadenza is a dramatic, gypsylike embroidery to a subsequent four-bar snippet of Diana Devereaux's sultry arioso ("I was the most beautiful blossom"). This brief passage is in C minor and is the only music in the overture rhythmically free: tempo *Rubato*.

Up to this point, the most climactic moment in the overture has been the dramatic D pedal and the sequence of chromatic chords perched atop it. The restless opening, the swirling and relentless "Because" passages, the climactic D pedal, the twofold hearing of the refrain of "Who Cares?," and the free paraphrase of Diana's arioso have perched the music at denouement and the listener on the seat-edge of high expectations.

The dramatic buildup, *a tempo* (no flats or sharps in the key signature), to the overture's climactic preview of the show's Big Tune is made up of these details:

1. Two bars; C minor moves up a half-step to D♭ minor; "Because" patterns return.

ANALYSIS 3.6

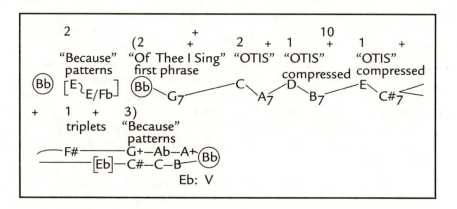

2. Four bars; two two-bar sequences move in the harmonic rhythm of the opening phrase of "Of Thee I Sing" (a sneak preview of the tune is heard above the musical fray); D minor moves up to E minor (see analysis 3.6.).

3. Four bars; two two-bar sequences (the musical pattern in each bar may be heard as an imperfect retrograde of the second and fourth bars of the preceding sequence pair—see detail 2); "Because" patterns. (The principal harmonies of the first three passages—circled in the analysis—inch up to B♭.)

4. Four bars (alternating meters $\frac{2}{4}$ and $\frac{1}{4}$ [!]); repeated hammering of B♭ (V) triads, supported by v_7/V, in the new key, E♭ major; "Because" patterns.

5. Two bars; compression of the preceding passage: three-beat patterns shortened now to two-beat patterns; E (F♭) major; "Because" patterns (see analysis 3.7).

6. Ten bars; sequence.

(The principal harmonies in this passage leave B♭ major only to inch up the scale back to B♭. The last four bars of the passage are faintly bitonal: two progressions converging simultaneously from opposite directions to B♭.)

ANALYSIS 3.7

EXAMPLE 3.3

marcato

A transitional passage marked *Alle breve risoluto*, $\frac{2}{2}$ time, follows directly, wherein the preceding climbing sequences find climactic resolution (would Bernstein say "inevitably"?) in a Bb-major triad as V in Eb major, the new and final key of the overture. The music of these four bars consists of repeated melodic hammerings on Bb and Db (example 3.3), accompanied by first-inversion triads slipping chromatically down by half-step from A$_6$ to Fb$_6$, and then dissolving to the Bb$_7$ dominant harmony. Rumbling octaves descending in eighth notes in the bass firm up Bb$_7$ as dominant, and the musical energies and great dramatic expectations of the overture are effectively funneled into Gershwin's revelation of the Big Tune.[6]

The Big Tune is "Of Thee I Sing," of course, set triumphantly, *Brightly (Allegro moderato)*, in Eb major.

A brief epilogue, three bars, *Molto allargando*, concludes the overture with a flourish: a sparkling sustained Eb chord, and busy bass octaves outlining Eb$_6$.[7]

The harmonic outline for the overture to *Of Thee I Sing* is simple and efficient:

Introduction
    —hints of "Wintergreen"   c
    —"Because" patterns   C
    —hints of "Of Thee I Sing"   to G major via V pedal
"Who Cares?"
    —with swirling "Because" filigree G
Interlude
    —"Because" patterns   G to C
"Who Cares?"
    —sheet-music version   C
Interlude
    —hints of "Wintergreen"   c
Diana's arioso
    —with violin obbligato   c
Interlude
    —"Because" patterns   c to . . .
    —"Of Thee I Sing" sequence Bb
Introduction to "Of Thee I Sing" Eb: V$_7$
"Of Thee I Sing"
    —the Big Tune   Eb

(See analysis 3.8.)

ANALYSIS 3.8

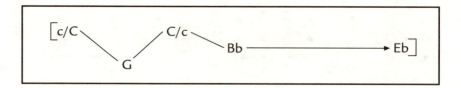

Only two years later, Gershwin created his greatest show overture, a work that reveals a maturing composer confident in the style of dramatic music-making. The overture to *Let 'Em Eat Cake* (1933) is a fascinating and complicated composition, consisting of introduction, three interludes, a coda, and previews of four of the show's songs. The introduction of the overture—the portion of music that precedes the preview of the first song, "Mine"—is in four sections, of decreasing length, and gradually clarified harmonic identity.

A lone snare drum, playing a two-bar march cadence, starts the show and the introduction's first section. (The show's military-political tone is thereby established immediately.) A brief, unaccompanied quotation of "The Girl I Left Behind Me" (an Irish folk song often heard as a brisk fife-and-drum march)[8] follows,[9] vaguely implying V_9^o (B–D–F–A) in C major. A twofold repetition of the drum cadence sounds next, this time punctuated by faintly bitonal percussive chords— $E_7^\flat + e_7^\flat$ over bass A —in the orchestra. Syncopation at the end of the second repetition neatly ushers in the bugle-call motive of the title song "Let 'Em Eat Cake," heard at important dramatic moments in the show, a motive repeated here in sequence over transposed percussive chords. (See example 3.4.)

Out of the chromatic "clutter" this passage effects a harmonic focus on G–B–D♯(E♭) and pedal G—V+ in C major.

In the next six bars, the countermelody of the song "Mine" alternates bar-by-bar with the bugle call and the opening phrase of the refrain of "Let 'Em Eat Cake"; C major abuts E♭ major. (See example 3.5.)

Gershwin chooses two motivic ideas from the opening phrase of the refrain of "Let 'Em Eat Cake," x and y— ♪♩. + ♩♩♪♪ —and combines them with snatches of the bugle call in the next half-dozen bars:

    1 + 1 + 1 + 1 + 1 + 1
"Cake" xy xy xx yy xx yy
bugle-call snatches throughout (See example 3.6.)

Harmonically, the motives of the "Cake" refrain, x and y, gravitate respectively to two tetrachords: E♭ F G♭ A♭/A B C D. The harmonies of the bugle-call snatch and the folk-song quotation—$V_{9\flat}^o$/V in C major (F♯–A–C–E♭) and V_9^o in C major (B–D–F–A) respectively—form "opposing" chords, the pitches of each duplicated in the tetrachords: E♭ F G♭ A♭/A B C D. At this

EXAMPLE 3.4

point in the music, then, both C and E♭ major have emerged strongly, along with two tetrachords—vaguely related to those keys—that are the source of two "opposing" seventh chords.

In the concluding portion of the first section of the introduction, Gershwin layers music upon music, systematically creating a bitonal, polyrhythmic "sandwich" of sound. (See example 3.7.)

- chugging eighth-note chords (various inversions) F♯–A–C–E♭, and
- bugle calls (one per bar) echoing in contrasting registers
- harmonies alternating between A♭ and D minor (or, in the tetrachord, E♭ F
  G♭ A♭/A B C D) (See example 3.8.)
- chugging quarter-note triplet repeated percussive chords D_7/d_7,[10] and

EXAMPLE 3.5

- A–B–C–D bass ostinato in eighth notes (the "yy" melodic pattern), and
- sixteenth-note filigree B♭ scale in upper register (last four bars), and
- sustained F-major triad played by trumpets (last bar only).

The B♭ filigree, the D$_7$/d$_7$ percussive chords, the F-major triad played by the trumpets, the A–B–C–D bass ostinato (rhythmically directed toward D), and the echoing A♭- and D-minor bugle calls from the previous four bars create a background, hovering, unresolved V$_7$ of E♭ major (B♭–D–F–A♭) in these closing bars of the first section of the introduction.

    The second section of the introduction suddenly dawns in clear G major, $\frac{2}{2}$ time, nine bars. (See analysis 3.9.)

EXAMPLE 3.6

EXAMPLE 3.7

EXAMPLE 3.8

ANALYSIS 3.9

EXAMPLE 3.9

This passage previews, in a "bassless" texture (chords in upper registers plus a "cello-line" tune), the opening phrase of the refrain of "Mine," the last part of which is repeated in a five-bar extension. The tune in these last five bars emphasizes the pitches of $V^\circ_{9\flat}$/V in the new key, G major (E–D♭–B♭–G); "dragging" triplets in the extension continue rhythmic patterns established in the foregoing musical "sandwich." Parallel harmonies chromatically clutter the extension; they are functional only in that they begin and end on G major.

The third section of the introduction is also in G major, $\frac{2}{4}$ time, fourteen bars; it melodically juxtaposes and compresses sustained notes (the x's in the following table), hints of the song "Union Square," and bits of the "epic" fanfare—in "dragging" triplets (see example 3.9)—that figures prominently in the finales of *Let 'Em Eat Cake*. (See analysis 3.10.) The passage modulates from G major to C major.

The fifth and final section of the introduction previews the six-bar introduction of floating parallel seventh chords, anchored on V_7 in C major, to "Mine," from the first act, published in the sheet-music version of the song.

No music is given in the Short Score MS of the overture for "Mine"; instead, a rubric instructs a copyist to write out "4 BAR VAMP AND C & E♭ CHO / MINE / 32 bars / 2nd Cho 30 BARS." Accordingly, the original version of the overture presented a twofold hearing of the song's refrain in precisely the two keys prepared by the introduction: C major and E♭ major. The E♭ repetition was later cut, an action that causes interesting structural consequences, to be discussed later.[11]

Interlude 1, which follows the preview of "Mine," is in two sections. The first consists of six bars of "bassless" music in $\frac{2}{4}$ time; the key signature is three flats, but neither C minor nor E♭ major is firmly established. (See analysis 3.11.) The first phrase of the song refrain "Comes the Revo-

ANALYSIS 3.10

1	+ 2	+1	+ 1	+ 1	+ 2	+ 1	+ 1	+ 2	+	2
x	"Union Sq"	x	fanfare	x	"Union Sq"	fanfare	x	"Union Sq"		"Union Sq"
G: I				F			G			G₇
G										C: V₇

ANALYSIS 3.11

(1 +	1 +	1 +	1	+	1	+	1)
"Comes the revolution"				~~~→			
$E^{\flat}$	$B^{\flat}_7$	$E^{\flat}$	$B^{\flat}_7$		$E^{\flat}$–G–B + F		E^{9}_{7} $\flat 5$
c_7	g_{11}	c_7	g_{11}				

lution" echoes in each bar—now in the lower, now in the upper register. The passage's first four bars telescope in miniature the E♭ major–C minor ambiguity of the overture to this point: a clear cadential progression in E♭ sounds simultaneously with a progression in C minor. Bar 5 contains the augmented triad heard earlier in the overture's introduction, but here coupled with F♮; the functional ambiguity of the augmented triad effects an enharmonic shift to the passage's concluding chord built on B, and modulation to a sharp key.

The second section of interlude 1 is in A major, $\frac{2}{4}$ time, ten bars. Harmonically, it is built upon a sustained dominant chord in A major. Textural figuration in the passage proceeds as follows:

Bar 1: swooping ascending scale in sixteenth notes; sustained chord below
Bars 2–3: "Comes the Revolution," first phrase, in "double time" (eighth notes and sixteenth notes); sustained chord below
Bars 4–5: the chord leaves off its sustaining and sounds in repeated, fanfare-like rhythms (related to those in "Comes the Revolution") while the upper-register filigree sustains in turn
Bars 6–9: descending arpeggiation in rhythmic figures related to those in "Comes the Revolution"; sustained chord below

Interlude 1 concludes on a Gershwinesque "blue" chord with fermata: E_7 + e_7 (V_7 + v_7 in A major).

A preview of "Comes the Revolution," thirty bars in A major, follows.[12]

Interlude 2, following directly the preview of "Comes the Revolution," is in two sections. The first section, which also acts as a codetta to the "Comes the Revolution" preview, is nine bars long, A major, $\frac{2}{4}$ time. The passage begins with four bars of clear pedal harmonies—I to V_7 (over I) to I to V_7 (over I)—supporting melodic snippets of "Comes the Revolution" echoing back and forth as in interlude 1; and ends with five bars of descending "chime chords" (stacked fourths, in quarter-note blocks and sixteenth-note arpeggiations) built over an implied tonic pedal, the whole cadencing with a rather precious trill to a concluding A-major triad.

The concluding section of interlude 2, in E major, $\frac{4}{4}$ time, previews the first six bars of the opening of act 2, followed by the two bars immediately preceding the refrain of "Blue, Blue, Blue" in that same scene (and in the sheet-music version of the song).[13]

ANALYSIS 3.12

$$
\begin{array}{cccccc}
 & & & 4 & & \\
(1 & + & 1 & + & 1 & + & 1) \\
\text{E–G–D} & & \text{F–C–B} & & \text{D–F–C} & & \text{E}\flat\text{–B}\flat\text{–A}
\end{array}
$$

E pedal ————————————————

E: I ————————————————————→ IV (?)

The preview of the refrain of "Blue, Blue, Blue," in E major, follows. It is twenty-three bars long, shy of a complete refrain by one bar; the music ends perched atop a V_7 chord sustained with fermata.[14]

Interlude 3, which follows the preview of "Blue, Blue, Blue," is in four sections. The first section of this last interlude consists of descending parallel triads in quarter notes over pedal E; the texture is reminiscent of that found in the music that introduces "Blue, Blue, Blue" in both the overture and act 2 opening. (See analysis 3.12.)

The second section of interlude 3 is seven bars long; its key signature shows no flats or sharps. A familiar friend—the percussive chord $\dfrac{E\flat_7 / e\flat_7}{\text{bass A}}$ —is sustained in the first two bars, over which blares the bugle-call motive ($E\flat/e\flat$–A–D). In the subsequent five bars, steady quarter-note chords strum in lower registers, while the first phrase of the refrain of "Let 'Em Eat Cake" sounds above. (See example 3.10 and analysis 3.13.)

The third section of the interlude, seventeen bars, $\frac{2}{2}$ time, in A minor, previews and develops the "millennium" music—the Russian-sounding "Trepak"—from the refrain of "Let 'Em Eat Cake." An opening A-minor triad, marked sforzando, gives way to perfect fifths (a–e) midregister in steady quarter notes, which continue throughout the passage. After a vamp bar of accompanimental, steady fifths, a canon of sorts begins at the fifth, with each entrance of the "millennium" tune falling into one of two interlocking pentachords: A–B–C#–D–E/E–F#–G–A–B. A stretto of the entrances occurs in the seventh bar. The tune is simplified four bars later to straight quarter-note motion that still outlines the basic shape of the "millennium" melody; the second bar of this simplified two-bar unit is combinable with the first, and all combinations are subsequently given in the music. The two-bar unit is compressed to one bar of eighth notes; the contrapuntal combinations are repeated. (See example 3.11.)

The last section of the interlude begins with ten bars of music similar to that found in the overture's introduction, first section. Snatches of the bugle-call motive, sounding now in the lower (A♭ minor), now in the upper (D major/minor) registers, surround a diminished seventh chord (F#–A–C–E♭) midregister (sustained, usually, but on one occasion a participant in imitation and echoing). A stretto of entrances of the bugle call builds excite-

EXAMPLE 3.10

ment; the bugle call itself is foreshortened. And here is the moment of truth in the overture, the dramatic denouement, the point at which a musical path must be chosen by the composer, a fate decided. The concluding ten bars of interlude 4 show that chosen path. (See example 3.12 and analysis 3.14.) Harmonically, the passage closes in on a V₇ of E♭ major; melodically, the music repeats and develops the first phrase of the refrain of "Let 'Em Eat Cake." The scalar filigree that swirls above these crucial ten bars also contributes to the climactic harmonic focus. (See analysis 3.15.) The pitches in

ANALYSIS 3.13

EXAMPLE 3.11

the scalar filigree are in retrograde order of those found in the tetrachord of
the introduction; the rhythmic emphasis of certain pitches in the tetrachord
and its transposition (marked with arrows in analysis 3.15) chord tones of
the concluding dominant harmony. That dominant harmony, in turn, dis-
places the dangling $F_{\flat5}^{7}$, or $C_{\flat5}^{\flat7}$, chord from the end of the second section of
interlude 3. The choice of E♭ major as a goal of harmonic denouement will
be discussed later.

EXAMPLE 3.12

ANALYSIS 3.14

2   +   2   +   (1 + 1)   (1   +   1   +   2)
"Cake" "Cake" "Cake" stretto   sustained chords only

(1x) ♩   (1x) ♩   (4x) ♪

F#–A–C–E♭ ──────────────── V9   V9♭   V7
                    (D–F–A♭–C) (D–F–A♭–C♭) (D–F–A♭–B♭)

B♭ pedal ──→

ANALYSIS 3.15

$$D\ C\ B\ A/A^b \overset{2}{\overbrace{}}\ G^b\ F\ E^b\ \overset{+}{}\ F\ E^b\ D\ C/B\ A \overset{2}{\overbrace{}}\ G\#\ F\#\ \overset{+}{}\ D\ C\ B\ A/A^b \overset{(1\ +\ \ \ 1)}{\overbrace{}}\ G^b\ F\ E^b\ B^b{}_7\ \overset{(1+1+2)}{\text{scale}}$$

$$E^b\ F\ G^b\ A^b/A\ B\ C\ D \qquad \text{transposed down a} \qquad \text{retrograde}$$
retrograde   minor 3rd

B–C–C^b–B^b
A^b
F
D

(from Interlude 3, second section: $\begin{bmatrix} F_{b5}^{\,7}\ \text{or}\ C^b{}_{b5}^{\,7} \\ V_{b5}^{\,7}/V\ \text{or}\ N_6 \end{bmatrix}$ B^b pedal → V$_7$

A preview of the refrain of "Let 'Em Eat Cake," the title song, follows, comprising forty bars in E♭ major. The first ending of the refrain is taken here; its scurrying eighth-note filigree (clearly the forebear of the overture's scalar noodling, which immediately precedes the song) leads directly to the coda.

The coda is in C major, three sections.

The first section, eight bars, *Grandioso*, $\frac{2}{2}$ time, reprises (or repreviews) "Mine"—in a very special way. The first four bars of the refrain of the tune —in augmentation to eight bars—are scored in upper brilliant registers, supported harmonically by a twofold statement of the vamp pattern associated with the tune. Moreover, in the bass line below, the first phrase of the refrain of "Let 'Em Eat Cake" sounds in octaves, two statements of four bars each. In short, Gershwin cleverly combined the beginnings of the refrains of "Mine" and "Let 'Em Eat Cake"!

In the second section of the coda, *Allegro*, $\frac{2}{2}$ time, the scurrying, linking eighth-note scalar patterns from the first ending of the refrain of "Let 'Em Eat Cake"[15] sound alone, with brief bits of "Union Square" (the middle patter section, beginning "Down with"), and with the opening phrase of "Cake." (See example 3.13 and analysis 3.16.) The rhythmic play on the

ANALYSIS 3.16

2	+	2	+	2	+	2	+	4	+
								16 beats: (3+3+3+3) + (3+1)	
pattern		pattern		"Down with"		"Down with"		"CAKE" ♪♩♩ etc.	
alone		alone		+ pattern		+ pattern		+ pattern	

+ 3	+ 1
pattern	pattern
alone	alone

EXAMPLE 3.13

EXAMPLE 3.14

opening phrase of the tune "Let 'Em Eat Cake" in this passage's middle bars
is similar to the melodic/rhythmic shifts in many of Gershwin's songs—
most famously the 1924 "Fascinating Rhythm." The harmony of this second
section of the coda fluctuates between C major and C minor, the result of the
cross-relation E–E♭ in the two-bar scalar pattern.

The overture concludes with a *Grandioso* statement of the first phrases of
"Let 'Em Eat Cake"'s refrain—at the words "Let 'em eat cake! / The land
of freedom / Is here once more!" This passage, lushly harmonized, served
the same function as a second ending of a typical Tin Pan Alley song: it pa-
rades the harmonic dramatis personae of the overture (especially $V^{\circ}_{9♭}/V$—
F♯–A–C–E♭) out for a curtain call, so to speak, but within the concluding
proscenium of the tonic. (See example 3.14.)

Overall, the overture to *Let 'Em Eat Cake* centers on the previewing of
certain songs from the operetta in a dramatically effective manner. Harmonically, the overture is "about" the conflict between C major and E♭
major, especially apparent when a simple diagram of the overture's principal keys, those of the songs, is charted. (See analysis 3.17.) "Comes the Revolution" in A major and "Blue, Blue, Blue" in E major form a middle pair of
tunes; the music immediately following "Blue" strongly suggests a return to
A major or A minor—percussive chords built on pedal A and the "Trepak"
music in A Dorian—and therefore the "inner music" of the overture forms
a symmetrical triptych of harmonies A–E–A. "Mine," the first song to be
previewed, is in C major; originally it was to have been repeated in E♭ major,
as discussed earlier. The title song, in the spotlighted concluding slot of the
overture, is presented twice, in the keys of "Mine," but in reverse order.
Harmonic skirmishes precede both "Mine" and "Cake," focusing on first C,

ANALYSIS 3.17

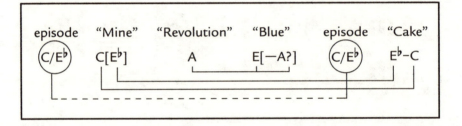

later E♭. The large sectional divisions of the overture, then, fall into lovely palindromic harmonic symmetries, one "inside" the other. The borders of the music are clearly C major, but the interior maps out E♭ major and the harmonic road—via fifths motion—to and from E major, both thirds away.

A deeper and fascinating look at the overture to *Let 'Em Eat Cake* and its creation is afforded by the happy survival of a treasure of manuscript material. The Short Score MS, frames 41–54,[16] is the principal musical source. Other single sheets of manuscript for the overture survive: inserts of varying lengths, carefully marked with Gershwin's instructions to copyists for placement in the principal manuscript, which is also marked with corresponding instructions. In addition, four pages of manuscript sketches survive, frames 65–68 of the Short Score MS, entitled "Notes for overture?"[17] These "notes" reveal those passages in the overture on which Gershwin spent some compositional experimentation; the contents of these pages are listed here in detail:

Frame 65
1. Lead-sheet (no flats or sharps; $\frac{2}{4}$ alternating with $\frac{4}{4}$; ca. nine bars; untitled) of music in the first section of the introduction to the overture—that complicated passage where the bugle-call motive echoes in contrasting registers over a harmonic sequence of percussive chords (bars 9ff.). The lead-sheet continues the sequence pattern two to three bars longer than the later version of the music.
2. Short score (G major; $\frac{4}{4}$, later $\frac{2}{4}$; twelve bars; untitled) of the second section and the beginning of the third section of the overture's introduction. The bass line figuration in the passage's opening bars is simplified in the later version of the music; Gershwin abbreviates ascending parallel triads by writing out only the first chord of each bar and simply drawing an ascending line to the next.

Frame 66
1. Short score (D major; $\frac{3}{4}$; two bars; untitled) of the first two bars of the parallel triads that occur in interlude 3, first section, of the overture (only the parallel triads are given; no pedal notes are written). The later version of this music is in E major: parallel triads over a tonic pedal.

2. Two-stave score (clefs and key not given, not inferable; $\frac{4}{4}$, later $\frac{2}{4}$; five bars; untitled) that appears to contain several experimental combinations of the first bar of the refrain of "Let 'Em Eat Cake" in various points of imitation, stretto, and so on. In the first two bars, Gershwin has written "x" note-heads instead of actual pitches: the purpose of the sketch seems to center on the timing of entrances, stretto, and vertical rhythmic patterns rather than harmonic considerations (such imitative texture is often heard in the overture to *Let 'Em Eat Cake*, most notably in the fourth section of interlude 3).

Frame 67

1. Short score (C major; $\frac{4}{4}$; two bars; untitled) of the first four bars (quarter note = half note) of the *Grandioso* combination of the refrains of "Mine" and "Let 'Em Eat Cake," in C major, at the beginning of the coda

2. Two-stave (presumably bass and treble clefs) score (C major?; $\frac{4}{4}$?; 1 bar + pickup; "Beheaded") of a single bar found in the "Trial of Wintergreen" from act 2 (the music occurs at the point where Kruger pronounces sentence on Wintergreen and the committee; Wintergreen responds, "Beheaded?"). Why this music should be included among short scores and lead-sheets to the overture is not clear; perhaps Gershwin wanted to incorporate the passage—which, after all, accompanies one of the most dramatic moments in the show—into the overture at some similarly dramatic spot, following the example of the *Leonore* overture, or certain overture-fantasies.

3. Short score (C major; $\frac{2}{4}$; nine bars; "Coda") of early thoughts on the second section of the overture's coda (quarter note = half note). The sketch shows an attempt to combine the repeating bass pattern with the bugle-call motive (two bars of pattern alone, two bars of pattern + bugle call, five bars of bugle call alone). Since the motive is a modulating one, its combination with a nonmodulating bass pattern is difficult at best; indeed, after four bars of bass pattern, the music apparently goes awry—Gershwin leaves off writing the bass pattern and continues writing only the bugle call (in imitation at the augmented second!). Evidently, the combination of bass pattern + bugle call was not considered worthy of further exploration; in the later version of the passage, Gershwin combines the bass pattern with snippets of the "Down with" patter from "Union Square."

Frame 68

Short score (E♭/c, later A major; $\frac{2}{4}$; fifteen to seventeen bars; untitled) of Interlude 3 of the overture. Two bars are crossed off; the rubric "Comes / The / Revolution" appears at the end of the short score. Generally, the music follows that of the later version.

In the analysis of the overture to *Of Thee I Sing*, I suggested that Gershwin composed the overture last, or at least after the show's principal songs had been composed. Since no primary source material has been located for that overture, any hypothesis concerning its composition cannot be fully supported. The rich cache of manuscript sources for the overture to *Let 'Em Eat*

Cake offers evidence that Gershwin did indeed create his overtures late in the composing of a show. Neither the principal Short Score MS nor the "Notes for Overture?" sources contain music for the songs previewed in the overture; instead, specific rubrics, naming songs and listing precise numbers of bars, instruct a copyist for their insertions. Obviously, such a system of compositional shorthand could work only if the songs were already written and titled.

Moreover, the "Notes for Overture?" manuscripts also confirm a notion regarding Gershwin's new 1930s operetta compositional style that might be self-evident: these short scores and lead-sheets are "workshop" sketches for precisely that music in the overture that involves counterpoint, imitation, the combination of tunes, and other compositional tours de force. George Gershwin is certainly not known as a master of counterpoint or compositional artifice; his spotty formal musical training in such devices was hardly a complete education in their use. Yet Gershwin's music in the 1930s contains canon, variations, fugues, mensural canons, invertible counterpoint, and other learned devices. The incorporation of such reflective music-making into a compositional style seemingly antithetic to artifice suggests a new musical maturity in the composer Gershwin. The manuscripts for the overture to *Let 'Em Eat Cake* do not reveal a naïve Gershwin dabbling with learned devices in emulation of "highbrow" composers; rather, they show us a diligent Gershwin seriously attacking new contrapuntal problems and adapting the results to his own artistic aims.

Much more than mere potpourris of show songs, the overtures to *Of Thee I Sing* and *Let 'Em Eat Cake* are dramatic music-making and surely two of Gershwin's finest compositions.

Finally, Gershwin's counterpoint, "modernistic" harmony, and other compositional devices in the connective tissue of the potpourri overture to *Girl Crazy* and especially the dramatic overtures to *Of Thee I Sing* and *Let 'Em Eat Cake* show his musical thinking to be conscious, purposeful, clever. Gershwin reveals and recollects his masterful songs in the most dramatic, sophisticated theater music of his day—whole overtures set on the traditional harmonic underpinnings of Tin Pan Alley, clothed in sleek, chromatic hues. There is method here, not a casual stringing together of songs; there is, in short, *composition*.

Notes

1. Leonard Bernstein, "Why Don't You Run Upstairs and Write a Nice Gershwin Tune?," *Atlantic Monthly* 195 (April 1955): 39–42; reprinted in Bernstein, *The Joy of Music* (New York: Simon & Schuster, 1959), 47–57. Pages given in notes refer to the reprint; the passage cited here is found on pp. 50 and 51.

2. Ibid., 52, 53.

3. Ibid., 53–54.

4. The Short Score MS of the overture to *Let 'Em Eat Cake*, discussed later, bears out this idea.

5. The piano-vocal score of *Primrose* (1924), the musical comedy Gershwin wrote for

EXAMPLE 3.15

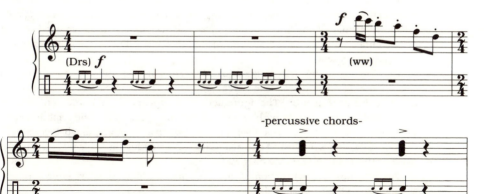

the London stage, prints no overture; instead, the show begins with the traditional big opening number. The entrance of the chorus in the opening is preceded by seventeen bars of introduction: tremolos and horn calls and chromatic fanfare figures over a pedal C that transform into sturdy eighth notes and clear dominant harmony for the chorus's first downbeat. Whether the exigencies of the London stage precluded an overture or whether an overture was written for the production and simply omitted from the piano-vocal score is not known.

6. This four-bar passage is heard later in the show in the finales to acts 1 and 2 always as introductory music to the title song. Clearly, Gershwin intended to associate this music with the title song wherever it appeared.

7. The epilogue also closes the operetta, at the end of the second act, effecting a neat musical closure between end of overture and end of operetta.

8. Doubtless Gershwin's quotation of this tune is its military incarnation. For more information on the song, see James J. Fuld, *The Book of World-Famous Music: Classical, Popular, and Folk* (New York: Crown, 1971), 242–44.

9. Just exactly when it follows is a matter of some dispute. The well-known "reconstruction" and orchestration of the overture by Don Rose casts the folk song in one bar of $\frac{3}{4}$ and one bar of $\frac{2}{4}$ time, thereby giving the opening passage a musical asymmetry. (See example 3.15.) While Gershwin was certainly not incapable of such "modern" metrical

EXAMPLE 3.16

shifts, the Short Score MS for the overture offers no evidence for this curious asymmetry. The manuscript clearly shows two bars of $\frac{2}{4}$, and overall—including the lone snare-drum cadence—a foursquare meting out of beats: 4 + 4 + 2 + 2. (See example 3.16.) Unfortunately, the Don Rose version of the overture has been recorded several times (Buffalo Philharmonic, Boston Pops), and this misreading of the manuscript has been publicly accepted.

10. This "dragging" triplet figure probably continues throughout the five bars in this portion of the musical "sandwich," although the Short Score MS is not clear about such a continuation. The figure definitely appears in bar 1, and definitely in bars 2 and 3, but possibly with an altered rhythm—♩♩♩ ♪ ♪♩—one reminiscent of *Cuban Overture*. The manuscript gives no indication that the figure, in whatever rhythmic guise, continues into bars 4 and 5, although, considering the "layered" style of the music at this point, it probably does.

The Don Rose reconstruction of the overture continues the "dragging" triplets through the five bars, unaltered.

11. In the Don Rose reconstruction, the thirty-two-bar refrain of "Mine" follows the four-bar vamp (from the sheet-music version), as indicated in the manuscript rubric. However, Don Rose additionally dovetails the first two bars of the vamp under the last two bars of the refrain, then finishes the vamp pattern, thereby creating a 4 + (30 + [2] + 2) structure. Moreover, a single bar of four quarter notes follows the extra vamp, and "pyramids" A–C–E–G into a I(6) or vi$_7$ chord, presumably acting as a musical bridge to the next music in the overture.

A better solution might simply be to follow Gershwin's instructions: perform the four-bar vamp and the thirty-two-bar refrain in C major (taking the second ending of the sheet-music version), then proceed directly into the following interlude. (The original version probably consisted of the four-bar vamp and the thirty-two-bar refrain, in C major—the final two bars of which modulated into E♭ major—and the first thirty bars of the refrain, in E♭. The song was presumably interrupted just before its final cadence—not an unusual gesture in overtures—and the music of the overture continued with the first interlude, which begins on an E♭(6), or c7, chord. The subsequent elimination of the E♭ refrain of "Mine" in the overture necessitates a leap to the first interlude from C major, thereby creating a less successful harmonic seam.)

The key of each song in the overture (the preview key; an exception is the E♭ repetition of the refrain of "Mine") is identical to the key of each song in the operetta (the premiere key).

12. The fact that this song is included in the overture is curious, for it was never published separately as sheet music. (Usually, of course, the songs previewed in the overture were hopefuls for hit status.) In fact, the song may have been so earmarked, but, for one reason or another, subsequently rejected. (The song's text, for example, is a bit gruesome, making it an unlikely favorite for informal music-making; see the published libretto of *Let 'Em Eat Cake*.)

13. That this music appears in the overture strongly suggests that Gershwin composed the overture only after most, if not all, of the operetta was composed. Not only songs but also introductory material and connecting music are previewed in the overture.

14. According to the Short Score MS, the overture to *Let 'Em Eat Cake* is divided into two parts, marked A and B. The dangling V$_7$ with fermata concludes part A. B begins on a fresh page. What this odd division suggests is not at all clear: perhaps additional sections of music originally fell between the parts, later removed by Gershwin himself or lost (for example, a preview of "On and On and On," the only published song from the show *not* included in the overture).

EXAMPLE 3.17

15. The two-bar scalar pattern is altered slightly from its guise in the refrain of "Let 'Em Eat Cake": the final note is changed from $\hat{4}$ to $\hat{2}$, so that it becomes infinitely repeatable. (See example 3.17.)

16. Frame numbers refer to the microfilm of the manuscript, available from the Library of Congress, Music Division.

17. Ira Gershwin's label.

the opening credits in *Damsel in Distress*. Also in the same film are the un-Gershwinesque quasi-English ballad "The Jolly Tar" and the madrigal "Sing of Spring." In another category are songs that were written for these productions but not used. "Just Another Rhumba," intended for *The Goldwyn Follies*, remained unpublished until 1959. As with the other *Goldwyn Follies* songs, the music for the verse was probably written or completed by Vernon Duke. The only manuscript known to survive bears this out in that the verse and refrain, though entered into copyright together, were plainly copied separately by two different copyists (examples 4.1a and 4.1b);[1] perhaps the refrain was copied without the knowledge that the verse even existed. "Hi-Ho," written for the opening scene of *Shall We Dance* and shelved because of staging costs, was known only to a few Gershwin friends until its publication in 1967. Both unused songs are of major proportions: "Just Another Rhumba" contains a trio section in addition to verse and refrain ("Swanee" is the only other Gershwin song with this feature); and "Hi-Ho," though without a verse (also unusual), has a commanding length of 118 measures.

Gershwin's last songs are indeed different, and in ways other than phrasing and structure. Carefully written accompaniments, contrapuntal bias, the thoughtful selection of key, a flirtation with quartal harmony, and the influence of Gershwin's studies with Joseph Schillinger mark the late songs in special ways. The following examples from this musical treasure trove give only a glimpse into their compositional richness and complexity.

Although general practice suggests that popular music be performed freely, clearly Gershwin wrote out his accompaniments as lavish instructions to the performer, as though they would be played largely as written. Many manuscripts of Gershwin's songs survive, representing as nearly as possible a composer's fair copy. Most are in pencil (the concert works are usually in ink), in what Wayne Shirley terms the composer's "informal" hand.[2] Often Gershwin's instructions never see print. For example, the 1924 manuscript of "Oh, Lady, Be Good!" (example 4.2a) includes dynamic markings more detailed than those in the published score (example 4.2b). But the most consistent discrepancies between manuscript and printed score, including those of "Oh, Lady, Be Good!," take place in the right hand. Gershwin had a large stretch, and his right-hand parts frequently contain four voices spanning an octave or a ninth, sometimes a tenth (example 4.2c). With few exceptions, these are changed in the published version (example 4.2d). Parallel octaves between the outer voices of the right hand, such as those at the start of the refrain of "Oh, Lady, Be Good!," are eliminated by deleting the right hand's lowest voice or by keeping it stationary. As for stretches larger than an octave, these are accommodated in either of two ways: by shifting the lower note up an octave, as in measure 5 of the verse, or by transferring it to the left hand, as in measure 10 of the verse. These practices continue in the late songs as well. A comparison of the fair copy and print of the opening of the "Foggy Day" refrain (examples 4.3a and 4.3b) show that, once again, the right

EXAMPLE 4.1a

EXAMPLE 4.1b

hand's lowest voice is cut out, taking with it the parallel octaves as well as the occasional ninths and tenths. While one assumes that Gershwin's manuscripts reflect his original and/or ideal intentions, one can also reasonably assume that the versions of songs published in his lifetime had passed his approval.

However, Gershwin's accompaniments reveal more than surface changes from manuscript to print. Gershwin tended to think in terms of counter-

EXAMPLE 4.2a

[tr. WJS]

point rather than the normal vernacular of "chords." Such thinking is already present, albeit less developed, in many of the earlier songs. In fact, Gershwin's contrapuntal bias is reflected throughout his work in so many ways that this study can barely scratch the surface. An apparently early lead-sheet for "I've Got a Crush on You," date unknown, is characteristic in its indication of the familiar descending chromatic inner voice at the start of the refrain (example 4.4). A striking similarity exists on a page from the *Tune Book* of 1933–37 (also known as the "Black Note Book") where, in what according to Ira Gershwin was probably the first sketch of "I Got Plenty o' Nuttin'" (simply labeled "Porgy" initially), the composer again takes care to show a chromatic inner voice (plus two bass notes) at a cru-

EXAMPLE 4.2b

cial point in the song—and that is the only thing written down other than the melody itself (example 4.5).

One of the relatively unknown post-*Porgy* songs is "(I've Got) Beginner's Luck," sung by Fred Astaire in *Shall We Dance* (example 4.6a). The introduction (not used in the film score and not altogether the same as in the composer's manuscript—a matter taken up later in this essay) quotes the main theme of the refrain in the dominant of D, the key of the verse, which is in turn the dominant of the refrain's G. (Gershwin's verses were sometimes

EXAMPLE 4.2c

Cho

1) D crossed out

[tr. WJS]

in the dominant, sometimes in the tonic.) The accompaniment to the syncopated, repeated notes of the verse, with bass D–D#–E counterpointed by
D–C#–b in the bottom voice of the right hand, reflects the composer's affinity for inversional balance.

The refrain of "Beginner's Luck" is in the AABA form of the standard
thirty-two-bar chorus. However, the first two A sections are six bars each,
not eight, so the song's total length, in the absence of a coda, is only twenty-
eight measures. Despite the musical inequality between the first two and the
last two sections, the stanzas are of an equal length of four lines each. In the
six-bar periods they are set as follows: line 1 (the song title and main observation), two measures of half and quarter notes; lines 2 and 3 (the specific
reasons for the observation), run together into three measures of syncopated eighths and quarters with a whole note at the end; line 4 (the comment), a single measure of quarter notes. Line 1 is the same for both stanzas,

EXAMPLE 4.2d

and the only rhyme is between the end of line 3 of stanza 1 and its coun-
terpart in stanza 2.

But the most interesting relationship is to be found between the last lines
of stanzas 1 and 2. The text is "Gosh, I'm lucky!" in the one, "Gosh, I'm fortunate!" in the other. Given that the Gershwins normally worked with the
music first, one could rightly expect a musical correspondence here, and indeed there is: "Gosh, I'm lucky!" is set to pitches d♯, e, a♯, and b, in that
order, while "Gosh, I'm fortunate!" has a♯, b, and e. The correspondence
might go unnoticed were it not for the fact that the verticals accompanying these pitches are exactly the same. In other words, if one assigns the
"Gosh, I'm lucky!" chords the numbers 0−1−2−3, the ordering for "Gosh,
I'm fortunate!" is 2−3−1.

The perennial question of whether Gershwin was himself aware of this

EXAMPLE 4.3a

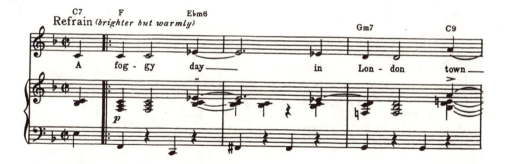

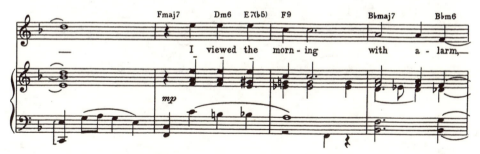

EXAMPLE 4.3b

REFRAIN

[tr. WJS]

kind of subtle relationship is answered, if only by implication, by the simple fact that it was not there initially. The sketch of the refrain on page 53
of the Black Note Book shows the "Gosh, I'm lucky!" measure (with the last
two beats as an eighth plus dotted quarter instead of two quarters) but not
"Gosh, I'm fortunate!" (example 4.6b). That the latter was added subsequently, presumably at a more studied pace, certainly suggests that the
composer knew about its structural relevance.

EXAMPLE 4.4

CRUSH ON YOU.

[tr. WJS]

The verticals themselves can be heard harmonically as a series of progressions from V of V to V, as indicated by the supposed roots shown here in brackets (example 4.7). Again using the numbers 0 through 3 in correspondence to the syllables "Gosh, I'm lucky!," one sees that verticals 0 and 2 and 1 and 3 are nearly intervallically identical in all voices, while the bottom three voices, forming (from bottom) a tritone plus a major third, are the same for all four. Horizontally, there are two main forces: first, the semitonal resolution of all four voices from verticals 0 to 1 and

EXAMPLE 4.5

Porgy-

1-9

1-9

[tr. WJS]

EXAMPLE 4.6a

2 to 3; second, the registrally fixed semitonal threads that tie all four together.

The link between these passages and the surrounding music is once again stepwise voice-leading, this time in the strand that begins with the descant in measure 1 of the refrain and then transfers to an inner voice: middle C in measure 2, going to B in measure 3, then back to d, then C♯ (measure 4), then C (measure 5). These are the same pitches emphasized in the verse by the inner voices that begin in contrary motion with the bass.

Quite a few of the late songs, including "Beginner's Luck," have been preserved—complete with introductions—in fair-copy manuscripts. Gershwin's attention to detail in these manuscripts is such that their differences

EXAMPLE 4.6a (*continued*)

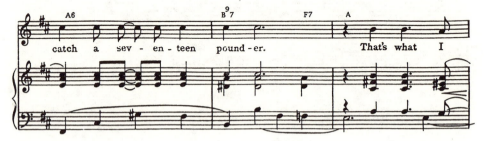

EXAMPLE 4.6a (*continued*)

EXAMPLE 4.6a (*continued*)

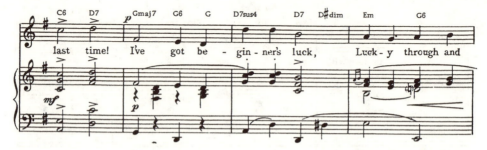

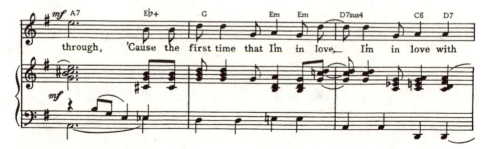

EXAMPLE 4.6b

[tr.WJS]

with the published score are magnified. Always it is the accompaniment that is affected, usually by presumed improvements in playability at the expense of voice-leading. In the majority of instances, changes from manuscript to print merely confirm the expected: simplified dynamics, the reduction or respelling of fisty chords, and the like. On rare occasions, however, the changes are substantial.

The four-bar introduction to "Beginner's Luck" is an example of the latter sort. The right hand is the same in both manuscript and published score; however, Gershwin initially counterpointed the opening c♯ not with e and a but with e♭ and a♭ (example 4.8). The chromatic relationship of e♭–a♭ with

EXAMPLE 4.7

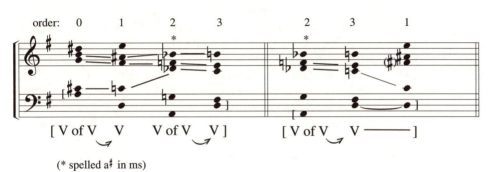

(* spelled a♯ in ms)

EXAMPLE 4.8

[tr. WJS]

e–a that occurs by implication (that which is heard versus that which is expected to be heard) is in effect extended into a series of chromatically descending, parallel perfect fourths, which reaches G♯–c♯ on the downbeat of measure 3, then deflects the lower note to G♮ a measure later while the bass enters with the dominant root A prefaced by E♭ (not E). The e♯ and b in the right hand in this same measure proceed, aided by crossed voices and a change in register, to f♯ and c♯, respectively.

The published introduction bears comparison. The left hand is still dominated by parallel perfect fourths, but now they are mostly diatonic and begin tonally, with e–a as expected. The second half of measure 2 shows the third B–d—possibly a misprint—where it could just as easily be the fourth B–e; either way, the resulting vertical has a dominant function to A. The latter follows in measure 3, supporting a six-four that then resolves to the altered A₇ in measure 4, the one measure that is identical in the two versions. Hairsplitting aside, the net result of these changes is an introduction that is more in the accepted popular song idiom and more accommodating to harmonic analysis (as shown in example 4.6); at the same time, the effect of the main contrapuntal idea is weakened.

Another traditionally flexible area in the world of popular song, along with accompaniment, is that of key. The transposition of a song to suit a given vocal range is, of course, an established practice in art as well as popular music, and a song may well be published in one key in a show score and in another in the separate sheet music. But if Gershwin wrote his songs with such evident care, then surely the keys in which he first set them down ought to be of some significance. In many cases they are the same as what ended up in print; in others, they are not. The fair copy and published score of "Beginner's Luck" are both in G, as is the first sketch of the refrain; however, the first sketch of the verse, which appears separate from the refrain and seventeen pages later in the Black Note Book, is in D♭—that is, a half step lower than in the fair copy and published score (recall that the verse is in the dominant).

Gershwin often chose and wrote in keys "difficult" or unusual for the popular-song idiom of his time, especially in his late songs. The original five-flat key of the verse of "Beginner's Luck," discussed earlier, is one ex-

EXAMPLE 4.9a

ample; others include the original keys of A♭ and E major, used in "Nice Work If You Can Get It" and "A Foggy Day," respectively. These were all transposed a half step in either direction for publication. A particularly interesting example of Gershwin's facile use of such a seemingly unlikely key as D♭ is "Mine" from the 1933 show *Let 'Em Eat Cake*, originally an exercise found in the notebooks of his studies with Joseph Schillinger (example 4.9a). The song, published in C, is probably best known for the patter that counterpoints its second refrain (example 4.9b). This countermelody (with its own lyric), which follows the progression of the topmost inner voice, is an improvement on the attempt shown in the notebook sketch, which straddles more than one inner strand and struggles in imperfect canon with the tune. The inner voices themselves, which combine to form a four-voice unit rich in stepwise motion, are the focus of attention in a series of suggested choral layouts in the sketch for male, female, and mixed voices, the last two of which are in D rather than D♭.

One might presume that an editor transposed these songs to more friendly keys in publication, but evidence suggests that in at least two instances it was Gershwin himself. The sketch of "I Got Plenty o' Nuttin'" (example 4.5) is in A; in the opera, however, it is in G, a key that works admirably both locally and with respect to the whole work. And on the first page of the manuscript of "A Foggy Day," in E, Gershwin wrote and circled "in F."

These details may be helpful in differentiating the style of Gershwin's late songs from the earlier ones. As I already suggested, a good portion of this difference is to be found in the accompaniments. The manuscript of

EXAMPLE 4.9b

EXAMPLE 4.10a

"Oh, Lady, Be Good!," a relatively early song, is remarkable in its completeness, yet its substance reveals no surprises, nothing that might not be considered idiomatic for a popular song of the 1920s. The same cannot be said of, for example, "Beginner's Luck"—with its abundant fourths and irregular period lengths punctuated by permutational devices—and the 1930s. And "Beginner's Luck" is not unique. "Things Are Looking Up," from *A Damsel in Distress*, has a verse replete with inner-voice fourths (example 4.10a) in which the choice of pitches echoes "Beginner's Luck" at

EXAMPLE 4.10a (*continued*)

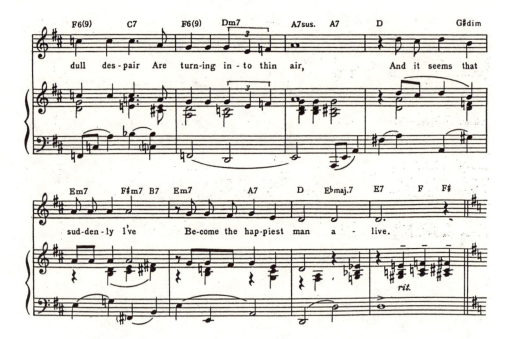

both beginning and end, a refrain whose first two A sections are ten bars each ("Beginner's Luck" was six), and settings of the title phrase that use the same notes in two distinct orderings (example 4.10b).

From the observations made thus far, it seems clear that Gershwin paid great attention to such things as introductions, turnarounds, and codas—literally specifying them down to the last grace note—and that this trait was not confined just to the late songs. Where the late songs do differ from the early ones is in the increasing role of other nontextual material, material that is less likely to be perceived as an appendage and consequently less easy to discard or, for that matter, to dismiss. In short, Gershwin's late songs show compositional touches over and above tune-plus-appropriate-accompaniment. "Shall We Dance," with its recurring inner-voice flourish, is one example (example 4.11). "They All Laughed" is another. There, in the refrain, while the first A section is the normal eight measures in length, the first stanza—only the first—is a line short, thus allowing the intervention of a two-bar instrumental interlude (example 4.12a). A more subtle, more deliberate touch are the two staccato eighth-note chords in the right hand that punctuate the first line; the same figure also appears at the end of the verse and before the refrain is repeated (example 4.12b). The manuscript, though mostly the same as the published score and in the same key, differs in that the eighth-note chords have one additional voice—that is, F#–A#–C–E to G–B–D–E instead of F#–A#–E to G–B–E. Moreover, the song's introduction is changed in a

EXAMPLE 4.10b

manner reminiscent of "Beginner's Luck" (example 4.12c). In the manuscript the left hand supports the right with parallel fourths, now in superposition, while in the published score this support is translated into a triadically based, harmonic progression. As in "Beginner's Luck," the fourth and last measure is the only one that is identical in both hands in the two sources. These flirtations with so-called quartal harmony owe substantially to Schillinger's influence, as does the occasional use of permutational devices: horizontal, as in the refrain of "Beginner's Luck" (discussed earlier), and vertical, as in the following passage from "Just Another Rhumba," which acts as a retransition from the trio section to the reprise of the refrain (example 4.13). Other devices and principles associated with Schillinger—stepwise voice-leading and recursive progressions, for example—were already part of Gersh-

EXAMPLE 4.11

win's vocabulary prior to the Schillinger years of 1932–36. In fact, Schillinger himself cites two pre-Schillinger Gershwin songs in *The Schillinger System of Musical Composition*, "The Man I Love" and "I Got Rhythm."[3] Conversely, the harmonic series of minor thirds from G through B♭, D♭, E, and back to G that opens the second part of *Rhapsody in Blue* can be described in Schillingerian terms as a scale of four tonics, one unit.[4] Perhaps the clearest uses of Schillinger techniques can be found in the *"I Got Rhythm" Variations*, the most ambitious in *Porgy and Bess*. In the post-*Porgy* songs the applications are freer, more subtle. And certainly the Schillingerisms in these songs are more isolated, as in the case of the introductions to "Beginner's Luck" and "They All Laughed," which were both revised for publication into something more conventional either by Gershwin himself or by an editor (presumably—in the

EXAMPLE 4.12a

nonposthumous songs—with Gershwin's consent). After all, these songs, for all their remarkable qualities, were still written in part from a commercial standpoint: it is likely that what was right for *Porgy and Bess* in the composer's mind would, upon second thought, not be quite right for *Shall We Dance.*

Even so, a review in *Variety* described the melodies in *Shall We Dance* as "not fashioned for popular acceptance in the hum-and-whistle category."[5] At the same time, in a letter to Isaac Goldberg, Gershwin expressed dissatisfaction with the way his songs were treated in the picture. "They literally throw one or two songs away without any kind of a plug," he wrote, uncannily echoing his early days on Tin Pan Alley.[6] As Gershwin's life was soon thereafter cut short, it would remain so: the Gershwin brothers' last

EXAMPLE 4.12b

EXAMPLE 4.12c

[tr. WJS]

songs, including some of their very best, would be written for a medium that they felt did not do them justice. Perhaps Gershwin's worries reflect his struggle between composing songs in the wake of *Porgy and Bess* and crafting songs within the exigencies of commercial cinema. Could his concern have been that the movies we know are just passing fancies? For all one can say negatively about them or about Hollywood, the miracle of film permits us to continue to enjoy the magic of Astaire performing those wonderful late Gershwin songs—complex, rich, and a little pensive—just as audiences did more than fifty years ago.

Notes

1. The manuscripts cited in this paper can be found in the Gershwin Collection, Library of Congress, Washington, D.C.

2. Wayne D. Shirley, "Scoring the Concerto in F: George Gershwin's First Orchestration," *American Music* 3 (Fall 1985): 297, n. 13.

3. Joseph Schillinger, *The Schillinger System of Music Composition*, 2 vols. (New York: Carl Fischer, 1941), 1: 111, 164, 179.

4. Ibid., 1: 151.

5. Quoted in Edward Jablonski and Lawrence D. Stewart, *The Gershwin Years*, 2d ed. (Garden City, N.Y.: Doubleday, 1973), 276, 281.

6. Quoted in ibid., 281.

EXAMPLE 4.13

Musings on "Nice Gershwin Tunes," Form, and Harmony in the Concert Music of Gershwin

LARRY STARR

Since the day he first set pen to music paper to compose a "concert" work, George Gershwin—that gifted and supposedly naive Tin Pan Alley tune-smith—has been a suspect figure in the world of "serious" music. Praise for Gershwin's melodic gift and rhythmic imagination, those characteristics that are so evident in his "pop" tunes and contributed so much to his success as a tunesmith, has always been lavish. But from the first reviews of *Rhapsody in Blue* through the early criticism of *Porgy and Bess* and up to the present day, connoisseurs and sophisticates, authorities and would-be authorities on Gershwin have claimed that he simply lacked the technique to construct convincing large-scale works. Critics have claimed that the *Rhapsody*, the Piano Concerto, *An American in Paris*, and even *Porgy* succeed, to some limited extent, virtually in spite of themselves—not because of their ambitious dimensions and "higher" aspirations but because Gershwin's talents as a tunesmith are abundantly evident in them. After reading such criticism, one can only conclude that enjoying Gershwin requires the lowering of one's sights.

In the celebrated 1955 essay "Why Don't You Run Upstairs and Write a Nice Gershwin Tune?,"[1] Leonard Bernstein summarizes and embodies the standard criticisms of Gershwin, describing point-blank deficiencies of the concert works. He exclaims: "Those tunes. Those beautiful tunes. But they still don't add up to a piece."[2] Of the *Rhapsody in Blue*, he remarks that "you can't just put four tunes together, God-given though they may be, and call them a composition."[3] And Bernstein remarks that "*American in Paris* is again a study in tunes, all of them beautiful, and all of them separate."[4] Bernstein's words carry considerable weight, of course, since—like Gershwin before him—he was one of those rare figures who moved easily between the worlds of "art" and "pop" music, and because he was a champion of American music and frequently performed Gershwin's concert works (which he claimed to love in spite of their deficiencies).

Critiques echoing or paraphrasing Bernstein's words continue to be heard, to an extent that such opinions function as a kind of "received wisdom" or even "party line" on Gershwin in academic and critical circles. The influence of these ideas is evident even in Richard Crawford's carefully written article on Gershwin in the *New Grove Dictionary of American Music*, where one finds statements like "The melodies of Gershwin's concert works are surely the chief reason the works hold their place in the repertory."[5] Later on in the same article, Crawford offers details about Gershwin's melodic style in his concert works, observing that "four-bar units are by far the most common" and that "tending towards symmetry . . . in the reliance on parallel units of two, four, and eight bars, Gershwin's melodic materials seem designed to impose regularity and coherence even in the ear of an inattentive listener."[6] Such statements point up resemblances between Gershwin the tunesmith and Gershwin the art-music composer, and Crawford's reference to an "inattentive listener," intentionally or not, helps reinforce suspicions that Gershwin was, at bottom, a not entirely "serious" composer who catered, in part, to a not entirely "serious" audience.[7] Unfortunately, the reader may embrace such suspicions without further evidence.

However, this is not the place for a survey of Gershwin criticism. I wish only to establish that certain attitudes toward Gershwin's concert music have become almost as commonplace as performances of the pieces themselves. We hear such views, I suspect, without questioning them, in much the same way most of us probably hear Gershwin's music these days, when we take the time to hear it at all—that is, without much sustained attention or a lively spirit of inquiry. In short, the "received wisdom" too easily gets in the way of truly *listening* to Gershwin's concert works. On the other hand, if we approach this music afresh and without preconceptions, we may discover that the traditional view offers a procrustean perspective that distorts and nullifies some of his music's most intriguing and delightful musical stylistic characteristics. To support this assertion, I will focus my discussion on Gershwin's two best-known and most frequently performed concert works: *Rhapsody in Blue* and *An American in Paris*.

I begin by asking some simple questions about what would appear to be the most obvious and noncontroversial aspect of this music: those wonderful "tunes." Just exactly where are the "tunes" in these works, what are their characteristics, and what is their function in the musical forms into which they are incorporated? Finding answers to these questions turns out to be considerably more complicated than one might think and opens up many issues concerning both the music and our perception of it.

First, a definition of "tune." This definition is particularly necessary because the standard descriptions of Gershwin's concert music seem to imply that the composer simply pulled some tunes out of his Tin Pan Alley trunk and pieced them together in an arbitrary and uninspired manner to create his big compositions. Defining a "nice Gershwin tune" is fairly easy since Gershwin created many unequivocal and great examples in their pure form —that is, as pop songs. The refrains of "The Man I Love," "Somebody Loves Me," "Someone to Watch Over Me," and many other wonderful songs provide a model of the typical form and content of a Gershwin tune. Such a tune is almost always a self-contained thirty-two-bar melody in four eight-bar phrases, with a clear internal form (AABA is the most common pattern, and ABAC also occurs frequently) and a straightforward harmonic sense and direction. The problem is that if one looks for these "nice Gershwin tunes" in Gershwin's concert music, one will encounter great difficulty finding them. A few—surprisingly few—melodies in the early *Rhapsody in Blue* reflect this model (compressed there into sixteen bars with four four-bar phrases), and they do not include the two best-known melodies in the work. In the later *An American in Paris*, moreover, the typical "nice Gershwin tune" has essentially disappeared.

Now clearly these works are "tune*ful*," in a general sense, and Gershwin's characteristic melodic style is clearly audible in them. Yet a work that has tuneful qualities is significantly different from one that is literally composed of *tunes*. Gershwin, unlike composers such as Tchaikovsky, Rachmaninoff, Borodin, or Chopin, did not slip into the American hit parade through the back door of instrumental concert music; he entered confidently through the front door (redefining the door in the process). If Gershwin wanted to write a successful pop tune—a "nice Gershwin tune"—he wrote one. He did not rely on his instrumental works as surrogates. When he wrote his concert music, Gershwin, an intelligent and practical musician, wrote in a manner quite different from that in his self-proclaimed tunes. Given Gershwin's talents and background, why did the melodies of *Rhapsody in Blue*, Concerto in F, and *An American in Paris* never become popular songs? The answer is disarmingly simple: these melodies never were, nor could they ever be, "nice Gershwin tunes." In fact, they make rather unsatisfactory pop tunes, which is why neither the composer nor anybody else has considered them pop-song material. Even if the definition of "tune" were loosened somewhat, clear, balanced, finished tunes are more common in the instrumental works of composers like Schubert, Mendelssohn, Tchaikovsky, and even Mozart and Haydn than they are in the concert music of Gershwin.

The opening of *An American in Paris* offers a good illustration. The initial idea of the composition is eight bars long, and whatever it may be, it's a pretty *bad* "tune." One could listen to this opening and never suspect that its composer could write a decent—let alone great—tune. (See example 5.1.) The repetitive, motivic character of this initial idea, combined with its registral shifts and large ambitus, mark it clearly as instrumental. In fact,

EXAMPLE 5.1

Gershwin wrote effectively for instruments in his instrumental works (as anyone who tries to sing accurately the opening of *Rhapsody in Blue* will testify) just as he wrote wonderfully for the voice in his songs. Furthermore, despite the arrival of the tonic F in the eighth bar, everything about the opening melody of *An American in Paris* suggests continuity and development rather than short, closed musical units. At the apparent "end" of this opening melody in the seventh and eighth bars, Gershwin creates a sense of sudden imbalance and asymmetry demanding continuation. Here the melody shifts abruptly to its upper register and presents two striking but neatly foreshadowed motives: the transformation of the recurring low-register e of bars 1–6 into a new, rapid, repeated-note motive; and the inversion of the rising major third c–d–e into a descending, rhythmically altered motive a–g–f. This concentration of energy and forward thrust at the conclusion of the eight-bar phrase strongly indicates long-range compositional intent. Moreover, Gershwin overlaps the end of the phrase with an asymmetrical extension—an extension that develops further the new descending-third idea, introduces new pitches, and finally creates a beginning "unit" eleven bars long.

Gershwin's concern with continuity and development may be observed as early as the fourth bar of the piece. Here, at the midpoint of the phrase,

Gershwin presents no relaxing or predictable gesture. Rather, he begins to play with the registral and rhythmic characteristics of his opening motive, perhaps preparing for the transformations introduced at the end of the second half of the phrase and in the following three-bar extension.

The opening eleven-bar "unit" of *An American in Paris* is reworked and developed further in the following longer "unit" of the work. The original eight-bar melody is repeated, but harmonic changes in the accompaniment of its second half further destabilize its "ending" on F (now heard as a seventh above a G-major triad). An elaborate extension follows, this time developing the repeated-note motive, and culminates in a *Vigoroso* passage that disrupts local meter and tonality. In short, whatever one may choose to call these compositional procedures, and however successful one may think them to be, they are not merely the stringing together of "tunes."

The opening of the earlier *Rhapsody*, Gershwin's first major instrumental concert work, owes even less to balanced units and parallel phrase construction than the opening of *An American in Paris*. As shown in example 5.2, the celebrated first melody of the *Rhapsody* (labeled A) is an asymmetrical nine-bar unit that changes key at its conclusion, and its cadential note overlaps the downbeat of the next melodic unit (labeled B). Since neither a repetition of A nor an "answering" phrase to it follows immediately, one might think on first hearing that A is simply an introduction to B, preparing the key of E♭ by emphasizing its dominant. In fact, however, Gershwin has more sophisticated things in mind: the ramifications of this opening passage lead to consequent issues of phrase structure, harmony, and form that affect and illuminate the entire composition.

Melody A, of course, turns out to be the most prominent idea in the first section of the *Rhapsody*, and Gershwin deliberately calculates the "unbalanced," modulatory character of its first appearance to establish paradigms for the rest of this section and the whole work. Uneven phrases of three and five bars are by far the most common compositional units in the first ninety (!) bars of *Rhapsody in Blue*. In fact, bars 77–84 present the first occurrence of consecutive four-bar phrases, and only at rehearsal 9 in the published score are traditionally balanced four-bar phrases arranged in such a way as to suggest a conventional "tune." (And only at rehearsal 9 is the tonality of the work stable for more than two phrases at a time.)

Example 5.2 reveals that the modulations of the opening phrases are anything but random and are clearly related to the harmonies underlying idea A. The modulation up a fourth in the initial melody, B♭ to E♭, engenders a series of harmonic motions by fourths: E♭ to A♭ at rehearsal 2, D♭ to G♭ at rehearsal 3. The fourth is also a central *melodic* interval of idea A, which suggests some congruence between the melodic and harmonic dimensions of Gershwin's musical language. The introductory swoop from F up to b♭ immediately highlights the two central melodic pitches in the first four bars of A, and the next bars ascend by fourths from f to b♭ to e♭ and finally a♭, the new tonic, at rehearsal 2. (The harmony in these bars also moves by

EXAMPLE 5.2

fourths, B♭ to E♭ to A♭, reinforcing the importance of this interval and fore-
casting modulations to come.) Moreover, the opening presentations of A
occur in keys that correspond to the first three pitches of the melody itself:
B♭ (beginning), A♭ (rehearsal 2), and G♭ (rehearsal 3). The progression by
whole tones downward from B♭ continues, after a passage of piano figuration, to the long pedal point on E, beginning in the fifth bar after rehearsal
4. This pedal point arrives via a progression in fourths from F♯ (enharmon-

EXAMPLE 5.2 (*continued*)

ically Gb) to B to E and, after ten bars, goes up another fourth to A—in which key the opening three bars of the A melody recur.

Once the key of A is reached, at three bars before rehearsal 5, the pattern of modulations by fourths finally breaks. Gershwin's choice of this tonality —one half-step removed from the opening Bb—to emphasize over the next forty bars of the piece is surely not accidental. Moreover, the extensive pedal point on E that precedes the arrival on A points to a resolution of structural significance. The answer may lie in the fact that *Rhapsody in Blue* is "about" the exploration of "blue" notes and their half-step relationships, and therefore underlining half-step relationships in the large-scale harmonic workings of the whole makes perfect sense.

The importance of A major in this next portion of the piece does not put an end, however, to modulation and tonal instability. The key of A moves toward C minor, a move that in turn prepares C major, the key that dominates the big second section of the *Rhapsody* (from rehearsal 9 to rehearsal 28). This second section begins with a new melody, the first real sixteen-bar "tune" in the work. However, this melody is heard only once; it heralds more even phrases (measures in multiples of twos), more balanced relationships among phrases, and the tonal stability that characterizes much of the second section. Immediately after the new melody cadences in C major (at rehearsal 11), Gershwin turns his compositional attention to idea B—heard here for the first time since the opening of the piece and now emerging as the second principal melodic idea to be explored.

As shown in example 5.2, idea B is four bars long and, unlike A, tonally stable. When first heard, however, it is apparently under the spell of A, for it is stated only once, its four bars extended to five, and its tonic immediately transformed into the dominant of the forthcoming key of A♭. Only in the second section of the *Rhapsody* does Gershwin thoroughly exploit the even phrase structures and "tune"-like harmonic stability of B—for here the composer sets up a musical contrast to the more rhapsodic behavior of idea A. The more "tune"-like behavior of B makes for a leisurely central section, alleviating—without entirely dissipating—the intensity set up by modulation and irregular phrases. In fact, B provides only contrast, not a norm, and one assumes that the characteristics of the opening section must eventually return.

Indeed, idea A even recurs within this more "tune"-like central section of *Rhapsody in Blue*, but here it shows itself to be under the musical influence of idea B. At rehearsal 22, A is heard in the form of two consecutive four-bar phrases, arranged neatly as antecedent and consequent and remaining unequivocally in the key of C. Eventually, however, the extension of A modulates out of C to E♭ by the fifth bar after rehearsal 23. Two bars later the *Rhapsody* dissolves into a long fanciful passage for solo piano, and the implied "tune"—never allowed to finish—is left behind.

The concluding section of *Rhapsody in Blue* begins, like the central section, by introducing a new melody (at rehearsal 28). Example 5.3 gives this famous melody and shows what a peculiar pop "tune" it would make. The first phrase of the new melody is eight bars long but divided into a strikingly asymmetrical pattern of 2 + 6 bars. Gershwin presents an ascending motive of three notes twice in steady quarter-note motion and then once in an extraordinary variant that simultaneously compresses the motive into ascending adjacent chromatic steps and expands the motive rhythmically into double whole notes. The feeling of quarter-note movement is kept alive against the double whole notes by an obsessive inner voice that inverts the motive's chromatic compression. The pitches d♯–d–c♯ recur again and again in the inner voice, arranged in a repeating rhythmic pattern that coincides exactly with the repeated pitch pattern only at three-bar intervals. Remarkably, Gershwin makes such complex, sophisticated developmental procedures sound spontaneous and effortless. (No wonder Schoenberg admired this composer!)

The second phrase of this new melody starts out repeating the first and continues as if a "balanced," consequent answer to the first, but it turns out to be only six bars long. The final c♯ of the a–b–c♯ double whole-note motive is an unexpected quarter note that also marks the beginning of the next phrase. This dovetailing of the motive with itself is a compositional device

EXAMPLE 5.3

that proves to be considerably important as the section progresses. Eight bars of development follow next (beginning four bars before rehearsal 29) and present brief, balanced, sequential phrases—once again, a restful contrast to an asymmetrical "norm"; the passage serves as a bridge back to the opening phrase of the melody. However—and here the significance of the dovetailing technique emerges—Gershwin has created a melody with a clear beginning but no clear ending, since the opening phrase receives no balanced, completing answers but only developmental continuation. Hence, the melody has no apparent choice other than to keep engendering itself and variants of itself, which is exactly what follows for over 100 bars. The melody's opening phrases, in their original key and characteristic 8 + 6 measure pattern, are heard verbatim only two times in these bars, while the development passages that follow them grow longer and longer.

The most remarkable development of this famous melody is the transformation of its ascending three-note motive into a rapid sixteenth-note figure beginning at rehearsal 33; this figure in turn becomes accompanying figuration to recurrences of the melody's opening phrase at rehearsal 34 and 35. Eventually, the basic motive's tendency to dovetail with itself creates a dizzy, tail-chasing climax at rehearsal 36, by which point the earlier lyrical character of the section has been completely changed to something fit for a rousing conclusion (see example 5.4). (Certainly it could not be accidental that C major blazes forth so suddenly and brilliantly at this climax; Gershwin makes a point of referring back to a key important in the central section of the *Rhapsody* before reiterating themes and keys from the opening section.)

The following conclusion to *Rhapsody in Blue* may seem too abrupt. Still, Gershwin pays respect to large-scale formal symmetry and harmonic rounding by ending with a restatement of the two opening ideas—in their original keys but in reverse order, so that idea B in E♭ leads to the final recurrence of idea A in the "home" key of B♭ major.

This brief overview of the *Rhapsody* demonstrates clearly that Gershwin's instrumental music is more thoroughly and shrewdly calculated in melodic, harmonic, and formal treatment than one might suspect after reading most of the critical literature on the work. A search for "tunes" leads not to small, isolated, closed structures but to rich, open-ended melodic ideas clearly designed for development over large spans of time—melodic ideas filled with harmonic and formal implications that their composer explored impressively.

Turning back now to *An American in Paris*, one can observe how the compositional procedures Gershwin used in the *Rhapsody* changed as he attempted more ambitious concert music and grew in artistic maturity. Like *Rhapsody in Blue*, *An American in Paris* falls into three main sections, the middle section (beginning with the *Andante* after rehearsal 45 and extending through the *Adagio* after rehearsal 68) a more symmetrically phrased and "tune"-ful contrast to the two outer sections. Despite this similarity between the two works, Gershwin appears to have completely rethought how

EXAMPLE 5.4

thematic presentation and recurrence affect formal balance in *An American in Paris*.

The overall form of *An American in Paris* is more convincing than that of the seemingly free-flowing *Rhapsody*. In the later work, the third section is exclusively recapitulatory: all the melodic ideas are introduced by midway through the work's middle section. Such a positioning of musical ideas creates a more balanced impression than one might receive from the *Rhapsody*, where the abrupt and constricted recapitulation can seem like an afterthought—although a harmonically and formally necessary one. Moreover, Gershwin deepens the formal complexity in *An American in Paris* by casting the big middle section in tripartite form, its ABA thematic structure reflecting in miniature the overall ABA shape of the piece.[8]

An American in Paris also reveals Gershwin's use of tempo to create overall formal coherence. Both the opening and concluding sections of the work are marked *Allegretto*. The big middle section of the work arrives not only with a new melody in a fresh key but also with a new tempo: *Andante ma con ritmo deciso*. And the tripartite form of this middle section is reflected in its own arrangement of slow-fast-slow tempi: *Andante* (five measures after rehearsal 45)–*Allegro* (rehearsal 57)–*Grandioso* and *Largo* (rehearsal 65 and 66). Moreover, Gershwin seems to foreshadow and recall tempi much as he does melodies. For example, the slow pace at the start of the middle section is forecast by two brief but striking passages within the opening section of the work, where the initial motive is presented in an abruptly curtailed tempo: at *Molto meno mosso* (rehearsal 19) and at *Calmato* (rehearsal 23). Furthermore, the central *Allegro* in the middle section functions as a reference back to the jauntier tempi that characterize the opening section (and as an anticipation of the final section), just as the *Grandioso* passage before the end of the work (just after rehearsal 76) makes a reference—in tempo as well as theme—back to the central section.

As in the earlier *Rhapsody*, the central section of *An American in Paris* is preceded by a melodic idea (rehearsal 29) that has more "tune"-like characteristics than anything heard before in the work. However, while the new idea in the *Rhapsody* (at rehearsal 9) never recurs, the corresponding idea in *An American in Paris* is pointedly recapitulated in that work's concluding section, thus assuring integration of this melody into the whole fabric of the composition. Significantly, the key of this new melody in *An American in Paris* is E major—a half-step below the tonic F—and Gershwin's apparent penchant for half-step harmonic relationships here reminds one of the importance he attaches to A major—again a half-step below the tonic—in the opening section of *Rhapsody in Blue*.

Gershwin avoids symmetrical and closed melodic structures in *An American in Paris* even more than he does in *Rhapsody in Blue*. The first "tune"-like structure, at rehearsal 29, suggests the conventions of a pop tune without ever fulfilling them. Very long notes at the ends of melodic phrases disrupt symmetry and predictability. The melody commences with two nine-bar phrases, arranged like antecedent and consequent. But the final note of the second phrase is an inconclusive sharped second degree of E major that seems to encourage and energize rather than balance and release the forward thrust of the first phrase (which ends on the *natural* second degree of E major). An asymmetrical "bridge" section of 6 + 8 bars follows and leads to a restatement of the opening two melodic phrases. But this restatement is inevitably inconclusive, rather than rounding or reconfirming, due to the open-ended nature of those two opening phrases. Not surprisingly, when the "bridge" material begins again at rehearsal 36, it leads to further expansion and development, not to resolution. The similarity here to Gershwin's presentation and extension of the big E-major melody in *Rhapsody in Blue* is apparent. Clearly, by the time he wrote *An American in Paris*, Gershwin was thinking in terms of self-generating, ongoing forms, not "tunes," in his concert works and was constructing his melodic materials accordingly.

The two memorable melodies in the middle section of *An American in Paris* generate development and avoid closure in distinctive ways. The first of them, given as example 5.5 (five bars after rehearsal 45), begins with a 4 + 4–bar antecedent-consequent structure. (As in the earlier melody at rehearsal 29, the two opening phrases differ only in their final notes: here, however, the concluding note of the second phrase resolves politely to the tonic. Does the new melody in fact function as a resolution to some of the tension that characterizes the earlier melody by presenting an alternative, tempering idea, one that eschews "irregularity" of pitch progression and phrase length?) The catch in this melody's traditional physiognomy, however, is the little "tag" Gershwin adds to the two phrases. While seemingly reinforcing and confirming the melody's cadence, the "tag" impudently refuses to come to a graceful stop and continues instead to modulation and asymmetrical phrases. This continuation dovetails back into a recurrence of the melody's opening phrase and, by now a familiar Gershwin technique, more development and expansion. After the melody's two main phrases are heard again, the "tag" inaugurates another harmonically restless passage, and consequently the next recurrence of the melody begins in a new key, G major (four bars before rehearsal 51). Here the "tag" sets off a remarkable development passage of modulating three-bar phrases (beginning at *Con moto* after rehearsal 52), culminating in a *Grandioso* series of downward-spiraling sequences derived from the basic motive of the melody.

The *Allegro* at rehearsal 57 introduces the last new melody in *An American in Paris*. Both the phrase structure of this snappy melody and the harmonic progression underlying it are derived from a twelve-bar blues pattern. The melody indeed comes to a tentative end in its eleventh bar on the third scale degree in the key of D, accompanied by clear D-major harmony, making this the most complete-sounding melody in the entire work. Nevertheless, the rhythmic energy of the melody's final two bars does not slacken, and the music drives forward into what promises to be a literal repetition of the twelve-bar "tune." The promise is broken, however, for the melody is foreshortened to ten bars and proceeds directly into an apparent "bridge" section of an AABA song form. But after twelve bars that should turn around to a final restatement of the main melody, the "bridge" dissolves into twenty-five bars of new material—a lush, sexy Charleston developing motives from the main melody. When that main melody finally returns, it avoids conclusion and becomes instead developmental transition to a recurrence of the earlier *Andante* melody that rounds out the middle section.

Like *Rhapsody in Blue*, *An American in Paris* shows clear evidence of large-scale harmonic shaping—more so, in fact, than the earlier work. A few examples, taken from the middle section of the piece, must suffice.

To begin with, Gershwin established the home tonality of F in *An American in Paris* much more thoroughly and systematically than the home key of B♭ in the *Rhapsody*; the opening and concluding sections of *An American in Paris* are anchored firmly in F. The middle section begins with the *Andante* theme in B♭, a fourth above the tonic, and ends with a recurrence of

EXAMPLE 5.5

that same melodic idea in C, a fourth below the tonic. Thus, the two framing keys of the middle section are symmetrically related to the tonic F in subdominant and dominant relationships.

Within the middle section, the progression of keys from B♭ to C owes less to conventional harmonic movement than to Gershwin's fascinating manipulation of the pitch relationships involving "blue notes" that occur so frequently in his melodic lines and their accompaniments. The "blue" third, d♭, is particularly prominent in the initial presentation of the *Andante* melody (see example 5.5), and the accompanying harmonies emphasize the "blue" seventh, a♭. However, the two most prominent pitches throughout this passage are unquestionably f and b♭. Can it be caprice that when this melody travels to new keys, its first stop is G—the key in which B♭ and F remain prominent in the texture as "blue" third and "blue" seventh? Moreover, in the move to G major, d♮ replaces d♭ and a♮ replaces a♭. Since the music eventually reaches an *Allegro* in D major, where d and a are important pitches in both melody and harmony, surely these evolving pitch relationships cannot be serendipitous.

And there are other examples of systematic harmonic movement in *An American in Paris*. The initial modulation in the middle section, down a minor third from B♭ to G, becomes a crucial harmonic template for the long developmental passage starting directly after G major is left behind (two bars after rehearsal 52). The sequence of keys here moves rapidly *upward* by minor thirds, from D to F to A♭ to B and to D again; a long pedal point on F supports the *Grandioso* climax before rehearsal 55. Finally, the new *Allegro* melody introduced at rehearsal 57 refers to the f♮ so prominent throughout the first part of the middle section (and, of course, throughout the entire work): Gershwin explicitly calls for the melody's trills in the sixth and seventh bars to involve the "blue" third of d. And the harmony throughout this passage emphasizes the "blue" seventh, C♮, the key heard at the end of the middle section. There are obviously compositional strategies at work here, strategies sensitive to the long-range relationships of certain crucial pitches.

Is Gershwin working with some specific melodic and harmonic *system* in his music? At this point, I cannot profess to know the answer to this question; it will take much listening, analysis, and study by many musicians to establish a credible answer. Yet the fact that the question even suggests itself says much about the level of compositional sophistication, complexity, and integrity revealed by even the abbreviated look at the music I have attempted here. That such characteristics should exist in Gershwin's concert music will surprise only those whose preconceptions about Gershwin have discouraged them from looking at this music seriously, or those who have hastily and inattentively mistaken the composer's authentic richness and complexity for lack of traditional constructive skill.

On the other hand, those who have tried to play a typical Gershwin song chart should not be surprised. They know that Gershwin's "pop" music reveals melodic and harmonic sophistication that sets it apart from comparable examples by any of Gershwin's contemporaries. Gershwin's music is *complicated* music; his great gift was to make it *sound* as if it isn't. (I confess I find the comparison to Mozart apt.) It only stands to reason that Gershwin would carry over his gifts for intricacy and complexity from his songs into his instrumental works, adding compositional interest in the formal possibilities afforded by the larger scope and greater freedom inherent in concert music. By the time he felt ready to undertake the work that would become the crowning achievement of his career, *Porgy and Bess*, Gershwin was prepared to combine the control of large-scale musical structures cultivated in his concert music with his preeminent skills as a songwriter; the resulting unique work synthesized all aspects of the composer's musical language and talents. Throughout his career, Gershwin revealed himself as a canny and craft-conscious composer. It is about time that he started to receive credit for those characteristics.

Nothing I have written here should be construed to imply that Gershwin's concert music is above criticism. *Rhapsody in Blue* is unquestionably an "immature" and somewhat rambling piece, although it is far from the formless morass described by Bernstein and others. *An American in Paris* is remarkably tighter than the *Rhapsody*; still, its big opening section may seem to wander a bit, especially when compared to its wonderfully compact and effective closing section. But meaningful criticism can only begin in an environment free of preconceptions. It can flourish only when an appropriate vocabulary has been developed for describing and analyzing the musical style of a composer and the musical forms of his oeuvre in a manner compatible with the musical data found in his scores. Clearly, such meaningful criticism of Gershwin's concert music has yet to be born.

Notes

1. Leonard Bernstein's essay "Why Don't You Run Upstairs and Write a Nice Gershwin Tune?," which originally appeared in *Atlantic Monthly* 195 (April 1955): 39–42, was reprinted in his *The Joy of Music* (New York: Simon & Schuster, 1959). The page references to *The Joy of Music* in this essay refer to its 1967 reprint (New York: Signet).

2. Ibid., 53.

3. Ibid., 52.

4. Ibid., 53.

5. Crawford's article is in H. Wiley Hitchcock and Stanley Sadie, eds., *The New Grove Dictionary of American Music* (London: Macmillan, 1986), 2: 199–205; the quoted passage is on p. 203.

6. Hitchcock and Sadie, *New Grove Dictionary of American Music*, 2: 203.

7. Crawford himself wrote tellingly about the perception of Gershwin in "serious" musical circles in his article "Gershwin's Reputation: A Note on *Porgy and Bess*," *Musical Quarterly* 65 (1979): 257–64.

8. Formal symmetry in *An American in Paris* extends even further. The B portion of the work's middle section is itself in a kind of tripartite ABA form. Furthermore, the internal proportions of the ABA forms on all levels are analogous: the opening A and the contrasting B portions always have approximately equal weight, while the final recapitulatory A portion is always much shorter in duration.

Gershwin's Blue Monday *(1922)* and the Promise of Success

JOHN ANDREW JOHNSON

By nearly all accounts, George Gershwin's "American folk opera" *Porgy and Bess* is among his greatest achievements, certainly his magnum opus, challenging for performers and audiences alike. The task of composing *Porgy and Bess* was unusually laborious for Gershwin as well, requiring more than two years of concentrated effort, due largely to the sheer size of the work — its lengthy libretto, big cast, and full-scale orchestration. The enormity of the undertaking even encouraged him to expand and develop his compositional technique with various teachers, including Joseph Schillinger. For Gershwin had a lot at stake in *Porgy and Bess*: fulfilling a public expectation to produce another musical coup d'ètat along the lines of his previous concert hall successes.[1] And *Porgy and Bess*, Gershwin's admitted "labor of love," posed a problem with which he would grapple considerably — the exacting of a faithful embodiment of his fascination with DuBose Heyward's story of Charleston blacks.[2] Fully ten years earlier, however, in "the heyday of the new jazz," when "Gotham was in the midst of a concurrent Negrophilia," Gershwin was already pondering opera and, earlier still, the role of black cultural expression in his own vernacular experience.[3]

The most important result of the composer's early thoughts on these issues is *Blue Monday*, a one-act "Opera Ala Afro-American," which Gershwin with lyricist B. G. DeSylva pieced together in five days for inclusion in George White's girlie revue *The Scandals of 1922*. It took persistence and

111

flexibility from composer and lyricist to gain the producer's approval, and even then White did little to promote this unusual skit.[4] The subtitle is first found in Will Vodery's 1922 orchestration (discussed later), where the heading atop page 1 reads: "*Blue Monday* (Opera Ala Afro American) by Geo Gershwin"; the line below reads: "*Scored by Will H Voder[y]*." (The last letter of Vodery's name was cut off when Gershwin bound the score later.) Since no program of the 1922 *Scandals* has been found, the positioning of *Blue Monday* in he show cannot be pinpointed. Wayne Shirley suggests "the finale of Act I," but that spot was clearly occupied by "I'll Build a Stairway to Paradise," elaborately staged (with costumes by chic designer Erté) as "The Patent Leather Forest."[5] Given White's initial objections to the complications posed by *Blue Monday*'s blackface garb, the "opera" must have followed the intermission, thus opening act 2, followed by Gershwin, DeSylva, and E. Ray Goetz's comic "Where Is the Man of My Dreams?" performed by Winnie Lightner.[6] DeSylva's melodramatic plot, essentially a gloss on Leoncavallo's *I pagliacci* (1892), was apparently too heavy for White and his audience.[7] Thus, despite a strongly supportive review following *The Scandals*'s tryout in New Haven, Gershwin's *Blue Monday*, its second-act opening feature, was dropped after a single performance once the revue opened on Broadway. Gershwin appears simply to have taken this early, critical defeat in stride and gone on to other projects and greater fame. If anything, he distanced himself from *Blue Monday*'s questions by simplifying the story of its premiere, evident in his description contained in his letter to Isaac Goldberg, dated 15–16 June 1931: "The show opened and the opera went well—its only drawback for the show being its tragic ending. . . . Mr. White took it out after that, because he said the audience was too depressed by the tragic ending to get into the mood of the lighter stuff that followed."[8] This account contradicts the idea, prevalent in the Gershwin biographies, although not always so strongly put, that *Blue Monday* was "a total failure."[9] Shortly after Gershwin's death, perhaps with an eye toward preserving his brother's legacy, Ira Gershwin reinterpreted Gershwin's recollections: "Lasting only one night it was eliminated not because it was ineffective artistically but because it changed the mood of the audience."[10]

But stylistic idioms prevalent in *Blue Monday* resurface in the composer's oeuvre: two years later in *Rhapsody in Blue* (1924) and finally in *Porgy and Bess*, which, in retrospect and in a very raw sense, seems an expansion of *Blue Monday*'s model informed by ten years of experience and study.

Kinship between *Blue Monday* and *Rhapsody in Blue* hinges on common use of Gershwin's characteristic jazzy, bluesy rhetoric of the 1920s—snazzy syncopated figures and ornaments, call-and-response patterns, bold skips in melodic lines, pentatonic collections juxtaposed against expressive blue notes, and novel choices of instruments—all features of early jazz appropriated for the theater and concert hall. Striking examples are found throughout the opening "Prologue" of *Blue Monday*.[11] (See examples 6.1a–c.) Elsewhere, Gershwin's 1920s style is not hard to locate. The title song from *Blue*

EXAMPLES 6.1a–c George Gershwin. Passages in "Prologue," from *Blue Monday* (1922), evocative of *Rhapsody in Blue* (1924): 1a) 1[+2]-1[+5]; 1b) 1[+14]; 1c) 2[-5]-2[-2]

1a: Opening theme

1b: Clarinet cadenza

1c: Bridge passage in strings

Monday, "Blue Monday Blues" (example 6.2a), for instance, is very similar to another Gershwin work, "The Half of It, Dearie, Blues" (example 6.2b), written with Ira Gershwin and premiered by Fred Astaire in *Lady, Be Good!* (1924).[12] Neither of these songs are true blues; rather, their texts and music evoke the blues. They are *bluesy* and demonstrate what Abbe Niles termed "blues song," pieces "in free form but with a liberal admixture of blues philosophy or musical tricks."[13] Such a description fits examples 6.2a–b perfectly, since each juxtaposes blues idioms against the conventions of Broadway song—although the harmonic language of example 6.2a contains distillates of an earlier age in its "barbershop harmony" of extended tertian sonorities. The songs' strongest claim to the blues genre is simply their titles, and in this regard "Blue Monday Blues" is more germane.[14] Each song seems to begin with a twelve-bar blues, but the blues pattern does not end

EXAMPLE 6.2a Gershwin, "Blue Monday Blues" (B. G. DeSylva, text), from *Blue Monday*: First refrain

			Mm.	Db
	A/A'			
Mike:	I must admit although I [b3]ª don't like Sunday	a	1–2	I–IV
	I have a fit when I go [b3] through Blue Monday	a	3–4	I–vi
	B1/B2			
	Monday's the one day that my dice lose—	b	5–6	II⁹–I
	They just re-[b7]fuse!	b	7–8	I–V
	C1/C2			
	That's when my cares are always bigger—	c	9–10	IV–iv
Mike:	Sweep on you lazy nigger!ᵇ	c	11–12	I–11⁷
	D			
Sam:	[b3]I got the Blue Monday Blues!	b	13–16	iv–I

a. The notes in square brackets refer to the text immediately following them.

b. Bassman's score changed this line to "His cares are always bigger" (cf. Gershwin/Bassman, "Blue Monday," 8). Other revisions of DeSylva's text will be discussed later.

EXAMPLE 6.2b Gershwin, "The Half of It, Dearie, Blues" (Ira Gershwin), from *Lady, Be Good!* (1924): First chorus

				Eb
	A			
Dick:	I've got the You-Don't-Know-the-Half-of-It-[b3]Dearie Blues	a	1–4	I–I
	A'			
	The trouble is you have so many from whom to choose.	a	5–8	I–I
	B			
	If you should marry	b	9	IV
	[b6 as b3]Tom, Dick or Harry,	b	10	iv
	Life would be the bunk—	c	11	I
	I'd become a monk.	c	12	V
	A			
	I've got the You-Don't-Know-the-Half-of-It-[b3]Dearie Blues!	a	13–16	I–I

in the "correct" place, the tonic. Instead, each ends with a half cadence on a dominant chord (II₇ and V respectively), setting up a four-bar tag in which the song's title, or slogan, is iterated. The pieces sound bluesy at points simply because their melodic lines contain many blue notes and their accompaniment follows the typical blues move from the subdominant to the tonic.[15] The texts of each song contain the rhyming patter of the blues, but the typical AAB blues text structure, where B represents a denouement, is subverted within the through-composed structure of "Blue Monday Blues" and the AA'BA form of "The Half of It, Dearie, Blues." Generally, however, it is the sentiments of the two texts that make them least blueslike, especially the later piece, with its Ira Gershwinisms (the Gilbert-like use of popular jargon).

For comparison, consider Antoine "Fats" Domino's version of the "blue Monday" idea in a "list song" (ironically, prevalent in Broadway and Hollywood film musicals in nonblues forms) titled "Blue Monday":

Introduction (two bars)

Measures 1–8:

Blue Monday, how are ya', Blue Monday?
Got to work like a slave all day.
Here comes Tuesday, oh hard Tuesday,
I'm so tired, got no time to play.

Measures 9–16:

Here come Wednesday, I be to my south.
My gal call, got to tell her that I'm out
'Cause Thursday is a hard workin' day
And Friday I get my pay.

Measures 17–24, the refrain:

Saturday mornin', oh Saturday mornin'.
All my tiredness has gone away.
Got my money, and my honey,
And I'm out on the stand to play.

Measures 25–32:

Sunday morning my head is bad,
'Though it's worth it for the time that I've had.
But I've got to get my rest,
'Cause Monday is a mess.

After an instrumental break, the refrain is repeated.[16] In short, these early-ish Gershwin songs evoke blues by mere intimations of sadness ("poor me" texts accompanied by major-minor rubs of melodic blue notes against major chords, and sudden shifts of modality from major to minor at the ends of phrases).[17]

The similarities and differences between *Blue Monday* and *Porgy and Bess* are even more striking. Both are based upon white men's views of black culture and were produced for predominantly white audiences. In light of these facts, many authors have found fundamental flaws in both works—in *Porgy and Bess* because it is billed as "an American folk opera," thus suggesting "authenticity" (most apparent in its black cast), and in *Blue Monday* because it plays up well-established hokum routines (most apparent in its use of blackface). Both works strive toward opera in their use of recitative rather than spoken dialogue. In *Blue Monday* these settings are stiff at best, whereas the recitatives in *Porgy and Bess* are full-blown attempts to maintain a truly operatic artifice where characters literally burst into song. One reviewer from the period, who obviously had not heard Scott Joplin's *Treemonisha* (1911), was perhaps more prophetic than he realized when he praised *Blue Monday*'s "new and free ragtime [not as currently understood, but as a catchall term for mixtures of early jazz and bluesy music, as well as ragtime itself] recitative."[18] And Gershwin, in his 15–16 June 1931 letter to Goldberg, seemed to be proud of this first attempt at recitative writing: "I believe this work was the first ever to use recitative in the 'blues' idiom."[19] Both scores contain true popular songs, but in the earlier work these are not so intimately tied to the action. Songs such as "I Loves You, Porgy" and "Bess, You Is My Woman Now," despite some memorable renditions over the years, are inextricably tied to the *Porgy and Bess* drama.[20]

Further, despite the shows' vast size differences, Gershwin demonstrates his ability to control the musical pace of each show in rather similar ways, balancing slow, minor-key moments of repose with up-tempo, jazzy numbers, setting the cast in motion and shaking up the audience.[21] Again, early moments in the *Blue Monday* score are instructive. Few would fail to recall the considerably more complicated (via crossing twos and threes) "African drumming" of *Porgy and Bess*'s "I Ain't Got No Shame" (examples 6.3b–d), for instance, when listening to the first two measures of *Blue Monday* (example 6.3a).[22] Gershwin's rhythmic thinking had developed considerably in the decade that separates these two works. Still, in both cases he turns to the startling sound of drums (in example 6.3d, the orchestra acts like a large drumming group) to grab the attention of the audience.

A quick glance at the hokum-inspired, happy-go-lucky air of the accompaniment segueing from the end of *Blue Monday*'s "Prologue" to the beginning of the dialogue, with cafe owner Sam's entrance (example 6.3e), suggests a similar spot in *Porgy*'s immortal "banjo song" (example 6.3f).[23] Clearly by the time Gershwin set about composing *Porgy and Bess* in 1933, having read DuBose Heyward's novel *Porgy* as early as 1926, his compositional mind had roamed over the musical landscape of *Blue Monday*, recalling passages that would suggest similar musical ideas in his later work.[24]

The scripts and characters of the two works are remarkably similar as well. Both are set, so to speak, on the "black side" of town: in *Blue Monday*, Harlem, and in *Porgy and Bess*, the tenements of "Catfish Row" (née Charleston's Cabbage Row) and "Kittiwah Island" (the Carolina sea island Kiawah).[25] Both stories have central female leads: Bess in *Porgy and Bess* is analogous to Vi in *Blue Monday*. Both women frequent seedy locales and cajole with low-down types. Both Bess and Vi are caught in love triangles between flawed men (Crown-Bess-Porgy, Joe-Vi-Sam), but they respond to their situations in very different ways. Out of jealousy, Vi murders her man Joe (that is *Blue Monday*'s simple plot). Bess, on the other hand, although nearly tempted to violence (for example, during Crown's advances following the picnic, and during Sporting Life's temptations with his infamous "happy dust" as she is trying to clean herself up), ultimately is subservient to men, turning her

EXAMPLE 6.3a Gershwin, "Prologue," from Blue Monday; 1-1[+1]

EXAMPLES 6.3b–d Gershwin, "I Ain't Got No Shame," act 2, scene 2, from *Porgy and Bess* (1935): 3b) 127[+17]-127[+20], 3c) 128[-6]-128[-3], 3d) 130[-2]-130[-1]

EXAMPLE 6.3.b

EXAMPLE 6.3c

EXAMPLE 6.3d

EXAMPLE 6.3e Gershwin, *Blue Monday*; 9-9[+2]

EXAMPLE 6.3f Gershwin, "I Got Plenty o' Nuttin'," act 2, scene 1, from *Porgy and Bess*: 13–13[+1]

rage inward in a fit of delirium.[26] Two of *Porgy and Bess*'s characters, Sporting Life and the on-stage pianist Jasbo Brown, are roughly paralleled in composite in *Blue Monday*'s Cokey Lou.[27]

Although they approach matters from opposite directions, both stories play upon perceived cultural differences between the urban East and the Deep South—inhabitants of the former as slick and exciting, of the latter as excessively sentimental and given to superstition and blind faith. In both stories, the characters work at menial jobs, wasting their pay on the whim of the alley crap game.

Not much of this information is new to Gershwin scholars, who have known and written about *Blue Monday* for years. All the Gershwin biographies, beginning with Goldberg's in 1931, tell the *Blue Monday*/*135th Street* story in varying degrees of completeness and accuracy due to source limitations and, sometimes, biases. David Ewen, whose discussion is based on Goldberg yet draws some interesting conclusions, mistakenly cites a "1936" performance of *135th Street*.[28] This error probably repeats that contained in Ferde Grofé's "George Gershwin's Influence," contained in the Armitage memorial volume.[29] Generally, views regarding *Blue Monday* have become more supportive as musicians have learned more about it. As Robert Kimball observed: "Occasional revivals have partly dispelled the impression that it [*135th Street*] was an immature work."[30] This stance is completely opposite Ewen's reading (p. 140) of the situation thirty years earlier. In 1973, Edward Jablonski and Lawrence Stewart called the music "often groping," whereas Jablonski's more recent view (referring specifically to the title song), "good if not great Gershwin," seems more tempered.[31] Deena Rosenberg's study, while not exhaustive in its treatment of *Blue Monday*, is up-to-date and largely unbiased, accurately summarizing that "while the libretto is simplistic and dated, the music is still dramatically suggestive."[32] Joan Peyser's book, while interesting and not without merit, is fraught with methodological problems. Regarding Al Jolson's interest in *Porgy*, for instance, Peyser states: "Jolson's persistent and continued interest in *Porgy* could have been precipitated by his concern that once blacks began to appear in shows created and produced by whites, Jolson's role as the most successful blackface in show business would be finished. He must have sensed this when he ordered George White to kill Gershwin's *Blue Monday Blues* back in the 1922 Scandals."[33] While there may be some truth to this assertion, *Blue Monday* did not compromise Jolson's profession but rather supported it. Jolson surely had associations with *Blue Monday*. "W. S.," in reviewing the first performance of the New Haven tryout, places Jolson there.[34] Also, Whiteman's 1925 performance cast Jolson's wife Blossom Seeley in the role of Vi. No evidence, however, confirms that Jolson was behind White's decision to cut *Blue Monday*, even if he was a financial backer of the revue. Further, it is embellishing to suggest that upon seeing a single performance of *Blue Monday* in 1922, or others in 1925, Jolson somehow knew *Porgy and Bess* was coming.

So even during Gershwin's lifetime, the piece did not fail to be revived after White's first staging. Paul Whiteman, whose Palais Royal Orchestra had turned out to be the real stars of the 1922 edition of the *Scandals*, was apparently so taken with Gershwin's little opera that he sought to foster his own career with *Blue Monday* as both credit toward Gershwin's compositional promise and as perhaps a work whose time was yet to come.[35] Whiteman's decision to solicit a "jazz concerto" from Gershwin (eventually *Rhapsody in Blue*) as the showpiece for his famous 1924 "Experiment in Modern Music" concern seems as much attributable to *Blue Monday*'s promise in Whiteman's mind as to the impresario's careful monitoring of Gershwin's growing publicity power. Goldberg, drawing upon Gershwin's letter, confirms the idea that *Blue Monday* led Whiteman toward *Rhapsody in Blue*: "To this day [ca. mid-1931], as Whiteman had told George, he likes the themes of the black opera better than those of the *Rhapsody in Blue*. When, then, he planned his ascent to Carnegie Hall [that is, presumably *from* Aeolian Hall or locales such as the Globe Theatre], he chose as *pièces de résistance* Deems Taylor's *Circus Days* and a slightly modified version of *Blue Monday Blues* that he rechristened, from its locale, *135th Street*."[36] Merle Armitage recounts things similarly.[37] Although Whiteman does not mention *Blue Monday* in his Armitage essay, he was clear (if problematic) about how he felt about Gershwin around this time: "I felt that George could write the thing I needed. Something that would show that jazz had progressed. Something that would illustrate that it was a great deal more than savage rhythm from the jungle."[38] In later years, Ira Gershwin confirmed the connection. Peyser quotes (without complete citation) his letter to the editor, dated 28 February 1949, of an unnamed newspaper: "If *Rhapsody in Blue* owes anything to anything it is to '135th Street,' a one-act blues opera my brother wrote in 1922. This work so impressed Paul Whiteman that two years later he asked my brother to write a piece for what turned out to be the (you'll pardon the expression) historic concert given at Aeolian Hall, Feb. 12th, 1924."[39] Most writings from Gershwin's lifetime, especially the reviews immediately following the performances, refer to the 1922 version of the work as *Blue Monday Blues*, not simply *Blue Monday*, as Gershwin's sketch-score has it. "135th Street" seems to have become the adopted (even by the Gershwin brothers) title to refer to the work after 1925. When Gershwin acquired Vodery's 1922 score he had it bound with a cover sheet (written in his hand) and spine reading "135th Street," and his examples for Goldberg also bear the heading "135th Street." This designation was perhaps a matter of simple preference, but it may have been chosen to avoid confusion with the most successful song of the show, "Blue Monday Blues." Moreover, Gershwin may have wished to distance the work from its 1922 flop status, moving it instead toward its more "serious" presentation at Carnegie Hall.

Thus, in 1925, when Whiteman sought to reproduce the success of his initial "experiment," he naturally returned to Gershwin, this time *Blue Monday* itself, now reorchestrated by Ferde Grofé (who had orchestrated *Rhapsody in Blue* the year before) and retitled *135th Street* (reflecting its Harlem setting), for a pair of performances, without sets and costumes, at Carnegie Hall.[40] Like *Blue Monday*, however, *135th Street* met with lukewarm responses.[41] No other productions of the work appeared during the composer's lifetime.

It is strange, then, that a work so seemingly insignificant (seven performances) in the context of Gershwin's professional career should have been given so much attention in the Warner Brothers' 1945 film biography *Rhapsody in Blue*.[42] As currently available on videocassette, the film contains 5'04" of *Blue Monday* and only 2'02" of *Porgy and Bess*, amounting to a patchwork of highlights from the former work and merely a reprise of *Porgy and Bess*'s "Summertime" (presumably Bess's, since Anne Brown is the singer here). The film does not use blackface of the Jolson-Cantor type; rather, the characters are made up with something on the order of a heavy dose of Quick-Tan. The film erroneously implies that *Blue Monday* was part of the *Scandals of 1924* (opened New York, 30 June 1924), a show that did not open before the Aeolian Hall concert it precedes in the film. The film *Rhapsody in Blue* is a fascinating document in many ways, much in need of scholarly attention.[43] One particularly strange moment occurs during *Blue Monday*'s mini-finale, the "spiritual" "I'm Going to See My Mother": white audience members, in orchestra seats, are seen grimacing as if the number were corny, yet a black couple, huddled in the balcony, are cameoed crying, presumably at the "honesty" of the number's sentimentality. In this storybook tale of Gershwin's life, *Blue Monday* is a more prominent feature than its clearly more remarkable progeny, *Porgy and Bess*. Why, and what can *Blue Monday* reveal about Gershwin's "serious" musical thinking in the early 1920s, before the string of successes in the concert hall, the roots of his meteoric compositional development? Getting at answers to these questions means setting *Blue Monday*'s record straight and, in the process, unpacking the implications of Gershwin's first opera during his lifetime and since.

Blue Monday's reputation has been tangled over the years due to two factors. First, like so many youthful efforts by other composers, early works are often low on the list of priorities for scholars, perhaps providing interesting anecdotes for those sketchy early years of the biography, but ultimately overshadowed by the proverbial later, greater works.[44] Gershwin's case is particularly problematic, however, since none of his works is truly "late" in the sense of reflecting a fully matured compositional mind.[45] Since Gershwin left so few completed pieces, all of them assume a greater role in appreciating his style. Second, the primary sources on which to build a scholarly analysis of *Blue Monday* have surfaced piecemeal over the years, so a thorough investigation of the work has not been possible. Fortunately, recent acquisition by the Library of Congress of the Gershwins' scrapbooks, along with some key sources for Whiteman's 1925 version and a production from the early days of television, makes wholesale assessment of the work, as Gershwin himself knew it, considerably less opaque, if still not wholly complete.[46]

The Sources

The extant sources for *Blue Monday* and *135th Street* fall into several chronological layers corresponding to the disparate productions of the work during Gershwin's lifetime and since.[47] The temporal distance between productions speaks much to the overt differences among the groups of sources, which survive as a kind of narrative: from the work's origins in blackface "vaudeville" to the so-called historical performance movement of today.[48] From the original 1922 original production, two important sources remain: (1) Gershwin's pencil sketch-score and, from this, "(2) Will Vodery's ink orchestration for Whiteman's *Scandals* orchestra.[49] Neither of these sources, unfortunately, contains a complete text. Therefore one cannot say definitively just what the 1922 script was.

A more complete collection of sources is available for Whiteman's 1925 version of the work as *135th Street*. Along with those sources cited earlier, which were clearly reused, these new items consist of Ferde Grofé's reorchestration of Vodery's score to suit a differently constituted Whiteman Orchestra; two copies (one of which is lightly corrected) of DeSylva's revised libretto, entitled "135th Street. A Glorified Mammy Song"; and a brief but valuable letter from DeSylva to Gershwin regarding this revival.[50] A third and last layer of primary material from the composer's lifetime dates from 1931, when Gershwin responded to Isaac Goldberg's query regarding this curious piece while Goldberg was working on his biography of the composer.[51]

Additional manuscripts correspond to three posthumous layers: the 1945 biopic *Rhapsody in Blue*; a 1953 CBS television production of the work, with yet another new orchestration and revised texts, both presumably the work of conductor George Bassman; and a 1976 copy of Bassman's score, with additional revisions in the text, deposited for copyright in connection with the premiere recording of the work by the Gregg Smith Singers. These sources are part of the Library of Congress's unprocessed Gershwin Collection cache (hereafter LC/GC-Un) cited earlier. An additional item in these folders is an 18 March 1953 letter to Ira Gershwin from William Spier of the Ford Foundation, who was the moving force behind Ford's *Omnibus* television production. Although the show reached a then exploding television audience, it aired only once (for a half hour) on a midspring afternoon (19 March 1953, 4:30–5:00 P.M.). Perhaps following concurrent success of *Porgy and Bess*, this performance used a black cast, including Jimmy Rushing (from the Count Basie band) as Joe and Warren Coleman (Crown in the 1940s Cheryl Crawford revival of *Porgy and Bess*) as Mike.[52] As Shirley has pointed out, it is through the Gregg Smith version that most listeners came to know *Blue Monday*—but this version is far afield from Gershwin's original, lacking, most of all, live bodies on stage.

Collectively, these sources reveal several things about the creation of *Blue Monday* and attempts to revive the work in spite of its dated material. Spier's letter cited in the preceding paragraph concerns revision of the script and concludes, "I think there can be nothing objectionable remaining." Aside from changes of key and minor alterations of the musical text (amounting to Bassman's so described "adaptation"), the changes reflected in these sources are textual. The 1976 Bassman score (a misleading label, given that the score was clearly produced more than twenty years earlier), a photocopy on 8.5" × 11" paper with no marginalia, revises (as described earlier regarding "Blue Monday Blues") De Sylva's 1925 text in interior sections of the work. The ca. 1953 version of the same score, a photostat on large orchestra paper, contains corrections in red that reflect and highlight (for reference purposes) those passages that have been revised. This score was clearly assembled early in the television production: it differs from an unattributed typescript (clearly copied directly from DeSylva, 1925), on blue paper, that takes the text revisions further. Spier's letter confirms that he is probably responsible for these revisions, and they appear to be in the same ink with which he signed his letter (for instance, on the title page, where DeSylva's "Glorified Mammy Song" subtitle has been typed in but struck through). These new changes now affect the "Prologue": "Mike's colored saloon" becomes "Mike's Harlem saloon," and "the white man's opera" becomes "every any [*sic*] old opera." The 1953 Bassman score was made with knowledge of the 1945 film text, since its title page contains the following note (beneath the "Libretto and Lyrics" credit): "Version used in this score is the same as that employed in the Warner Bros. production 'Rhapsody in Blue.'" So DeSylva's 1925 text was revised by the time of the 1945 film. In 1953, these socially conscious corrections were taken further. The 1976 recording picked up the process but strangely restored "the white man's opera" passage, here playing up the work's blackface roots despite the fact that Smith's liner notes state, "We make no attempt at creating a 'Black Opera.'"[53] Gershwin's 1931 recollections about the work's genesis explain the appearance of the 1922 items: the rough character of the sketch-score looks like "five days and nights" of hurried work. Yet the formal nature of the scores, at least by *Scandals* standards, demonstrates at least some prior planning and consideration.[54]

Concluding that Gershwin had loftier-than-usual intentions with *Blue Monday* requires some qualification. Regardless of how it was labeled, *Blue Monday* was written for a revue, where pastiche is the rule, not the exception. Nonetheless, several "classical" idioms appear in the sketch-score. First, Gershwin quotes Mendelssohn's "Wedding March" in a number that was subsequently cut by the time of Vodery's orchestration.[55] Second, and far more unusual and significant, Gershwin decided to reuse one of his "serious" compositions, namely the *Lullaby* for string quartet (ca. 1919), in various ways: as a brief release of tension in the opening "Prologue" when the thrust and tone of the text changes; prominently as the accompaniment for Vi's solo "Has Anyone Seen My Joe"; and perhaps as a melodic wellspring for the show's single "spiritual," Joe's "I'm Going to See My Mother," which occurs at the nexus of the story and returns as the work's finale.[56] The melodic affinities between the main themes of *Lullaby* as quoted in *Blue Monday* and "I'm Going Home to See My Mother" (cf. in Gershwin/Bassman, "Blue Monday," rehearsal 7 and rehearsal 56 respectively) amount to their plaintive qualities (each begins on $\hat{3}$ and moves toward $\hat{6}$), which result from largely conjunct motion (thirds in "I'm Going" give it its folksy, "spiritual" quality) and lack of melodic chromaticism, except toward their centers (rehearsal 7 [+3] and rehearsal 56 [+10]), where melodic spikes (major seventh and major sixth, pivoting up to an augmented second to E major; and augmented fourth, abruptly shifting up a minor second to C major) are used to turn the phrases toward their conclusions. If, as I suggested earlier, Gershwin was fond of the *Lullaby* theme, it would not be surprising that he would derive the finale-spiritual from his first opera from it—after all, the soothing qualities of most lullabies and spirituals are ideologically similar.

Gershwin's usual practice of drawing upon his famous "tune books" for songs (especially hits) appears nowhere in evidence between the *Blue Monday* sketch and the early tune books, but this lack of evidence does not preclude his having followed this Broadwayish practice.[57] Aside from the borrowings, then, *Blue Monday* appears to be a new composition from top to bottom.[58] A third instance of allusion to serious idioms arises in DeSylva's libretto, where an opening "Prologue" clearly evokes and must satirize *I pagliacci* and other works of *verismo*.[59] For this passage Gershwin provided a handful of quasi-leitmotifs, although their treatment is more incidental than dramatically weighted and, perhaps due to the brevity of the work, they are not developed significantly later in the score.

Vodery's orchestral score was secured by Gershwin sometime following the 1922 production. In fact, Gershwin kept Vodery's score in his library, presumably as "the" *Blue Monday* score, binding it in the same leather-edged, gold-embossed covers that characterize his archiving of the autographs of his other concert works. Clearly, Whiteman's 1925 concert performances drew upon Vodery's orchestration and slightly revised libretto by DeSylva. Grofé's score follows Vodery's closely, save for some dramatic changes in orchestration.[60] DeSylva's new script, however, attempts to reconstruct the original text as closely as possible, as DeSylva described to Gershwin in a letter dated one month prior to the Whiteman concert:

> Dear George:
> Just a line, as I take my hasty departure, to beg you to take what I send you and make it fit your excellent music. The thing isn't all I wanted to make it, but lack of time prevents me improving it.
> As you will notice, I was unable to remember bits of it and re-wrote it as best I could.
> I hope it goes over—particularly for Paul's sake.
> See that Mr. Coppicus gets the missing lines so that he can extract the parts for rehearsal. . . .
> You are surely on the crest of a wave. . . .
> Buddy[61]

So when DeSylva directs Gershwin to "fit" this revised libretto to his music, and look up the "missing lines," he is apparently referring to the composer's sketch-score, since on page 3 of DeSylva's libretto a note reads, "For lines that go here, see score," and the lines are indeed found hastily penciled in the score at the appropriate spot.[62] Seemingly, then, Gershwin's sketch was still, at least for him, a working document for the 1925 production, and some of the corrections found there may correspond to this later performance, not the 1922 original. Despite his other commitments, Gershwin was apparently still involved with the Whiteman production by mid-December. The photograph reproduced in Robert Kimball and Alfred Simon's *The Gershwins* shows Taylor, Whiteman, Grofé, Seeley, and Gershwin peering over a score that could be Gershwin's sketch-score. The paper seems about the right size and thickness. A bold circular mark at the tip of Whiteman's pen in the photograph, however, does not seem to correspond to any point in the sketch. Whiteman may be doodling on a separate piece of paper atop the score, or they may be looking at an entirely different piece.[63] Peyser quotes from contemporaneous diary entries of Pauline Heifetz (sister of Jascha) that confirm this involvement: "Go with Chotzie [Samuel Chotzinoff, pianist, her husband] to George's rehearsal of the 'Nigger Opera'" (17 December 1925), and "Go with mother to George's 'Nigger Opera'—Whiteman—George & C. [apparently Chotzinoff again] to Reubens."[64] In any event, all of these sources dating from the composer's lifetime (the sketch-score, the orchestrations by Vodery and Grofé, and De-

Sylva's revised script) were brought together in George Bassman's 1953 reconstruction.

The Bassman score gives the most complete "version" of *Blue Monday*, in the format of a piano-vocal score. It contains all of the music found in the manuscripts (except, of course, Vi's discarded number), coupled with a re-revised setting of DeSylva's revised text. The score is useful because it fits DeSylva's "Prologue" text to that section's music, a situation not found in Gershwin's sketch-score or the Vodery or Grofé orchestrations. Bassman's reconstruction seems perfectly plausible. The intended relationship between text and music are clear. Bassman's score is, however, an "adaptation," which is most apparent in terms of orchestration. It is a very sketchy "short score," essentially a piano-vocal score with a few key instruments indicated at various points throughout. In short, it is a script of the performance staged for television in 1953, subsequently recorded by Gregg Smith in a studio production in 1976. A recent recording under the direction of Marlin Alsop re-creates the orchestrations from the 1920s but uses the later, "sanitized" versions of the text.[65]

As Ira Gershwin noted, the greatest textual difference between the *Blue Monday* of Gershwin's day and the *135th Street* revivals is that "nigger" has been purged from the text and the character "Cokey Lou" has lost his drug-user connotation in favor of the more innocuous street name "Sweet Pea."[66] This first layer of social reform is apparent upon comparing the text for "Blue Monday Blues" as found in the Bassman score to DeSylva's 1925 version of the text—Mike's chiding "Sweep on you lazy nigger!" is replaced by a kind of placating response to Sam's previous line: "That's when my cares are always bigger. . . . His cares are always bigger." Most of the changes in the text dating from the early 1950s take this form, removing the boldly objectionable term "nigger" and some of the derogatory tone of the remarks among the characters.[67]

Although all of these changes bring the text more in line with the social mores of their times, none of them confronts the fundamental blackface demeanor of the work. The problem of casting future stage productions of *Blue Monday* thus remains to be addressed. Appreciating the work as Gershwin knew it, however—that is, in terms of the social norms for New York entertainment in the early and mid-1920s—requires one to consider the work with all its objectionable elements in full view. In this way, the distance and similarity between *Blue Monday* and the considerably more progressive *Porgy and Bess* are thrown into sharper relief.

The Reviews

Period reviews and press notices of *Blue Monday* and *135th Street* (table 6.1) say much more about Gershwin's work than has been previously pointed out in Gershwin studies. By and large, scholars have tended to cast *Blue Monday* as an early, experimental failure. The work was surely all of these things, but most of the 1922 reviews were positive. Charles Darnton's report

TABLE 6.1 *Blue Monday* (1922) and *135th Street*: Summary of Press Notices and Reviews

	Pro	Con	Pro/Con	Labels[a]
S., [New Haven] (8-22?-22)[b]	x			real American opera one-act musical piece "Blue Monday Blues"
"White's Scandals," *NYTimes* (8-27-22)	—	—	—	—
"The New Plays," *NYTimes* (8-27-22)	—	—	—	—
"White's Scandals," *NYTimes* (8-28-22)	—	—	—	—
Darnton, *NYWorld* (8-29-22)		x		"Blue Monday Blues" black-face sketch
S[avage], *NYPost* (8-29-22)	x			"Blue Monday Blues" number
"Scandals," [New York] (8-29?-22)	x			colored grand opera "Blue Monday Blues" a tragedy of colored folks grand opera a fine bit
Woollcott, *NYTimes* (8-29-22)	—	—	x	—
"Glorifying," *NYHerald Trib.* (12-27-25)	—	—	—	an opera[...]in black face "135th Street"
"The Man of the Week," *NYWorld* (12-27-25)	—	—	—	"135th Street" the one act jazz opera
"Paul Whiteman," *Morn.Tele.* (12-27-25)	—	—	—	"135th St." a one-act jazz opera
"Whiteman," *NYTimes* ? (12-27?-25)	—	—	—	l-act jazz opera "135th St."
"2nd 'Experiment'," *NYTimes* (12-27-25)			x/pro	"jazz opera" "135th Street" "opera"
Riesenfeld, *NYEveningWorld* (12-29-25)	—	—	—	—
Kaufman, *NYTelegram* (12-30-25)	—	—	x/con	one act jazz opera
"Paul Whiteman," *NYSun* (12-30-25)	—	x	—	"135th Street" "one act jazz opera" publicity blown opera sad story old hokum vaudeville skit jazz opera

TABLE 6.1 (*continued*)

	Pro	Con	Pro/Con	Labels
"Paul Whiteman Gives," *NYTimes* (12-30-25)	—	—	x	"135th Street" "grand opera" one-act "135th Street" swift tragedy
Downes, *NYTimes* (12-31?-25)	—	—	x	"135th Street" jazz opera "operetta"
Kitchen, *NYEveningWorld* (12-31-25)	—	—	—	"jazz opera"

a. Material in quotation marks is so found in the sources—particularly interesting in the later reviews, since there the various labels or buzzwords seem to have become questionable for the writers.

b. Uncertain dates and titles reflect the fact that some of the clippings in the scrapbooks are inadequately labeled regarding their source.

Sources. The abbreviated titles or descriptions here correspond to the following: W. S., "White's Scandals of 1922 Score Triumph," unidentified New Haven newspaper, 22? August 1922; George White's Scandals" (advertisement), *New York Times*, 27 August 1922; "The New Plays; George White's Scandals of 1922," *New York Times*, 27 August 1922; "George White's Scandals" (advertisement), *New York Times*, 28 August 1922; Charles Darnton, "'George White's Scandals' Lively and Gorgeous," *New York World*, 29 August 1922; C.[harles] P.[ike] S.[avage], "'Scandals of 1922' Is Most Pleasing; George White Heads a Clever Company in Singing, Dancing, and Fun; 'The Gingham Girl' at the Earl Carroll Theatre Highly Entertaining," *New York Post*, 29 August 1922; "Scandals of 1922 Outscandals Everything; New White Production at Globe a Wonderful Collection of Scenery and Jazz, Mostly Jazz, " unidentified New York newspaper, 29? August 1922; Alexander Woollcott, "The Play, A Dancer's Revue: George White's Scandals of 1922," *New York Times*, 29 August 1922; "Glorifying American Jazz" (photograph), *New York Herald Tribune*, 27 December 1925; "The Man of the Week" (captioned illustration), *New York World*, 27 December 1925; "Paul Whiteman and His Greater Concert Orchestra; Presenting a One-Act Jazz Opera by Gershwin and DeSylva, '135th Street' (Happened on Blue Monday) with Blossom Seeley, and Deems Taylor's Colorful Suite 'Circus Day;' Also Latest Popular Numbers Done in the Whiteman Manner" (advertisement), *Morning Telegraph*, 27 December 1925; "Paul Whiteman Himself! and His Orchestra" (advertisement), *New York Times*?, 27? December 1925; "2nd 'Experiment in Modern Music,'" *New York Times*, 27 December 1925; Hugo Riesenfeld, "Off-Stage Views of Stage People," *New York Evening World*, 29 December 1925; S. Jay Kaufman, "Round the Town; Whiteman Up," *New York Telegram*, 30 December 1925; "Paul Whiteman Concert at Carnegie Hall," *New York Sun*, 30 December 1925; "Paul Whiteman Gives 'Vivid' Grand Opera; Jazz Rhythms of Gershwin's '135th Street' and Deems Taylor's 'Circus Day' Delight," *New York Times*, 30 December 1925; Olin Downes, "Music; Paul Whiteman's Novelties," *New York Times*, 31? December 1925; Karl K. Kitchen, "Up and Down Broadway," *New York Evening World*, 31 December 1925. All of these items can be found in the Gershwin Scrapbooks—those from 1922 in LC/GC-GS1, and those from 1925 in LC/GC-GS2.

in the *New York World*, by far the most often cited in the secondary literature, is far and away the most caustic. The handful of other reviews are supportive. Even in 1925, when the criticisms do tip in a negative direction, most of these are of the "pro and con" variety: their primary objections are with the staging (or lack thereof), not Gershwin's music.[68]

Certain aspects of these two rather different collections of reviews need to be kept in mind. First, reviewers of the *Scandals* were drama critics, whose pens wielded considerably more financial power (to help kill a show, a star, or a number, for instance) than those of the 1925 music critics, whose primary responsibility was aesthetic and technical.[69] Largely, although perhaps encumbered by DeSylva's libretto, Gershwin's youthful work passed both tests: as a dramatic work, if perhaps too short-winded and out-of-place in the venue of a popular revue; and as a musical work, generally sparkling, drab in its treatment of the dialogue, yet containing at least two universally liked numbers.[70]

Second, and more telling than the critical votes on *Blue Monday* and *135th Street*, are the many labels used to describe the piece. Clearly, in 1922 critics could not agree, their terms ranging from "grand opera" to "real American opera," from "tragedy" to "skit." An American operatic paradigm was lacking. Shortly after the premiere of the *Rhapsody in Blue* in February 1924—that is, in the two years preceding the *135th Street* revival in December 1925—Gershwin's name began to appear as a possible, even probable source for "the great American opera," for which a dizzying array of possible subjects was offered.[71] One feature of this slurry of news reports is clear and consistent: that an American opera must reflect distinctly American locales, and that the musical idiom of jazz is the logical first choice for such a work. Henrietta Malkiel was clear about the relationship of jazz and American opera: "The great American opera, the idyl of the wide open spaces, has come down to earth. It has come to Broadway. The dream of an American Wagner has passed with the days of Indian librettos. It is now the jazz opera that waits for a composer and a plot."[72] Gershwin seems to have responded to this idea when he told an interviewer in 1928: "Jazz is the real American contribution to art. Previously, everything in American art was borrowed from Europe. I hope to help place jazz among the classics of all time."[73] Earlier, he had reached more profound conclusions: "Jazz is not Negro but American. . . . Jazz is, in short, not an end in itself, but rather a means to an end."[74] Similar reports continued throughout the 1920s, eventually coming to rest with announced plans for a Gershwin setting of S. An-Ski's popular *Dybbuk* story.[75] When this venture fell through and the Gershwins moved on to other projects, the hype of a Gershwin opera receded from the headlines, at least for the next few years. In light of these descriptions, in which *Blue Monday* is mysteriously never mentioned, *Porgy and Bess* appears as a thoroughly logical response to the public's earlier expectations.

Blue Monday's Promise

Gershwin was a young man when he came upon the idea of *Blue Monday*, with few published works under his belt and little in the way of completed "serious" compositions. But he was far from inexperienced, despite his youth. Indeed, Gershwin was precocious and prolific, especially through the 1920s, and it is this popular image of him that is highlighted in the film version of his life, which probably explains the emphasis the film places on *Blue Monday*. Only during the 1930s, really, did he begin to confront compositional roadblocks.[76] In 1922, he was only on the brink of success, not yet faced with its burden. *Blue Monday* was thus a large step forward, bold indeed for the ragtime composer of *Rialto Ripples* (1916–17) and tunesmith of "Swanee" (1919) fame.[77] His pattern of employment on Tin Pan Alley and Broadway explains why Gershwin offered *Blue Monday* to George White. White was where his contacts were. A youthful miscalculation, perhaps, since White expected entertainment first and, in this regard, *Blue Monday* did not deliver the right kind. Its story was too ponderous, it lacked the requisite theatrical payoffs, and, most of all, it cast black characters (here, importantly, whites in blackface rather than black performers, as in *Porgy and Bess*) in often sympathetic and largely serious (if sometimes sappy) roles.[78] In short, in 1922 *Blue Monday* did not fit into an established niche of American popular entertainment: it was a long way from minstrelsy and not exactly vaudeville. Moreover, it was fundamentally flawed as a serious work about blacks, perpetuating certain black stereotypes while simultaneously stepping away from such stereotypes and grappling with serious, universal human emotions (love, jealousy, rage, guilt). *Blue Monday* is flawed, too, like many would say of *Porgy and Bess*, because it presents degrading (and racially derogatory) situations without providing social commentary, a prerequisite for what Duke Ellington termed an "honest negro musical play."[79] The work had serious aspirations but relied on conventions of popular entertainment. In *Porgy and Bess*, these dualities are more skillfully balanced. But, importantly, in the person of Will Vodery, in 1922 Gershwin was already working with one of the finest African American musicians of the day, a situation that shaped the success of *Porgy and Bess*. Clearly, *Blue Monday*, in spite of its obvious flaws, demonstrated the possibilities of opera to Gershwin, and the work's reviews urged him on.[80] He had embraced his subject matter and was beginning to find his compositional voice. He needed a better story, however, and a surer compositional hand.

Although a fantastic life lay ahead, many elements of Gershwin's cultural experience were in place by 1922, and his choices throughout the rest of his career demonstrate an ever more acute sense of the limitations and possibilities of the complex equation of his musical gift. Viewing young Gershwin as a "modern" man ("one of us"), not merely a "modernist," demystifies *Blue Monday*, makes it real, revealing its promise alongside its weaknesses.[81] Gershwin grew to understand his fame and his role as a leader of American music.[82] The differences between *Blue Monday* and *Porgy and Bess* illustrate this understanding. *Blue Monday* is not "the first real American opera," but it does reflect "the spark of musical genius."[83] Compared to *Porgy and Bess*, it pales in many ways. But like all of Gershwin's works (early or late), *Blue Monday* is pivotal in his compositional maturation, the first of several conversely shaky and sure steps in fresh directions. Here is a failed experiment, yes, but bold-like-genius, and without it his later greater contributions would not reflect the scope that they do.

Blue Monday, "Opera Ala Afro-American," from Act 2 of George White's *Scandals*, musical revue in two acts (1922)

Book:	B. G. DeSylva
Lyrics:	B. G. DeSylva
Orchestration:	Will Vodery
Musical director:	Max Steiner
Orchestra:	Paul Whiteman and His Palais Royal Orchestra
Conductor:	Paul Whiteman
Stage Designer:	Herbert Ward and/or John Wegner
Costume designer:	? (not Erté)
Choreographer:	George White
Producer:	George White
Director:	George White
Cast	
Vi:	Coletta Ryan
Joe [sings "Prologue"]:	Jack McGowan
Tom:	Richard Bold
Cokey:	Richard Bold
Sam:	Lester Allen
Mike:	Franklyn Ardell?
Tryout:	Schubart Theatre, New Haven, Conn. 21? August 1922
Broadway opening:	Globe Theatre, 28 August 1922
Number of performances:	New Haven (4); New York (1)

Comments: New Haven performances hypothesized from single review in LC/GC-GS1: (1) M, 8/21/22; (2) T, 8/22/22; and (3–4) W, 8/23/22 (matinee and evening performances); show/revue scoring (see Shirley, "Notes," 9): 2 fls. (1 pic.), ob. (Eng. hn.), 2 cls., bsn., 2 hns., 2 trp., 2 trmb., perc., hrp., str. (vln. 1–2, vla. 1–2, vlc., db.).

135th Street, "one-act jazz opera," concert performance (1925)

Book:	B. G. DeSylva (revised)
Lyrics:	B. G. DeSylva (revised)
Orchestration:	Ferde Grofé, after Vodery, 1922
Orchestra:	Paul Whiteman and His Orchestra
Conductor:	Paul Whiteman
Stage designer:	?
Costume designer:	if any?
Choreographer:	if any?
Producer:	Paul Whiteman
Director:	F. C. Coppicus
Cast	
Vi:	Blossom Seeley
Joe:	Charles Hart
Tom [sings "Prologue"]:	Jack McGowan
Cokey Lou [Cokey]:	Francis Howard
Sam:	Benny Fields
Frank [Mike]:	Austin Young

Opening:	Carnegie Hall, New York, 29 December 1925
Number of performances:	2

Comments: 2 performances (T, 12/29/25 and F, 1/1/26); an additional rehearsal performance (without singers) for invited critics, either before the first performance or between the two (on W, 12/30/25) (see Downes, "Music"); along with Whiteman and His
Orchestra, Jack McGowan the only member of the 1922 cast to perform here (although,
perhaps, in the role of Tom rather than Joe); Downes refers to "Mike" (as in the 1922 production) rather than Frank; presented as part of Whiteman's "Second Experiment in
Modern Music," which also featured premieres of works by Grofé (*A Tone Journey: Mississippi* [a.k.a. *Mississippi Suite*]), Carpenter (*A Little Bit Of Jazz*) and Deems Taylor (*Circus Day* [orch. by Grofé]); "jazz orchestra" scoring (see Shirley, "Notes," 10; and Smith,
liner notes): cl. (E♭, B♭, alto and bass), sax. (sop., alto, tenor, bari.), ob., Eng. hn., bsn.,
fls. (pic.?, alto?, bass?); all of these instruments covered by "four or five pit men" (Smith,
liner notes), Goldberg, *George Gershwin*, 218, provides a cast list, referring to "Frank" as
"Harlem Mike," and "Cokey Lou" as "Cookey Lou."

Blue Monday (Blues), as part of *Rhapsody in Blue*, film (Warner Brothers, 1945)

Book and lyrics	B. G. DeSylva, 1925?, revised by Howard Koch and Elliot Paul
Orchestration:	Ray Heindorf, after Grofé, 1925?
Vocal arrangements:	Dudley Chambers
Musical director:	Le Roy Prinz
Orchestra:	Warner Brothers Orchestra
Conductor:	?
Stage designer:	?
Costume designer:	?
Choreographer:	Le Roy Prinz
Producer:	Jesse L. Lasky
Director:	Irving Rapper
Assistant director:	Robert Vreeland
Cast	
Vi:	?
Joe:	?
Tom:	?
Cokey:	?
Sam:	?
Mike:	?
Release:	Hollywood, June 26, 1945; New York, 27 June 1945

Comments: 5'04" excerpt, erroneously presented as part of *Scandals of 1924*, not *Scandals of 1922*, but before the *Rhapsody in Blue*.

135th Street, "a one-act opera," television broadcast (1953)

Book and lyrics:	B. G. DeSylva, 1925, revised by George Bassman, Paul Feigay, and William Spier
Orchestration:	George Bassman, after Vodery, 1922, and Grofé, 1925

Orchestra:	CBS Orchestra
Conductor:	George Bassman
Stage designer:	Valerie Bettis?
Costume designer:	?
Choreographer:	Valerie Bettis
Producer:	William Spier
Associate producer:	Paul Feigay
Director:	Valerie Bettis
Cast	
Vi:	Etta Warren
Joe:	Raun Spearman
Tom:	Lorenzo Fuller?
Sweetpea [Cokey Lou]:	Lorenzo Fuller
Sam:	Jimmy Rushing
Mike:	Warren Coleman
dancers:	15 performers
Number of performances:	1

Comments: Ford Foundation Workshop/*Omnibus* series broadcast (CBS television, 3/29/53, 4:30–5:00 P.M.); reconstructed from Vodery's 1922 orchestration ("an orchestration"), Grofé's 1925 reorchestration ("a conductor's score"), and DeSylva's 1925 revised script(s) ("a couple of hentracked [*sic*] pages of Mr. Sylva's words") by *Omnibus* associate producer Paul Feigay and George Bassman, with the assistance of Ira Gershwin; prior to reconstruction, "no instrumental parts, no vocal parts and no composer's notes" (see Allison, "'New' Gershwin Opera on TV," 6); production probably assembled with some internal connections to the 1945 film reconstruction.

135th Street, concert performance (1968)

Book and lyrics:	B. G. DeSylva, 1925, revised by Bassman, Feigay, and Spier
Orchestration:	[Skitch Henderson?, after George] Bassman, after Vodery, 1922, and Grofé, 1925
Orchestra:	Skitch Henderson's Orchestra
Conductor:	Skitch Henderson
Number of performances:	1

Comments: Philharmonic Hall, New York, 20 May 1968; recorded (Penzance Records 43); a complete list of production credits has not been located.

Blue Monday, studio recording (1976)

Book and lyrics:	B. G. DeSylva, 1925, revised by Gregg Smith, after Bassman et al., 1953
Orchestration:	Gregg Smith and Edmund Najera, after Grofé, 1925, and Bassman, 1953
Orchestra:	chamber orchestra of 17 players
Conductor:	Gregg Smith
Cast	
Vi:	Joyce Andrews
Joe:	Thomas Bodgan
Tom:	Jeffrey Meyer

APPENDIX (*continued*)

Sweet Pea:	Jeffrey Meyer?
Sam:	Walter Richardson
Mike:	Patrick Mason

Comments: (Turnabout TV-S 34638); recorded spring 1976; orchestra, rescored (reduced and simplified) from Grofé, consists of 5 winds (fl., cl., ob., sax., and bsn.) + 12 strings; orchestration prepared without the use of Vodery, 1922: "That orchestration has disappeared, to the best of our knowledge" (Smith, liner notes); lyrics, and perhaps additional features of the orchestration, adapted from Bassman et al., 1953 (note Bassman's contemporaneous, 1976 copyright deposit); no "Gregg Smith–*Blue Monday*" material located on LC or any other collection.

Blue Monday, "a one-act jazz opera," "world premiere recording" (1993)

Book and lyrics:	B. G. DeSylva, 1925, revised by?, after Bassman et al., 1953/1976
Orchestration:	after Vodery, 1922; Grofé, 1925; and Bassman, 1953/1976
Orchestra:	Concordia
Conductor:	Marlin Alsop
Cast	
Vi:	Amy Burton
Joe:	Gregory Hopkins
Tom:	William Sharp
Sweet Pea:	William Sharp
Sam:	Arthur Woodley
Mike:	Jamie J. Offenbach

Comments: (Angel CDC 7 54851 2 7); recorded 10/19/92 and 1/10/93, Manhattan Center Studios, New York; slight revisions in the Bassman, 1953/1976 lyrics; "world premiere recording" somewhat a misnomer given the 1976 Smith recording, yet the two recordings are at least different, although neither re-creates either the 1922 or 1925 versions verbatim.

Note: These listings will remain incomplete until certain documents come to light, esp. the following: (1) programs for the 1922 and 1925 performances; (2) detailed production notes from the Warner Brothers studio files; and (3) further information regarding the 1968 Henderson performance.

Notes

1. In the "Gershwin Memorial Concert" broadcast from the Hollywood Bowl (8 September 1937), commentator Louie A. Whitten stated: "Gershwin's *An American in Paris* constituted what is often referred to as a *musical coup d'état*." A complete recording of the concert is commercially available (Cambria Records C133A-B).

2. Gershwin's often quoted phrase "labor of love" originates in his letter to DuBose Heyward, dated 9 September 1932, where he distances his designs on Heyward's novel from those of Al Jolson, then making news: "The sort of thing I have in mind for PORGY is a much more serious thing than Jolson could ever do. . . . It would be more a labor of love than anything else." Copies of the Gershwin-Heyward correspondence are found in the Gershwin Collection (box 17, item 13) of the Music Division, Library of Congress (hereafter as, for example, LC/GC-b17, i13). The originals are held by the South Carolina Historical Society in Charleston. Also, "fascination" does not seem too strong a descrip-

tion given the pattern of Gershwin's interest in *Porgy*. See Gershwin, "Rhapsody in Catfish Row: Mr. Gershwin Tells the Origin and Scheme for his Music in That New Folk Opera Called 'Porgy and Bess,'" *New York Times*, 20 October 1935, sec. 10, p. 1.

3. Isaac Goldberg, *George Gershwin: A Study in American Music* (New York: Simon & Schuster, 1931), 120.

4. On White's uneasiness, see ibid.

5. Wayne Shirley, "Notes on George Gershwin's First Opera," *I. S. A. M. Newsletter* 11 (May 1982): 8.

6. Regarding "Stairway to Paradise" (also known as "New Step Every Day," with lyrics by DeSylva and Ira Gershwin under his pre-1924 pseudonym, Arthur Francis), see Ira Gershwin, *Lyrics on Several Occasions* (New York: Knopf, 1959), 294–96. For a description of Lightner's "Man of My Dreams," see Charles Darnton, "The New Plays, 'George White's Scandals' Lively and Gorgeous," *New York World* (29 August 1992; LC/GC-GS1). For the remainder of this essay, except where noted otherwise, all reviews will be cited per their location in the (consistently chronological) Gershwin Scrapbooks ("GS") in the Gershwin Collection, Library of Congress—far and away the easiest source in which to access most of them. As mentioned in note 2, all other LC/GC primary documents will be referred to using similar abbreviations.

7. Many writers have made the *Pagliacci* connection. Shirley states: "The libretto does, in fact, read somewhat like freeze-dried *Pagliacci*" ("Notes," 9). Joseph Smith was more explicit: "The opera runs one third as long as *I Pagliacci*, the libretto's obvious model" ("Blue Monday," liner notes accompanying *Blue Monday* [Angel CDC 7 54851 2 7], p. 3).

8. Reprinted in Shirley, "Notes," 10.

9. Charles Schwartz, *George Gershwin: His Life and Music* (Indianapolis: Bobbs-Merrill, 1973), 61.

10. Ira Gershwin, "My Brother," in Merle Armitage, ed., *George Gershwin* (New York: Longmans, Green, 1938), 19.

11. No attempt is made in these examples to point out any literal reuse or modeling of material; rather, general stylistic features are highlighted. Following the model established by Charles Hamm for the *Porgy and Bess* text, rehearsal numbers are used to refer to specific points in the score: thus, "rehearsal 1 [+2]–rehearsal 1 [+5]" and "rehearsal 2 [-5]–rehearsal 2 [-2]" refer to 2 through 5 measures after rehearsal number 1, and 5 through 2 measures before rehearsal number 2, respectively. See Hamm, "The Theatre Guild Production of *Porgy and Bess*," *Journal of the American Musicological Society* 40 (Fall 1987): 520, n. 43. Examples 6.1a–1c are drawn from George Gershwin and B. G. DeSylva, "Blue Monday (135th Street Blues)," adapted by George Bassman (copyright 1953; New York: New World Music Corporation, 1976), unpublished copyright deposit (LC, M1503.G376/G422, 1976). Bassman's score (hereafter referred to as Gershwin/Bassman, "Blue Monday") is discussed later.

12. This example is collated from two sources: (1) Gershwin/Bassman, "Blue Monday," 7–9; and (2) George Gershwin and B. G. DeSylva, "Blue Monday" (sketch-score, 1922; LC/GC-Bound), 6–7, discussed later. Gershwin's original is in B♭ but contains no text; Bassman's reconstruction contains text but transposes the number to D♭. A third key (A♭) is found in the manuscript page of "themes" Goldberg included (p. 219) in his Gershwin biography. Gershwin no doubt produced these illustrations long after the fact, probably copying them from Vodery's score. None of the songs from *Blue Monday* was ever published as sheet music.

"The Half of It Dearie Blues" is from *Lady, Be Good!* (New York: New World Music, 1924). For alternate versions of the text, see Robert Kimball, ed., *The Complete Lyrics of Ira Gershwin* (New York: Knopf, 1993), 52–53.

13. Abbe Niles, "The Story of the Blues" (1949), in W. C. Handy, ed., *Blues: An Anthology* (New York: Macmillan, 1972; reprint, New York, Da Capo, 1985), 40. Niles also stated: "The blues spirit appealed to each of the three leading white song writers of the period following the publication of Handy's first tunes [beginning with "The Memphis Blues" (1912), generally regarded as the first published blues]: Irving Berlin, George Gershwin, and Jerome Kern" (p. 36); and he continued, "Among the leaders, George Gershwin, an acknowledged devotee of the blues and admirer of Handy, had too many kind things to say to confine himself to blues language, but it speaks strongly in his long orchestral pieces and his piano preludes as well as in *Porgy and Bess* and the one-act tragedy *135th Street*" (p. 40). The 1926 (first) and 1949 (revised) editions of Handy and Niles's collection will be discussed later.

14. The long-winded title of "The Half of It, Dearie, Blues" was not without precedent on Broadway. Anne Caldwell and Jerome Kern's "Left-All-Alone-Again-Blues," written for *The Night Boat* (1920), really began this trend among white composers. See Niles, "The Story of the Blues," 39. Niles also points out that Kern's "Can't Help Lovin' Dat Man (of Mine)," from *Show Boat* (1927), is "perhaps the only such example [of a true blues verse] ever published by a white composer" (p. 39). The assertion is debatable. The first edition of Handy's book (New York: A & C Boni, 1926) contained a curious collection of pieces by white composers not reproduced in later editions: Kern and Caldwell's "Left-All-Alone-Again-Blues" (pp. 165–67); Berlin's 1921 "The Schoolhouse Blues" (168–70); an excerpt from John Alden Carpenter's "jazz ballet" *Krazy Kat* (1924), highlighting its quotation of the "Kat-nip Blues" (171–73); the Gershwin piece under discussion as "The Half of It, Dearie, Blues (Duet)" (174–76); the first page of *Rhapsody in Blue* (177); and an excerpt from the second movement of the Concerto in F (178–80). The version of "The Half of It, Dearie, Blues" found there is noteworthy because its accompaniment is rewritten in spots (cf. in the chorus, mm. 3–6, 9–12, and 19–24). This rewritten accompaniment captures Gershwin's pentatonic improvisations (clearly recalling *Rhapsody in Blue*) when he recorded the piece with Astaire during the London run of *Lady, Be Good!* in April 1926, a record that contained the following "warning" on its label: "This recording contains actual dancing [!]" As Ira Gershwin's note accompanying Gershwin's copy of Handy's *Anthology* (now in LC/GC-Bound; inscribed by the authors "August 12, 1926") relates, "Niles had heard the English recording. . . . He asked George to put down the $\frac{2}{4}$ intervals [♪s] of the recording." The Gershwin-Astaire performance of "The Half of It, Dearie, Blues" can be found most recently on *Gershwin Plays Gershwin* (Pearl GEMM CDS 9483).

15. One might recall also the prominent ♭3s and ♭7s in the chorus of "I'll Build a Stairway to Paradise," the weighty ♭3s in the chorus of "Somebody Loves me" (written for the 1924 edition of White's *Scandals*), and other similarly bluesy gestures among many other Gershwin songs of the 1920s.

16. Transcribed from Imperial 5417 (1956).

17. These comments are not meant to be pejorative. Both songs were written for Broadway stage characters, thus the crucial element of autobiographical believability (e.g., in the contemporaneous performances of country blues masters Papa Charlie Jackson and Blind Lemon Jefferson) is inherently lacking in them.

18. W. S., "White's Scandals of 1922 Score Triumph," unidentified New Haven newspaper (22? August 1922; LC/GC-GS1).

19. Quoted in Shirley, "Notes," 10.

20. Consider, for instance, Billie Holiday's 1948 "Porgy" (née "I Loves You, Porgy) (Decca 24638); instrumental renditions by Miles Davis (1958), Oscar Peterson (1959), and the Modern Jazz Quartet (1964); and countless others over the years. Many could eas-

ily enlarge this list to include those numbers that do not contain character names in the title (esp. "Summertime" and "I Got Plenty o' Nuttin'," but also "A Woman Is a Sometime Thing," "My Man's Gone Now," "It Ain't Necessarily So," and "There's a Boat Dat's Leavin' Soon for New York").

21. In this line of thinking, *Porgy and Bess*'s scenes are simply much longer, containing more action (and text). The size of *Porgy and Bess*, moreover, and Gershwin's more developed sense of musico-dramatic organization yielded the network of motives that help to hold the work together. In *Blue Monday*, such ideas have little time to acquire meaning.

22. Gershwin's sketch-score does not contain these first two measures. The example here is reproduced from Gershwin/Bassman, "Blue Monday," 2.

Examples 6.3b–d are from George Gershwin, DuBose Heyward, and Ira Gershwin, *Porgy and Bess* (New York: Gershwin Publishing/Chappell, 1935), 277–79.

23. In his sketch-score (p. 6), Gershwin indicates "Banjo acc." at the beginning of "Blue Monday Blues," which suggests that *Porgy and Bess*'s later musical complex (i.e., example 6.3f) perhaps developed from these earlier thoughts. In any event, both spots yielded singularly successful numbers.

The location of example 6.3e is derived from Gershwin/Bassman, the example itself from Gershwin and DeSylva, "Blue Monday" (sketch-score), 5, which does not contain rehearsal numbers. This spot in the sketch raises a question regarding the 1922 text, since Gershwin has Mike (indicated with a large M above the staff) saying "Paul . . . Paul" rather than "Sam . . . Sam," as in all other sources.

Example 6.3f is from Gershwin, Heyward, and I. Gershwin, *Porgy and Bess*, 197.

24. Of course, countless other prominent features of *Porgy and Bess* are nowhere in evidence in *Blue Monday*: notably, the crap-game fugue and the canon of the wake (both resulting, at least partly, from Gershwin's studies with Joseph Schillinger), the choral writing, the orchestration, and the general expanse of *Porgy and Bess*, with its exhaustive use of motives-of-reminiscence. All these features will be discussed in my forthcoming dissertation, "Gershwin's 'American Folk Opera': The Genesis, Style and Reputation of *Porgy and Bess* (1935)."

25. Harlem, like all American cities, is rougher now than it was in 1922. Charleston's Cabbage Row, with eighteenth-century aristocratic roots, is no longer a tenement, having been restored, in radiant pastels, to its former white splendor. For clarification, "Kittiwah" approximates Carolina sea island Gullah pronunciation of "Kiawah," now a resort community.

26. Cf. act 2, scene 3. Bess's delirium upon returning from the picnic could be explained as withdrawal from cocaine ("happy dust"), not to mention post-traumatic stress following Crown's rape, in addition to her guilt over being unfaithful to Porgy.

27. Goldberg, *George Gershwin*, has the name as "Cookey Lou" (cf. p. 218), which is quite a difference. This name is not found in any other source and is probably a printer's error, but it may support DeSylva's initial conception of the character as a drug user (unlike Sporting Life) rather than a drug peddler (like Sporting Life). Sometimes the character is referred to simply as "Cokey," which supports the consensus reading of him. He is always described as a cafe pianist. Gershwin did not write any music for Lou analogous to *Porgy and Bess*'s "Jasbo Brown Blues."

28. David Ewen, *A Journey to Greatness: The Life and Music of George Gershwin* (New York: Henry Holt, 1956), 93.

29. Armitage, *George Gershwin*, 27.

30. Robert Kimball, "The Roots of 'Porgy and Bess,'" in liner notes accompanying *Porgy and Bess* (London: EMI Records CDS 7 49568 1/2/4), p. 15.

31. Edward Jablonski and Lawrence D. Stewart, *The Gershwin Years,* 2d ed. (Garden City, N.Y.: Doubleday, 1973), 72; and Jablonski, *Gershwin: A Biography* (New York: Doubleday, 1987), 51.

32. Deena Rosenberg, *Fascinating Rhythm: The Collaboration of George and Ira Gershwin* (New York: Dutton, 1991), 47.

33. Joan Peyser, *The Memory of All That: The Life of George Gershwin* (New York: Simon & Schuster, 1993), esp. 238–39.

34. W. S., "White's Scandals of 1922 Score Triumph."

35. Charles Pike Savage stated: "The greatest hit of the evening was Paul Whiteman and his orchestra, which 'jazzed' Schubert and Beethoven symphonies to applause that was loud and long" ("'Scandals of 1922' Is Most Pleasing," *New York Post* [29 August 1922; LC/GC-GS1]). Another review went even further: "If you go once, you'll go again, if only to see 'The Patent Leather Forest' [Gershwin's "Stairway to Paradise"] or to hear Whiteman's music, or the colored grand opera" ("Scandals 1922 Outscandals Everything," unidentified New York newspaper [29 August 1922; LC/GC-GS1]). Charles Darnton, who had little good to say about *Blue Monday,* called Whiteman's group the "best of all jazz bands" ("The New Plays").

36. Goldberg, *George Gershwin,* 218.

37. See Merle Armitage, "George Gershwin and His Time," in Armitage, *George Gershwin,* 7–8.

38. Paul Whiteman, "George and the Rhapsody," in Armitage, *George Gershwin,* 25.

39. Quoted in Peyser, *The Memory of All That,* 125.

40. Schwartz, *George Gershwin,* 62, reaches similar conclusions regarding Whiteman's motives for reviewing the work.

41. In both cases, mostly warm responses to Gershwin's music were cooled by consistently negative reactions to DeSylva's script.

42. The seven performances are as follows: in 1922, four performances at the Schubart Theatre in New Haven (21–23 August, with matinee and evening performances on the last date), and the famous single performance at New York's Globe Theatre (28 August); and in 1925–26, two performances at Carnegie Hall (29 December and 1 January). For an overview of all productions of the work over the years, see the appendix, "*Blue Monday* (1922)/*135th Street* (1925): Production Credits," at the end of this essay.

43. See *Rhapsody in Blue* (MGM/UA Home Video M301149). Also see Charlotte Greenspan's essay in this collection. A fourth posthumous (concert) production was mounted by Skitch Henderson for a single performance at Philharmonic Hall in New York City on 20 May 1968. Like the *Omnibus* production (discussed later), from where it doubtless got its score and parts, Henderson's version used an African American cast. This production was recorded (Penzance Records 43), although it has long been out of print and is now nearly impossible to locate. To my knowledge, no film exists for either the *Omnibus* or Henderson productions.

44. Performers, however, have done much to revive *Blue Monday/135th Street.* Over the years, both Ira Gershwin and Edward Jablonski advocated some sort of instrumental arrangement of "selections from" the work. Such a notion has recently come to fruition. See George Gershwin, *Blue Monday,* arranged for piano solo by Alicia Zizzo (New York: George Gershwin Music and Warner Brothers Music, 1993). Zizzo's arrangement is curiously subtitled "An Afro-American Setting."

45. This is a precarious way of stating the obvious, simply suggesting (as most would) that Gershwin's style would have continued to develop had he lived longer. Although "late" does not necessarily mean "great," most creative figures, and certainly those of Gershwin's singularity, continue to grow artistically well past age thirty-eight.

46. Three important documents are lacking: (1) a musical sketch of the opening "Prologue" in Gershwin's hand, (2) a copy of DeSylva's 1922 version of the text, and (3) a program from the *Scandals* listing scenes and numbers of the revue. Most of these items can be estimated, however, with extant, albeit sometimes chronologically later, documents.

47. See the appendix at the end of this essay.

48. In Gershwin's 1931 letter to Goldberg, he refers to *Blue Monday* as "this one-act vaudeville opera" (quoted in Shirley, "Notes," 10).

49. Both sources are now in the Music Division, Library of Congress, as "Gershwin Collection-Bound" (hereafter LC/GC-Bd). Ira Gershwin deposited the Vodery score in 1970; Gershwin's sketch was acquired in 1982, sparking Wayne Shirley's previously cited article of the same year.

50. Excepting Grofé's orchestration (a copy of which has long been in the New York Public Library), these materials are now in LC/GC, but as of this writing they have not been formally processed. DeSylva's "correction" is simply a rewording, not a significant change in content: a single sentence where Joe describes his desire to return to his mother after years away from her.

51. See note 8.

52. For background on this production see Gordon Allison, " 'New' Gershwin Opera on TV; Long-Lost '135th Street' to Be Presented Today," *New York Herald-Tribune*, 29 March 1953, pp. 1, 6. For a (largely negative) review see Jack Gould, "Television in Review: '135th Street,' Written by Gershwin at 22 [*sic*], Is Offered by 'Omnibus' in Local Premiere," *New York Times*, 30 March 1953, p. 18, which is cited in Schwartz, *George Gershwin*, 62.

53. Gregg Smith, liner notes accompanying *Blue Monday* (New York: Turnabout TV-S 34638).

54. "Buddy DeSylva and I discussed for some time the possibilities of writing an opera for colored people. . . . After five days and nights we finished this one-act vaudeville opera" (in Shirley, "Notes," 10). Gershwin's phrase "for colored people" is curious, since he must have understood that White would expect performers in blackface. Perhaps he was bringing a 1930s attitude to the work.

55. Cf. Gershwin and DeSylva, "Blue Monday" (sketch-score), 34–35b. See Shirley, "Notes," 9, where this number is first discussed.

56. Gershwin's *Lullaby* was composed as a composition exercise for Edward Kilenyi around 1919. Its two-page, piano-score manuscript (LC/GC, B12–19) is (mis)titled "Lulluby." Although performed several times soon after its completion, the work was not published until 1968. See Richard Crawford and Wayne Schneider, "Gershwin, George," in *The New Grove Dictionary of American Music*, ed. H. Wiley Hitchcock and Stanley Sadie (London: Macmillan, 1986); Schwartz, *Gershwin*, 43; and especially Ira Gershwin, "My Brother's Manuscript," in George Gershwin, *Lullaby* for String Quartet (New York: New World Music, 1968), [2]. An interesting anecdote relating *Lullaby* and *Blue Monday* is found in "2nd 'Experiment in Modern Music,'" *New York Times*, December 1925 (LC/GC, GS2): "The piece [*135th Street*] was sketched out seven years ago [ca. 1918], and one of its principal melodies has lain in the composer's wallet since that time."

57. None of the Tune Books (early or late) at LC appears to contain *Blue Monday* material. In his letter to Goldberg, Gershwin recalled: "Two or three weeks before the show opened, he [White] came to us and said he would like to try it [*Blue Monday*] anyway. So De Sylva sat down with his pencil and I dug down and found a couple of suitable tunes and we began writing" (in Shirley, "Notes," 10). Gershwin's phrase "dug down" may suggest an image of the composer improvising at the piano rather than sift-

ing through tune books. On the early Tune Books, see Jablonski and Stewart, *The Gersh-win Years*, 70.

58. Gershwin's use of *Lullaby* in *Blue Monday* apparently usurped the former's existence as an independent composition in his mind, as Ira Gershwin noted: "I can't recall why George borrowed the opening theme of his string quartet for the beginning of an aria in *Blue Monday*. Maybe it was the urgency of the assignment, or perhaps by then George had come to regard 'Lullaby' as merely an exercise. But borrow the opening bars he did, and that, so far as the composer was concerned, was the end of the string quartet, as I've no recollection of his ever mentioning it again" ("My Brother's Manuscript," 2).

59. In the *New Harvard Dictionary of Music*, Charlotte Greenspan defines "verismo" as follows: "The settings are contemporary; the characters are often rural and generally impoverished; the passions run high and lead to violence. There is a tendency in these works to wed the sordid with the sensational" (*The New Harvard Dictionary of Music*, ed. Don Michael Randel [Cambridge: Harvard University Press, 1986]). *Blue Monday* has most of these traits: contemporary setting, impoverished characters, violence, and the wedding of the "sordid" (i.e., Tom) with the sensational (Vi shoots and kills Joe in front of a host of onlookers). Satire in DeSylva's script and Gershwin's setting is not hard to locate either: compare the transition in the "Prologue" from the typically veristic "Love! Hate! Passion! Jealousy!" phrase through the quotation of Gershwin's *Lullaby* theme (at "In this little plot . . . "), to the razzmatazz dance sequence (beginning "And it's all on account of a woman's intuition gone wrong") that follows.

60. These changes are described in Shirley, "Notes," 9–10. The changes are "dramatic" in that the 1925 score thins the texture considerably, yielding the sound of a typically tinny mid-1920s "sweet" band rather than that of a theater orchestra (with doublings from "classical" instruments).

61. B. G. DeSylva, typewritten letter (carbon) to George Gershwin, 25 November 1925 (LC/GC-Un). Gershwin was indeed "on the crest of a wave" in December 1925. He premiered his Concerto in F with Damrosch and the New York Symphony on 3 December, then saw three shows premiered on three successive nights: *Tip-Toes* (Liberty Theatre, 28 December), *135th Street* (Carnegie Hall, 29 December), and *Song of the Flame* (Forty-Fourth Street Theatre, 30 December). See "The Man of the Week" (captioned illustration), *New York World*, 27 December 1925 (LC/GC-GS2); and Karl K. Kitchen, "Up and Down Broadway," *New York Evening World*, 31 December 1925 (LC/GC-GS2). "Mr. Coppicus" must have been F. C. Coppicus, who directed the concert.

62. The passages are as follows: DeSylva, "135th Street" (typescript, 1925; LC/GC-Un), 3; Gershwin and DeSylva, "Blue Monday" (sketch-score), 19–20.

63. Robert Kimball and Alfred Simon, *The Gershwins* (New York: Atheneum, 1973), 53. The photograph is now in LC/GC-30/11-10.

64. Quoted in Peyser, *The Memory of All That*, 114. If one concurs with Peyser's interpretation that Heifetz's use of quotation marks around "Nigger Opera" suggests that this was Gershwin's phrase, then interesting questions arise regarding Gershwin's racial views at this early stage in his career. Appreciating the meaning of this highly toxic term over time is well beyond the scope of this essay. Suffice it to say, however, that while the term may have been more prevalent seventy years ago, it was always racially derogatory and patronizing.

65. In the "Prologue" passage used for comparison earlier, one finds "Mike's *uptown* saloon," "a *lover's* tragedy," and "like the *grand* opera" (my emphasis).

66. Ira Gershwin's summary can be found in his explanatory notes accompanying the *Blue Monday/135th Street* materials at LC. In B. G. DeSylva/[George Bassman and William Spier], "135th Street" *Omnibus* script, 1953; (LC/GC-Un), 3, the last four words of the fol-

lowing stage direction have been marked through: "Sweet Pea sits at a piano and plays a few bars then takes a sniff." Obviously, changing the character's name was not enough; stage actions reinforcing his Sporting Life–like character (i.e., the devil in disguise) had to be changed, too.

67. For instance, Tom's question to Vi regarding Joe, "What do you see in that crap-shootin' nigger anyway?" (cf. DeSylva/[Bassman and Spier], "135th Street," 2, and Gershwin and DeSylva, "Blue Monday," 13), has been changed to "that crap-shootin' rascal" (DeSylva/[Bassman and Spier], "135th Street," 4). Although he may feel it, Porgy never goes so far regarding Bess and Crown.

68. Olin Downes is most enlightening in this regard: "In the score itself there is excellent material. The writer was fortunate in hearing it rehearsed by orchestra without singers or actions. . . . There was also the great disadvantage of a concert platform for what should have been seen on a stage. A few chairs and table, with an apology for a bar, gave no suggestion of the scene described in the libretto" ("Music," New York Times, 31 December 1925 [LC/GC-GS2]). David Ewen recalled (seemingly first-hand) that "the distraction of watching Whiteman conduct behind the stage action was disturbing" (A Journey to Greatness, 140).

69. Woolcott, for instance, far and away the most important of the 1922 reviewers, does call "I'll Build a Stairway to Paradise" a "smart and spectacular finale," but he never mentions Gershwin (aside from the production credits) and does not even hint at a reaction to Blue Monday.

70. Except by Darnton, who called the work "the most dismal, stupid and incredible black-face sketch that has probably ever been perpetrated" and whose review has become the negative germ spread throughout the Gershwin biographies. The two successful numbers were clearly "Blue Monday Blues" and Vi's "Have One of You Seen Joe?" (also known as "Has Anyone Seen My Joe?"). In "Paul Whiteman Concert," the New York Sun reviewer concludes: "The music was skillfully scored, but with the exception of two clever songs it served simply as an unimpressive accompaniment for an old hokum vaudeville skit."

71. Ranging from Bret Harte's "Outcasts of Poker Flat" to Woollcott's idea of "the life of Irving Berlin" to what Carl Van Vechten called a "Negro 'Scheherazade'" (which some may see as a fitting description of Porgy and Bess).

72. Henrietta Malkiel, "Scheherazade in West Virginia: Jazz Opera on Its Way," Musical America 42 (25 April 1925): 3.

73. "Critics Look to Harlem Composer to Write Music for Opera Portraying American Life," Home News, early? 1928 (LC/GC-GS1).

74. Gershwin, "Our New National Anthem: Broadway's Most Popular Modern Composer Discusses Jazz as an Art Form," Theatre Magazine, 41 May 1925: 30. (LC/GC-GS2). See also Richard S. Greenhalgh, "When We Have Jazz Opera: An Interview with Mr. George Gershwin," Musical Canada 6 (October 1926): 13–14.

75. Virgil Thomson's discussion of "the cult of jazz" reflects the debate raging over jazz as a source material for "serious" composition in the later 1920s. See Thomson, "The Cult of Jazz," Vanity Fair 24 (June 1925): 54, 118. See also Percy Grainger, "What Effect Is Jazz Likely to Have upon the Music of the Future?," Etude 2 (September 1924): 593–94; "[Irving] Berlin Says Jazz Is Dying," New York Times, 15 April 1926; John Alden Carpenter, "Jazz Is Assuming Prominence as an American Music Idiom," Musical Digest 11 (23 November 1926): 3; and "Sousa Expects Jazz to Wane: Denies It Is Truly American," New York Times, 26 April 1928. The rights for Dybbuk were secured by Italian composer Lodovico Rocca. Gershwin's connections to Dybbuk and its affinities with Song of the Flame (1925) will be discussed in my dissertation. But see "Gershwin Plans Serious

Works," 15 July 1926; F. P. Dunne, "Gershwin Shelves Jazz to Do Opera; Tin Pan Alley's King Composing One for Metropolitan; Based on 'The Dybbuk'; At Kahn's Request, He Admits, Saying He'll Be Back," unidentified clipping, after spring 1929 (LC/GC-GS2); "Gershwin Plans American Opera after Good Rest," *Business Telephone*, spring 1929? (LC/GC-GS2); and Schwartz, *Gershwin*, 26.

76. Even this biographical event is tainted by a spurious trope of scholastic fancy, as Ira Gershwin observed, in a letter to the editor: "In *Newsweek*, Sept. 25, the Schillinger System is discussed. I have nothing against the system. But I do object to a couple of the writer's statements. When he says 'George Gershwin, for example, came to the system in desperation. He had written hundreds of songs; he feared he had run dry,' he goes in for a stratospheric flight of musical fancy. I collaborated with my brother, on and off, for some twenty years and never did he (or I, or anyone else, for that matter) feel he had 'run dry'" ("Gershwin on Gershwin," *Newsweek*, 23 October 1944, 14). Gershwin studied with Schillinger, on and off, between ca. 1932 and ca. 1936.

77. *Rialto Ripples* was written in collaboration with fellow Remick staffer Will Donaldson. Jablonski sums up the piece succinctly: "It patently reflects Gershwin's tricky piano style and was probably Remick's answer to the current popularity of E[uday] L. Bowman's *Twelfth Street Rag* and Felix Arndt's 'Nola.' *Rialto Ripples* merged the money-making elements of the two: the traditional rag and the piano novelty number" (Jablonski, *Gershwin*, 21). "Swanee," originally written for the *Capitol Revue* (New York, 24 October 1919), did not become a hit until Al Jolson incorporated the song in *Sinbad* and, especially, recorded it for Columbia Records (8 January 1920).

78. The show's single "spiritual" (so labeled by Gershwin in Goldberg, *George Gershwin*, 219), Joe's "I'm Going to See My Mother," is the main source of sap in the show. Still, S. Jay Kaufman found that "Charles Hart's 'Mammy Mine' was effective and tuneful and old-fashioned and 'got over' notwithstanding" (Kaufman, "Round the Town; Whiteman Up").

79. Quoted in Robert Garland, "Negroes Are Critical of 'Porgy and Bess,'" *New York World-Telegram*, 16 January 1936, p. 14. *Blue Monday* is also problematic in the sense that African Americans, especially in the Harlem of the 1920s, did not merely push brooms, peddle dope, shoot craps, and kill their friends.

80. Gershwin read his reviews, and he (or Ira Gershwin) kept them in scrapbooks. He quoted from the New Haven review of *Blue Monday*, the most supportive of all, in his 1931 letter to Goldberg.

81. See Saul Bellow, "Mozart: Work Transformed into Play," *Bostonia* 1 (Spring 1992): 42–47, in which Bellow finds that "the essence of 'modern' is to demystify" (p. 47).

82. Gershwin appears to have anticipated this role early on, submitting (anonymously) "O Land of Mine, America" (lyrics by Michael E. O'Rourke, pseudonym of Kern collaborator Herbert Reynolds) as an entry in a national anthem context sponsored by the *New York American* in 1919. See Ewen, *A Journey to Greatness: The Life and Music of George Gershwin*, 84–85, among others.

83. New Haven's W. S.: "Although Mr. White or any of his confreres may not be aware of it they will have done one thing which will, or ought to, go down in history: they have given us *the first real American opera* in the one-act musical piece 'Blue Monday Blues'" ("White's Scandals of 1922 Score Triumph," my emphasis). Dolly Dalrymple, "Pianist, Playing Role of Columbus, Makes Another American Discovery; Beryl Rubinstein Says This Country Possesses Genius Composer," unidentified newspaper, 6 September 1922 (LC/GC-GS1): "What I do mean is that this young fellow George Gershwin, now only 25 [sic], has *the spark of musical genius* which is definite in his serious moods" (my emphasis).

II

Reception

CHARLOTTE GREENSPAN

Rhapsody in Blue: The Story of George Gershwin was made at the Warner Brothers studios in 1945, eight years after the composer's death. Produced by Jesse Lasky and directed by Irving Rapper, the film starred Robert Alda as George Gershwin, Herbert Rudley as Ira Gershwin, and Charles Coburn as Max Dreyfus; the female leads were taken by Joan Leslie and Alexis Smith, both playing fictional characters invented for the film.

The film was a critical and commercial success. The musical directors of the film, Ray Heindorf and Max Steiner, received an Academy Award nomination for musical direction. Praising the film as a whole but expressing reservations about its biographical accuracy, *Variety* stated that "those who knew George Gershwin and the Gershwin saga may wax slightly vociferous at this or that miscue, but as cinematurgy designed for escapism and entertainment, no matter the season, *Rhapsody in Blue* can't miss."[1]

Musicologists concerned with George Gershwin have almost nothing good to say about this film. It is not so much that they criticize the movie; rather, they tend to dismiss it. The recent biography of the Gershwins, Deena Rosenberg's *Fascinating Rhythm*, refers to *Rhapsody in Blue* as a "pseudo-biography," although the author acknowledges that Ira "provided guidance and input" for the film.[2] Edward Jablonski and Lawrence Stewart seem to echo the *Variety* review when they state that "in 1945 Jesse Lasky released his *Rhapsody in Blue*, an inaccurate and highly romantic conception of George's life; it was prepared at a time, however, when the world

145

needed escape, romance, and music, and this film circled and recircled the globe."[3]

These writers are complaining, with good reason, about the fanciful mixture of fact and fiction that unfolds in this film. The movie is not the story of George Gershwin or his music but a story in which some aspects of Gershwin's life and music make up a part. As the review in *Halliwell's Film Guide* suggests, this semifactual treatment of a life story can be taken as typical: "No more trustworthy on factual matters than other Hollywood biopics of its era, this rather glum saga at least presented the music and the performers to excellent advantage."[4]

Film biographies cannot tell the whole truth in the space of a few hours, and they have no intention of giving the audience nothing but the truth: this is a cardinal fact about the genre. The most useful critical question to ask about a biographical film is not how truthful it is but how truth and fiction are blended. The most intriguing critical questions ask where the fictions come from and what purposes they serve.

The Warner Brothers' staff involved with the production of *Rhapsody in Blue* was in fact quite proud of the veracity of some aspects of the film. A 1945 publicity puff announces that "for the sake of realism, many of George Gershwin's personal possessions were loaned to the studio by his brother and lyricist, Ira Gershwin. These included the composer's 13 volume scrapbook, his combination desk and work-table, the silent piano keyboard he always carried with him as a practice instrument, and six original paintings from the George and Ira Gershwin collection."[5] This appropriation of props may be considered truthfulness, or realism, on the level of artifacts, and certainly these details contribute to the documentary value of the film.

Furthermore, the same publicity booklet comments that

> when Hollywood produces a film based on the story of a contemporary personality, in which many well-known celebrities of screen, stage and radio must be portrayed, the producer is faced with a serious casting problem. Audiences are quick to catch any slight difference between the appearance and actions of the actor and the real life person he portrays. In "Rhapsody in Blue," . . . Warner Bros. solved the problem by having seven of the twenty real life characters played by themselves. Paul Whiteman, Oscar Levant, Al Jolson, George White, Anne Brown, Hazel Scott and Tom Patricola play themselves.[6]

Unfortunately, such authenticity on one level causes an inaccurate impression on another level. For example, Al Jolson, born in 1886, was a dozen years older than George Gershwin. When he played himself in the film he was 58 and, of course, looked a full generation older than Robert Alda, who played Gershwin. Although, as the film suggests, Jolson was an established star when he gave the young Gershwin's career a jolt forward with a performance of Gershwin's "Swanee," these two men were more nearly contemporaries than the film suggests. Nevertheless, the performances of the "real life characters . . . played by themselves" gives the film a significant documentary value.

To be sure, a film biography is more than the sum of its artifacts, and a biography of a composer involves more than the performances of his works—however authentic those performances may be. One hopes to become acquainted with or even have the illusion of understanding the subject of the biography and to get a sense of the personality as well as the accomplishments of the person. The story the biography tells is essential.

The screenplay of *Rhapsody in Blue* was not carelessly thrown together. According to David Ewen, "Hollywood paid Gershwin the highest accolade it could bestow on a composer by filming his biography, *Rhapsody in Blue*. Ira Gershwin had prepared an outline for the film biography and it was rejected; so was a three-hundred page script prepared by Clifford Odets."[7] The screenplay that was used for the movie, written by Howard Koch and Elliot Paul, was based on a story by Sonya Levien, who had become a friend of the Gershwins in 1930, when they had worked together on the musical film *Delicious*. (Levien wrote the screenplay for that film with Guy Bolton.)

One can give *Rhapsody in Blue* good marks for presenting a fairly accurate picture of Gershwin's early life and career. He himself recalled that "one of my first definite memories goes back to the age of six. I stood outside a penny arcade listening to an automatic piano leaping through Rubinstein's *Melody in F*. . . . To this very day I can't hear the tune without picturing myself outside that arcade on One Hundred and Twenty-fifth Street, standing there barefoot and in overalls, drinking it all in avidly."[8] This memory is the basis for the opening sequence of the film, although the young man the audience sees is closer to a teenager than a six-year-old. Moreover, according to one biographer, when Gershwin's mother "attended the premiere showing of *Rhapsody in Blue* . . . in 1945, she was heard to remark that they were never as poor as depicted."[9] Nevertheless, the beginning of the film is essentially accurate, perhaps because Gershwin's early life conveniently conformed to the rags-to-riches formula. It is true, as the film shows, that the Gershwins grew up in New York City, that they were initially in modest circumstances financially, that the father changed jobs several times, and that the family moved several times to different locations in New York. It is true that George and Ira supported and encouraged one another and eventually worked as a successful team together. And it is true that George was more precocious than Ira at getting his career started.

Many facts about Gershwin's career are presented accurately in the film. George worked as a pianist in the Tin Pan Alley firm of Jerome H. Remick. He also worked as an accompanist for vaudeville acts. Some time after he left Remick's, Gershwin signed a contract with Max Dreyfus to write songs for the T. B. Harms company, publishers of songs by Victor Herbert, Rudolph Friml, and Jerome Kern, among others.[10] Other musical and biographical landmarks of Gershwin's career duly recorded in the film are the success of "Swanee" as Al Jolson performed it; the failure of *Half Past Eight*; the success of Gershwin's scores for *George White's Scandals*, *Rhapsody in Blue*, and the Concerto in F; the lukewarm initial reception of *Porgy and Bess*; George's move to Hollywood; and his premature death there. In fact, one could watch the film with the "Highlights of Gershwin's Life" from Charles Schwartz's *George Gershwin: A Selective Bibliography and Discography*[11] in hand and not suffer from disorientation.

Are the critics of this film nitpicking, then, when they complain about its inaccuracies? Not really. The film veers away from fact in dealing with Gershwin's relation to his music, particularly when and how certain songs were composed. It also waxes fictional in describing Gershwin's relations with other people, mainly because many of the people George "relates to" in the film are fictitious. The principal offenders in this category are the two presumed romantic interests in Gershwin's life, Julie Adams and Christine Gilbert, and his purported music teacher, "Professor" Otto Frank.

A close look at a brief scene gives a clearer idea of how *Rhapsody in Blue* stirs together truth and fiction. Early in the film (about thirty minutes after the opening credits) a scene shows Gershwin composing. The camera pans in on a street sign of 103d Street and Riverside Drive: the Gershwin family is obviously moving up in the world. Dissolve to the interior, where George's father, Morris, is playing cards with three of his friends. The friends comment on the Gershwins' comfortable new surroundings and Morris acknowledges that it is George's success as a songwriter that has afforded them these greater comforts.

Morris: His songs are selling like hot corns, and always new ones coming. Listen.

[Sounds from the piano are heard in the background. Bits of phrases start, stop, and continue with slight changes.]

Morris: You hear that? George is in the act of composition.
Card player: Composition?
Morris: Sure, counterpoint.
Card players: Counterpoint, oh.
Morris: A song is being born. Excuse me.

[He walks across the room and opens the door to another room, in which George is seated at the piano. George plays a repeated note and a falling fourth, then a repeated note and a falling major third. Morris whistles the motif of a repeated note and a falling minor third—the first three notes of "'S Wonderful."]

Morris: Does that help you, Georgie?
George: Thanks, Pop.
Morris: Don't mention it. It's all in the family.

[Morris leaves and George begins playing the completed version of "'S Wonderful."]

Morris: Boys, that song is for a new singer he found. Some tea somebody?
Card player: No thanks.
Morris: Such a fine girl.
Card player: Who is she?
Morris: Her name is Julie Adams.
Card player: George is writing the music for a show?
Morris: Yeah, a musical show.

Card player: What's it called?
Morris: *Half Past Eight*.

This is the kind of scene that makes knowledgeable viewers either chuckle or groan. Most films about composers show them, at some point, in the act of composition. For a movie biography such a scene presents certain problems. For one thing, on some level the act of composition is mysterious —in some cases, especially to the composer. Where ideas come from, how they are put together, how a composer recognizes when a piece has taken its final form—these matters are not readily accessible to the analytical, conscious part of the mind. So it is probably beyond anyone's expectations to think a biographical movie will give an accurate picture of a composer's process of creation. Moreover, the act of composing is probably not externally dramatic—there is not much of interest to watch. Thus, the inclusion of such a scene—the composer composing—may be a conventional necessity, but the deck is stacked against such a scene being factually accurate. And, indeed, this scene presents three biographical falsehoods regarding "'S Wonderful"—when it was composed, with whom, and for whom.

Although George composed songs for *Half Past Eight* in 1918 (that is, early in his career, as the film suggests), the song "'S Wonderful" was composed in 1927 for *Funny Face*. Morris Gershwin may or may not have been around while George was composing "'S Wonderful," but the family member who certainly was there—but is not shown in this scene in the film— was Ira, who wrote the lyrics. Isaac Goldberg, close friend to George and Ira, gives an account of the composition of "'S Wonderful" in his biography of George: "George has been rambling over the keys and has come upon a sensuous, gliding music that expresses insidiously the general notion of ecstasy in love. (What, by half, is all song?) He plays it to Ira; he plays it, in fact, to everybody who'll listen. That's George. Ira is soon humming the tune unaided. He feels, better than an outsider would feel, the very psychology of the music; and, as he points out, words may suit a specific rhythmic outline and yet be false to the essential meaning of the tune."[12] Finally, the Gershwins composed "'S Wonderful" to be sung by Adele Astaire and Allen Kearns, not by Julie Adams, a character invented for *Rhapsody in Blue*.

But perhaps the film's most egregious liberties are the characters concocted for Gershwin's love life and musical training. Julie Adams, played by Joan Leslie, represents cinematic innocence and unfulfilled love. She and George meet early in the film—he is an aspiring songwriter, working as a song plugger at Remick's, and she is an aspiring singer. Their careers ascend together—he writes hit songs and she sings them. Adams seems ripe for a romantic attachment to Gershwin as well, but he seems to view her only as a friend and professional associate.

Gershwin's romantic interest is stirred in the film by the other invented female part, Christine Gilbert, played by Alexis Smith. Whereas Julie Adams stands for youth and naïveté, Christine Gilbert represents experience and sophistication. George meets Christine while he is in Paris. He is already a well-known composer; she is an American socialite with a strong interest in but not a first-rate talent for painting. The film suggests that George becomes interested in painting through Christine's influence. Actually, the impetus to paint came from the self-effacing Ira.[13] What is very interesting about the Christine Gilbert character is that it could have been a drawn-from-life sketch of Linda Lee Thomas, who met Cole Porter in Paris and married him in 1919. Indeed, when Warner Brothers approached Cole Porter with a proposal to do a film biography based on his life (the film was to be *Night and Day*, released in July 1946, one year after *Rhapsody in Blue*), one of Porter's conditions was that the part of Linda be played by Alexis Smith.

In *Rhapsody in Blue*, Gershwin courts Gilbert, and she follows him to New York but—to Gershwin's disappointment—leaves him to take up painting again in Mexico. Her motivation is not entirely clear, but apparently Gilbert recognizes that she would be playing second fiddle to George's music and this would not be enough for her. "You don't need anyone or anything," she tells him. "Everything you touch turns to gold."

Although the roles of Julie Adams and Christine Gilbert are in some ways stereotypical, this film is an atypical musical in that neither romance works out for Gershwin. Apparently it is within the assumed, unwritten, allowable limits of the genre to invent romances for the protagonist but beyond the pale to invent a marriage partner for him or her. Gershwin was unmarried when he died—in fact and in the film.

The third invented character, Professor Frank, is a less typical role. Although George Gershwin did not have a formal musical education equal to that of Jerome Kern or Cole Porter, he was an avid music student and studied privately, at different times, with a number of musicians, including Charles Hambitzer, Rubin Goldmark, Wallingford Riegger, Joseph Schillinger, and Henry Cowell. He also solicited instruction from Maurice Ravel and Arnold Schoenberg, but both these composers had the wisdom to assure Gershwin that he had no need of lessons from them.

With a large number of real teachers to choose from, why did the script writers invent Professor Frank? In a sense he is the designated representative of all of Gershwin's teachers. Further, he represents not only people but also ideas: that is, like Julie Adams and Christine Gilbert, who represent different types of romantic experience, Professor Frank operates not as a person in a biography but as a symbolic character in an allegory.

Professor Frank represents European high art. He has lived in Vienna and was a friend of Brahms. Frank encourages Gershwin, but he hopes George will be a classical composer—another Schubert. The professor's opposite number in this film is Max Dreyfus, who urges George to stick to writing standard popular songs. Incidentally, Frank is shown to be Gershwin's piano teacher, not a teacher of composition. One suspects that the filmmakers wanted the activities of a composer to seem more intuitive and spontaneous—more mysterious, perhaps. They do not wish to show composition as a craft to be learned, as piano playing is.

To the implied ground rules allowing the invention of a sweetheart but not a spouse, the death of Professor Frank adds the apparent license to kill off characters who never really existed in the first place. In a bathetic scene, George comes rushing to Professor Frank's home after the premiere of *Rhapsody in Blue*, to share his triumph with him, and learns that Professor Frank has just died. While romance is a conventional necessity for the musical genre, death scenes are not. In *Rhapsody in Blue*, George dies at the end of the film; he is present at his father's deathbed; and, as if this were not enough, the fictional Professor Frank dies just as his pupil achieves success. Is the film suggesting that great art comes at a heavy price? Or does the fact of Gershwin's death at age thirty-eight shadow the entire film, giving it its distinctive somber color and elegiac mood?

Finally, one seemingly minor bending of the truth I discussed earlier—placing the composition of "'S Wonderful" in 1918 rather than 1927—brings up, in fact, the most important issue in this film: what music was chosen to represent the composer and how this music was presented in the film. On the one hand, the film succumbs to the temptation to make the movie popular by choosing to highlight some of Gershwin's most popular tunes. For example, although the show *Half Past Eight* figures prominently in the film's narrative of Gershwin's early career, none of its songs was published, none was a hit, and none was used in the film. Indeed, with the exception of "Swanee" (1919), performed in the film by Al Jolson, *Rhapsody in Blue* uses only works Gershwin composed in 1922 or later. Hit songs—in addition to "Swanee"—given full productions in the film include "'S Wonderful" (1927), "Somebody Loves Me" (1924), "Oh, Lady Be Good!" (1924), and "Delishious" (1931). All of the popular songs featured in the film are listed here in order of their appearance in the film with their dates of composition:

Swanee (1919)
'S Wonderful (1927)
Somebody Loves Me (1924)
Stairway to Paradise (1922)
Oh, Lady Be Good! (1924)
Blue Monday (1922)
   Blue Monday Blues
    Has Anyone Seen My Joe?
    I'm Going to See My Mother
The Man I Love (1924)
Clap Yo' Hands (1926)
Fascinating Rhythm (1924)
I Got Rhythm (1930)
Yankee Doodle Blues (1922)
Liza (1929)
Someone to Watch Over Me (1926)
Bidin' My Time (1930)
Embraceable You (1930)
Delishious (1931)

Porgy and Bess (1935)
   Summertime
   It Ain't Necessarily So
Love Walked In (1937)

On the other hand, both from the evidence within the film and from the publicity released with it, Warner Brothers clearly considered *Rhapsody in Blue* not merely a work of entertainment but a work of patriotism. (In fact, the film was shot during World War II. Warner Brothers' previous biography of a composer, in 1942, was a life of George M. Cohan—*Yankee Doodle Dandy*.) Gershwin is meant to be seen not simply as a successful and popular composer but as an expression of the American spirit. Professor Frank tells George: "You can give America a voice." Later Max Dreyfus says: "George is an American. He writes of America for America." Christine Gilbert declares that George is "America personified." Before his death George says he would like to set the Gettysburg Address to music. The speaker addressing the audience in Lewisohn Stadium at the end of the film declares that George "gave voice to the America he knew and loved so well." *Rhapsody in Blue* is not simply a biography of Gershwin but a glorification of him, a kind of hagiography. Likely, on the part of the Hollywood moguls there was more than a little projection and identification with a person who, while appearing to create popular culture, was in fact doing something greater: giving America a voice.

In the process of choosing the music to be included in the film, the scales were tipped heavily toward pieces that demonstrated Gershwin's "greatness" and showed him as an innovator or, better, pioneer of American music. The publicity booklet accompanying the film proclaims that "twenty-nine of Gershwin's compositions, including all of his more serious works and his most popular song hits, provide the picture's musical framework. Eighteen of the compositions receive featured treatment. The music used was selected from 160 Gershwin works available, and represent his finest efforts."[14] "All of his more serious works" translates as his more symphonic works—*Rhapsody in Blue*, *An American in Paris*, *Cuban Overture*, and Concerto in F. *Porgy and Bess* is represented by "Summertime," which receives featured treatment, and "It Ain't Necessarily So," which is played as background music for a conversation. Interestingly, the early and unpublished *Blue Monday*, in some ways an adumbration of *Porgy and Bess* and relatively unknown, is given a fairly extended treatment, with presentations of its three songs—"Blue Monday Blues," "Has Anyone Seen My Joe?," and "I'm Going to See My Mother." (This is the first "recording" of *Blue Monday*, a fact that further increases the documentary value of the film.)

Although the film goes out of its way to showcase Gershwin as an American original, *Rhapsody in Blue* shows an ambivalent, not to say distrustful, attitude regarding the accessibility of these serious works for the film audience. In fact, they are all presented in condensed versions. *Rhapsody in Blue* (the composition) takes less than nine minutes in the film (instead of an uncut fifteen minutes); it gets a three-minute reprise at the end. *An Amer-*

ican in Paris, played against an elaborate montage of sights of Paris, lasts only four minutes; *Cuban Overture* and Concerto in F get even shorter shrift.

Although I have pointed to abbreviated versions of works as I have pointed to biographical errors, I do not wish to construct a case against the film but to suggest the complex mixture of motives that went into its creation. In presenting Gershwin's music poised between high art and popular art, the filmmakers of *Rhapsody in Blue* projected their own aspirations and insecurities. In telling Gershwin's life, biography played a part, but so did myth, allegory, hagiography, and even other films. (*Citizen Kane*, released in 1941, may have provided impetus for the theme that Gershwin's life, though filled with professional success, was scarred by a lack of romantic satisfaction.) Gore Vidal has observed that "much of what we take to be true is often seriously wrong, and the *way* that it is wrong is often more worthy of investigation than the often trivial disagreed-upon facts of the case."[15] This essay has attempted not only to investigate some of the ways *Rhapsody in Blue* is right and wrong but also to suggest models more appropriate than scholarly biography for the evaluation of film biographies.

Introduction to a Guide to Musical Cues in *Rhapsody in Blue*

There are nearly sixty cues for music in the film *Rhapsody in Blue*, ranging in length from a few seconds to about eight and a half minutes for a condensed performance of *Rhapsody in Blue*. Most of the music in the film is by Gershwin. But excerpts of works by Anton Rubinstein, Chopin, Beethoven, Schubert, Wagner, and Brahms, and a few non-Gershwin popular songs, such as "Sidewalks of New York," by Charles Lawlor and James Black, and "Smiles," by J. Will Callahan and Lee G. Roberts, are also used, mostly at the beginning of the film, when Gershwin's musical personality is being shaped.

As in most musical films, music in *Rhapsody in Blue* is heard both diegetically, in which the people on screen are aware of the music that the film audience is hearing, and nondiegetically, or as what is loosely called background music. The musical directors, Ray Heindorf and Max Steiner, taking a page out of Richard Wagner's book, decided to treat some of Gershwin's songs as leitmotifs. For example, "The Man I Love," sung in French by Hazel Scott in the nightclub in Paris where Gershwin and Christine Gilbert first meet, is played nondiegetically four other times, including the scene when Gershwin reads Gilbert's farewell letter to him. "Embraceable You," first sung by Julie Adams at a party at which she first sees Gershwin with Christine Gilbert, returns the two times Adams rejects Gershwin after he has been left by Gilbert. *Rhapsody in Blue* is not only presented twice diegetically— once as a performance in Aeolian Hall with Gershwin as piano soloist and once in Lewisohn Stadium with Oscar Levant as piano soloist; it is also used as background music at crucial moments in Gershwin's life, such as the deaths of Professor Frank and Morris Gershwin.

Table 7.1, drawn up after several viewings of a videotape of the film, is

TABLE 7.1. Musical Cues in *Rhapsody in Blue*

Cue no.	Type	Description	Action	Performance remarks	Approx. duration
1	ND	*Rhapsody in Blue*	Opening credits	Inst.	13"
		"The Man I Love"		Inst.	19"
		"Embraceable You"		Inst.	19"
		"I Got Rhythm"		Inst.	26"
		"Love Walked In"		Inst.	26"
2	D	Melody in F (Anton Rubinstein)	G. G. listening to a player piano	Inst.	24"
3	ND	"Sidewalks of New York" (Charles Lawlor & James Blake)	Scene change to outside Gershwin home	Inst.	39"
	ND	Melody in F		Inst.	24"
	ND	something Yiddish		Inst.	26"
4	D	Melody in F	G. G. plays the piano "without even a lesson"	Inst.	26"
5	ND/D	5-finger exercise	Montage showing	Inst.	12"
		Etude, Op. 25, No. 9 (Frederic Chopin)	G. G.'s progress as a piano student	Inst.	20"
6	D	Nocturne, Op. 9, No. 2 (Chopin)	G. G., grown up, plays piano at home	Inst.	46"
7	D	???	G. G. accompanies Groucho Marx in a vaudeville act	Inst.	24" + 8"
8	D	Prelude, Op. 28, No. 7 (Chopin)—all but last measure	G. G. at piano lesson with Professor Frank	Inst.	28"
9	D	"Smiles" (J. Will Callahan & Lee Roberts)	G. G. and a trio of singers on a truck, plugging songs	Voc.	24"
10	D	Collage of several songs of the time	In the offices of Remick & Co.	Voc. and Inst.	20"
		"When You Want 'Em You Can't Get 'Em"	G. G. plays something of his own for a tap dancer	Inst.	26"
11	D	"Smiles"	J. A. seeking music for an audition	Voc.	21"
	D	"Swanee"		Voc.	1'2"
	D	"Back to My Shack"	in background	Voc.	1'29"
12	ND	"Swanee"	Scene changes to Harms office	Inst.	5"

TABLE 7.1. (*continued*)

Cue no.	Type	Description	Action	Performance remarks	Approx. duration
13	D	"Swanee"	G. G. plays for Max Dreyfus	Inst.	2'
14	D	"Swanee"	Performance by Al Jolson	Voc.	3'6"
15	D	"Swanee"	Salesman demonstrating new hit record	Voc.	8"
16	ND	Unfinished Symphony (Franz Schubert)	Professor Frank tells G. G. about great	Inst.	26"
		Overture to *Rienzi* (Richard Wagner)	composers who were not initially commer-	Inst.	22"
		Symphony No. 5 (Ludwig van Beethoven)	cially successful	Inst.	19"
		"Swanee"		Inst.	28"
		Lullaby (Johannes Brahms)		Inst.	19"
		proto-*Rhapsody in Blue*?		Inst.	28"
17	ND	something Yiddish	Change of scene to apartment on 119th St.	Inst.	8"
18	D	"'S Wonderful"	G. G. is composing while his father is playing cards	Inst.	1'
19	D	"'S Wonderful"	Production number with J. A. dancing and chorus singing	Inst. and voc.	1'
20	ND	"'S Wonderful"	End of number segues to J. A. consoling G. G. for failure of show	Inst.	24" + 1'17"
21	ND	something Yiddish	Change of scene to Turkish bath	Inst.	9"
22	D	"Somebody Loves Me"	Production number with J. A. and Tom Patricola	Voc.	3'22"
23	D + ND	???	Montage of G. G.'s hits	Inst.	11"
		"Stairway to Paradise"		Voc.	13"
		"Oh, Lady Be Good!"		Inst. and voc.	52"
24	D	*Blue Monday*	Staged production	Voc.	5'4"
25	ND	???	Change of scene to outside Aeolian Hall	Inst.	48"

TABLE 7.1. *(continued)*

Cue no.	Type	Description	Action	Performance remarks	Approx. duration
26	D	*Rhapsody in Blue*	Performance with G. G. at piano and Paul Whiteman conducting	Inst.	8'36"
27	ND	*Rhapsody in Blue*	G. G. learns that Professor Frank has	Inst.	15"
		Lullaby (Brahms)	died	Inst.	1'26"
28	ND	*Rhapsody in Blue*	Change of scene to Paris	Inst.	11"
29	D	"The Man I Love"	Hazel Scott performs in a	Voc. (in French)	1'16"
		"Clap Yo' Hands"	Parisian nightclub	Voc.	16"
		"Fascinating Rhythm"		Voc.	26"
		"I Got Rhythm"		Voc.	55"
		"Yankee Doodle Blues"		Voc.	1'13"
30	ND	???	G. G. and C. G. at an art exhibit	Inst.	1'46"
31	D	"Liza"	G. G. and Ravel discuss music, ignoring C. G.	Inst.	51"
32	ND	"The Man I Love"	G. G. and C. G. have tea	Inst.	1'2"
33	ND	"The Man I Love"	G. G. invites C. G. to return to New York with him	Inst.	2'4"
34	D	"Somebody Loves Me:	Party thrown by	Inst.	11"
		Rhapsody in Blue	Max Dreyfus for	Inst.	3"
		"Someone to Watch Over Me"	G. G.'s return to New York	Inst.	12"
		"I Got Rhythm"	O. L. and G. G. at	Inst.	31"
		"Bidin' My Time"	two pianos	Voc.	1'
		"My One and Only"		Inst.	49"
		"Embraceable You"	Sung by J. A., who breaks into tears at end	Voc.	1'17"
35	ND	"The Man I Love"	C. G. rejects G. G.'s proposal of marriage	Inst.	3'1"
36	ND	"The Man I Love"	G. G. returns to J. A.	Inst.	3'27"
		"'S Wonderful"	but she too rejects		
		"Embraceable You"	him		
37	ND	*Rhapsody in Blue*	Newspaper announces G. G. returns to Paris	Inst.	18"

TABLE 7.1. (*continued*)

Cue no.	Type	Description	Action	Performance remarks	Approx. duration
38	ND	*An American in Paris*	Montage of Parisian scenes	Inst.	4'41"
39	ND	*Rhapsody in Blue* "Oyfen Pipichik"	G. G.'s father dies	Inst.	1'39"
40	ND/D	*Cuban Overture*	Montage of G. G.'s concert tour	Inst.	52"
41	D	"Mine"	G. G. and O. L. are kidding around together	Voc.	1'
42	ND	*Rhapsody in Blue*	Dreyfus advises G. G. to woo J. A. again; G. G. complains of headaches	Inst.	1'2"
43	D	"Delishious"	J. A. performs in a nightclub in Florida	Voc.	1'3"
44	ND	"Embraceable You"	G. G. proposes to J. A.; she claims she is engaged to someone else	Inst.	2'19"
45	ND	"'S Wonderful"	J. A. admits to her friend that she lied to G. G.	Inst.	21"
46	D	"Summertime"	Performance of *Porgy and Bess*	Voc.	2'1"
47	ND	"It Ain't Necessarily So"	G. G. discusses the disappointing reception of *Porgy and Bess*	Inst.	36"
48	ND	???	G. G., I. G., and O. L. are traveling by train to California	Inst.	1'20"
49	D	Concerto in F	Performance with G. G. at piano	Inst.	3'12"
50	ND	Concerto in F	G. G. incapacitated by headaches	Inst.	1'41"
51	ND	Concerto in F	I. G. tries to reassure their mother	Inst.	38"
52	D	"Love Walked In"	G. G. playing piano at home	Inst.	35"
53	ND	Concerto in F	G. G. in pain but wants to continue composing	Inst.	1'15"

TABLE 7.1 (*continued*)

Cue no.	Type	Description	Action	Performance remarks	Approx. duration
54	ND	*American in Paris* "'S Wonderful"	J. A. phones G. G. from New York; she wants them to be together again	Inst.	30" 1'30"
55	D	"Love Walked In"	G. G. rehearses with singer but collapses near end of song	Voc.	1'7"
56	ND	Concerto in F	Newspaper announces G. G. is ill	Inst.	16"
57	D	Concerto in F	Performance, with O. L. at piano, is inter-rupted to announce the death of G. G.	Inst.	1'30" then 2'5"
58	D	*Rhapsody in Blue*	Performance at Lew-isohn Stadium with O. L. at piano and Paul Whitman conducting	Inst.	3'13'
59	ND	"Embraceable You" "Somebody Loves Me" "Oh, Lady Be Good!" "Swanee"	Closing credits	Inst. Inst. Inst. Inst.	14" 11" 8" 18"

Note: D = diegetic; ND = nondiegetic; Inst. = instrumental; Voc. = at least some portion of the lyrics of the song are sung; G. G. = George Gershwin; O. L. = Oscar Levant; J. A. = Julie Adams; C. G. = Christine Gilbert

admittedly sketchy. I have not been able to identify the Yiddish-sounding music in several scenes, the music used when Gershwin is a relief pianist for Chico Marx, or the music used for the tap dancer at Remick's. Nor have I found it possible, for purposes of the guide, to sort out the various strands of melodic material woven together for several sequences of background music. Doubtless a study of the complete film score in conjunction with the production notes for the film would allow for a more complete table. In addition to identifying the music I have noted whether the music is used diegetically or nondiegetically, who performs the piece, whether it is presented vocally or instrumentally, what is happening on screen when the music is played, and how long the music lasts. In almost all cases, when a song is performed, even in the longest production numbers, the verse is omitted and only the chorus is sung one or more times. The one exception is Jolson's performance of "Swanee."

Notes

1. Reprinted in *Variety Movie Guide* (New York: Prentice Hall, 1992), 503.

2. Deena Rosenberg, *Fascinating Rhythm: The Collaboration of George and Ira Gershwin* (New York: Dutton, 1991), 395.

3. Edward Jablonski and Lawrence Stewart, *The Gershwin Years* (Garden City, N.Y.: Doubleday, 1958), 281.

4. Leslie Halliwell, *Halliwell's Film Guide*, 7th ed. (New York: Harper & Row, 1989), 852.

5. "Filming 'Rhapsody in Blue,'" unsigned article in unpaginated *"Rhapsody in Blue": The Jubilant Story of George Gershwin and His Music* (Hollywood: Warner Bros., 1945).

6. "Filming 'Rhapsody in Blue.'"

7. David Ewen, *George Gershwin: His Journey to Greatness*, 2d ed. (New York: Ungar, 1986), 305–6.

8. Isaac Goldberg, *George Gershwin: A Study in American Music* (New York: Simon & Schuster, 1931; reprint with supplement, New York: Frederick Ungar, 1958), 54.

9. Alan Kendall, *George Gershwin: A Biography* (London: Harrap, 1987), 15.

10. The film is not specific about time. According to Jablonski, Gershwin worked for Remick from May 1914 until he quit in March 1917. He signed with Harms in February 1918. Edward Jablonski, *Gershwin: A Biography* (New York: Doubleday, 1987), 16–17, 27–28.

11. Charles Schwartz, *George Gershwin: A Selective Bibliography and Discography* (Detroit: College Music Society, 1974), 15–19.

12. Goldberg, *George Gershwin*, 199.

13. According to Jablonski in *Gershwin: A Biography*, "Under his brother's influence, George began dabbling in art, beginning with a set of watercolors he had received from Ira on his . . . birthday" (p. 184).

14. "Filming 'Rhapsody in Blue.'"

15. Quoted in Michael Kammen, "What He Learned at the Movies," *New York Times Book Review*, 30 August 1992, p. 27.

8 Gershwin on the Cover of Rolling Stone

SUSAN RICHARDSON

Scholarly studies and especially biographies of George Gershwin have been wide-ranging in content and, because of the continuing success of such works as *Rhapsody in Blue* and *Porgy and Bess*, have appeared rather consistently since his death. But surprisingly little attention has been paid to his position as a popular music figure per se. Yet Gershwin was exactly that: a new kind of popular musician. He bridged "serious" and popular music and found himself squarely within the complexities of the emerging twentieth-century music business. Moreover, he was a cultural figure who transcended specifically music circles and was "famous" in society at large.

This broader view questions how Gershwin relates to twentieth-century popular music in general and, in particular, to its most powerful incarnation in this century—rock and roll. Obviously, both Gershwin's music and his social context are very different from those of, say, Chuck Berry, Bob Dylan, Prince, or Salt'n'Pepa. Each of these musicians' worlds is distinct, and literal or simplistic ties between rock musicians and Gershwin pay little scholarly dividend.

However, in spite of their different times and places, an examination of Gershwin and rockers, each in light of the other, suggests two areas of thought. First, Gershwin has influenced rock mostly through occasional covers of his tunes, usually as a stylistic or career aside when a rock singer branches off into pop standards from the show-tune tradition. Second, and perhaps most important, Gershwin's power as a popular figure is not yet fully understood, and some aspects of his career, such as the function and influence of royalties in his creative life or society's general perception of him during the 1920s and 1930s, call for further study. In short, Gershwin heralded a new breed of popular musician.

Gershwin's influence on rock and roll is, paradoxically, either profound or superficial. On the one hand, his body of work has so permeated culture as to become an inseparable part of pop-music vocabulary. On the other hand, few Gershwin songs per se have made their way inherently into the rock/pop repertory. Rock singers—as opposed to jazz or "standards" artists, who perform his work more often—cover Gershwin songs only occasionally, and those covers rarely make their way into public awareness, let alone the pop music charts.

   Those singers who have taken Gershwin on come from a variety of backgrounds and musical styles. Various singers, such as Big Joe Turner and Ray Charles, who were bridging the crossovers among R&B, popular standards, and rock as early as the 1950s, looked to Gershwin at various points in their careers, perhaps because of their proximity to the jazz and standard pop traditions.[1] Singers as diverse as Etta James ("Embraceable You"), Booker T and the MGs ("Summertime"), and Willie Nelson ("Someone to Watch Over Me") have chosen to record Gershwin's songs over several decades of pop-music history.[2]

   Some musicians used Gershwin as a means to explore different pop genres in an effort to find their own best idiom. The young Aretha Franklin covered "It Ain't Necessarily So" with Columbia, her first record company, in 1960.[3] She was backed by a small jazz combo that could barely contain the swooping soul singer who would later emerge, stylistically unfettered, in the early Atlantic recordings of 1967. Sam Cooke, on the brink of pop stardom after leaving the gospel quartet The Soul Stirrers, cut an experimental secular demo, expecting Side A, "Summertime," to be the success; Side B, "You Send Me," took off instead.[4] Other artists have more than perform a Gershwin tune—they have reinvented it, giving it their own identifiable thumbprint. R&B singer Billy Stewart sang "Summertime" with a sexy, Latino backbeat, while Janis Joplin crafted a sultry, urgent bluesy version of the same song.[5]

   Some performers that are far from the musical mainstream have covered Gershwin as well. In a notable but little-known effort, the band When People Were Shorter And Lived Near The Water extracted a cycle of songs from *Porgy and Bess*. Calling the cycle simply *Porgy*, this latter-day garage band gave Gershwin's opera an eclectic reading that brought the musical and textual implications of the original well into the 1990s, drawing on musical styles from R&B to grunge.[6]

   Occasionally rock and roll singers have performed Gershwin songs for film soundtrack music or compilation albums. A recent example is the 1987 film *Someone to Watch Over Me*, which opens with a version of that song by Sting and closes with Roberta Flack singing the same. Elton John sings "But

Not for Me" on the soundtrack of *Four Weddings and a Funeral* (1994). Also in 1994, Mercury Records released an unusual compilation album of rock stars covering Gershwin songs. Entitled *The Glory of Gershwin*, it was produced by former Beatles associate George Martin and features Larry Adler on harmonica.[7] The album's roster of singers includes Peter Gabriel ("Summertime"), Elton John ("Someone to Watch Over Me"/"Love Is Here to Stay"), Jon Bon Jovi ("How Long Has This Been Going On?"), and Lisa Stansfield ("They Can't Take That Away from Me"). The collection is uneven, encompassing effective new interpretations, such as Elvis Costello's "But Not for Me" and Larry Adler and George Martin's *Rhapsody in Blue*, as well as more incongruous combinations, such as Meatloaf's "Somebody Loves Me" and Cher's "It Ain't Necessarily So," where singers not known for stylistic flexibility take an unexpected turn.

Finally, occasionally rock music evokes Gershwin himself as a musical icon. A recorded version of *Rhapsody in Blue* played over speakers has preceded some Billy Joel concerts, and the impact on rock performers of Gershwin's image as a suave pianist-singer-songwriter seems real and worth exploring. Surely pianist-balladeers such as Elton John pay homage to stylistic forbears in the tradition that includes Cole Porter, Hoagy Carmichael, and George Gershwin.

In sum, a variety of rock singers have occasionally strayed into Gershwin territory. Further study into the reasons behind individual covers might not only uncover revealing or historically significant anecdotes but also provide a clearer understanding of Gershwin's direct impact on rock singers. For instance, Bob Dylan, one of rock's most influential and enigmatic musicians, was the only rock musician to attend the Gershwin Gala, honoring both George and Ira, held at the Brooklyn Academy of Music in March 1987. Dylan even performed his guitar-and-harmonica version of "Soon." Yet nothing in Dylan's background or espoused heroes explains either his choice to attend or his decision to perform.

But in general, the factors behind rock musicians' covers of Gershwin seem to be varied, suggesting some mix of business and musical motivations. Some singers may have recorded a Gershwin tune at the encouragement of a manager or fellow band member, and some because they heard the tune or remembered it from childhood and liked it. So even though Gershwin has not been a staple of rock balladeering, singers have dipped into that repertory for stylistic or career asides, and several notable covers have been created.

If Gershwin's effect on rock has been subtle, rock's "influence on Gershwin" remains largely unexplored. In other words, awareness of popular composer-performers in the late-twentieth-century music business casts a slightly different light on Gershwin as a popular figure, suggesting a greater historical role for him than is usually acknowledged.

Gershwin encountered factors common to much twentieth-century popular music and especially to rock. In particular, his career is analogous to those of later popular musicians in its combination of the following factors: his early life and ethnic/cultural background on the fringes of mainstream America, his rapid rise to great popularity not only as a songwriter but also as a performer and cultural figure, his conscious incorporation of musical materials drawn from the African American community into the popular music of his day, and, finally, his position squarely within the technology and legalities of the emerging twentieth-century popular music business.

First, Gershwin came from a working-class minority background that placed him outside mainstream musical culture. His family was Jewish and had only recently immigrated; his parents arrived in the United States from Russia around 1893. The Gershovitz family settled on New York City's lower east side, a largely immigrant neighborhood. Consequently, the young Gershwin was connected to the city streets and to the world around him, not to a specialized learning environment. By all accounts, George Gershwin was a tough kid in a tough neighborhood: "With a little less luck he might have become a gangster, for the neighborhood in which his father's first restaurant was situated was also the neighborhood that bred Lefty Louie and Gyp the Blood."[8] Gershwin himself recalled that "there is nothing much I can really tell . . . except that music never really interested me, and that I spent most of my time with the boys on the street, skating and, in general, making a nuisance of myself."[9]

Gershwin's formal musical study was patchy and irregular. His most important studies were with Charles Hambitzer (piano; beginning in 1912), Edward Kilenyi (harmony, orchestration, and form; between 1919 and 1921), and Joseph Schillinger (theory, composition, and orchestration; from 1932 to 1936)—though there were brief stints with such notable musicians as Rubin Goldmark, Henry Cowell, and Wallingford Riegger. Yet according to biographer Charles Schwartz, even Gershwin's studies with Schillinger—his most extensive formal study—"were in a sense makeshift measures, generally subordinate to Gershwin's lucrative assignments for Broadway and Hollywood."[10] In a musical culture characterized by a widening gap between popular and "serious" music, Gershwin's natural proclivity for popular music, such as ragtime and Tin Pan Alley tunes, fueled his formal study rather than the reverse.

Though that cultural gap had existed in American music during the nineteenth century, factors early in this century—such as the momentum of modernism and the increased accessibility of published and recorded music—came together in such a way as to emphasize and entrench the differences between "high" and "low."[11] As the nineteenth century turned to the twentieth, concert composers were all too aware of these distinctions. Victor Fell Yellin, Nicolas Tawa, and MacDonald Smith Moore demonstrate that the generation of composers born around the turn of the century, a generation that included Gershwin and Aaron Copland, was the first to depart from the nineteenth-century "Yankee" tradition of composers such as George Chadwick and Edward MacDowell.[12] This generation of young composers left behind, or "contaminated," established American musical culture in several ways: intercourse with popular materials, whether through the incorporation of jazz elements into concert music, or, as in the case of Gershwin, wholehearted embrace of the popular idiom; status as members of recently immigrated families; Jewish heritage; a different approach to family life, exhibited in their decision not to marry; and, finally, a shift in musical focus from Boston to New York City.

The older generation of composers who had thus far defined the notion of the American composer saw itself positioned clearly within the classical concert tradition, and that generation regarded popular materials with, at best, suspicion. When Chadwick and Theodor Presser cofounded the Music Teachers National Association, Chadwick presented a paper entitled "The Popular Music—Wherein Reform Is Necessary."[13] Yellin considers one of the paper's key ideas not only to sum up Chadwick's stand on this issue but also to reflect generally his musical aesthetic: "I do not ask you to make popular music classical—I ask you to make classical music popular."[14] Noting the differences between younger composers and their nineteenth-century predecessors, Yellin observes that those differences were based on factors other than purely musical ones and, in fact, were part of larger social shifts within the United States:

> The antipathies generated by ethnic fears and economic rivalry spilled over into social and aesthetic realms. People began to fear dilution of traditional American values, which the nativists tried to prevent by founding such organizations as the Sons of the American Revolution. . . . Ultimately, Congress passed the first comprehensive Immigration Act of 1924 to stem the flow of non-Protestant populations, the multiplication of foreign linguistic enclaves, and people with darker skins. In music the popularity of ragtime, jazz, and melodies and performers with Jewish mannerisms was seen as the result of an insidious conspiracy to infect and destroy the white, Anglo-Saxon melos. Even on more elevated planes of discussion, conservatives rallied against modernist tendencies in music as typified by Debussy, Stravinsky, and Schoenberg and spread by the new immigrant-dominated generation as an indication of the breakdown of long-held aesthetic principles.[15]

MacDonald Smith Moore reinforces the idea of a relationship between contemporary racial perceptions and early-twentieth-century popular music, underlining the association of African Americans and Jews with jazz and the dilution of "proper" Yankee culture. In their desire to define the terms of American music, most of the older composers, with the possible exception of Ives, were antimodernism, anti-Semitic, and "negrophobe."[16] In the 1920s, racial terms became increasingly embedded in national ones as the struggle for national identity gathered steam, and as Europe became enamored of jazz, the Yankees' own prototype became even more confused. The older composers thought of ragtime as "frivolous . . . spiritual slumming."[17] Moore suggests that the Yankees considered jazz the opposite of responsibility and self-control. Jazz was seen, even by its supportive white critics, as elemental, sensual, sexual. African American performers were trapped, stereotyped as either simplistic or animalistic, and such views affected the way jazz was perceived.[18] Some, like Daniel Gregory Mason, went so far as to see jazz as the manifestation of the emerging consumerism and materialism in American culture. "Writers of every stamp associated Jews with the success of jazz, with the fusion of jazz and classical music, with the domestic avant-garde movement, and with an overall challenge to Yankee leadership of musical culture."[19] The 20 July 1925 issue of the then-new *Time* magazine, which included a cover article on Gershwin, referred to him as a "young Jew," a "famed jazzbo," and described his youth in ripe, patronizing prose: "He skinned his knees in the gutters of this street; he nourished himself smearily with its bananas; he broke its dirty windows and eluded its brass-and-blue clothed curator."[20] Such reportage implied an association between Jews and the "adulteration" of pure Yankee culture, all part of a growing racialism in early-twentieth-century America.[21]

John Ryan, in his study of the similarities in background of those who ran the American Society for Composers, Authors, and Publishers (ASCAP), has observed that during the 1930s and 1940s that organization was dominated by publishers and composers who were of Jewish immigrant backgrounds. The turn-of-the-century waves of immigration in the United States had created a xenophobia, a marginalizing in American culture of various minorities, including Jews. ASCAP and the rapidly developing entertainment industry provided a haven and a union for the talents of this particular group, a means of both income and impact "in much the same way that U. S. and British working-class youth would use it [ASCAP] in the 1950s and 1960s—as a means of effecting upward mobility."[22]

Finally, Gershwin rejected traditional notions of family, never married, and fostered the reputation of being something of a ladies' man. Different biographers provide varying accounts of Gershwin's personal life. Schwartz, in particular, emphasizes Gershwin's ambivalence toward women: Gershwin claimed to have many but was truly comfortable with few.[23] Although Gershwin may have idealized marriage and remained hopeful that he would find a union, the perfect woman seemed elusive, especially as a consequence of his deep connection to his work. Author S. N. Behrman recalled that "George was becoming one of the most eligible bachelors in America; there was curiosity among his friends from the beginning as to who the girl would be." When a potential match, a woman for whom George supposedly cared very much, married, Behrman broke the news to him.

> His brown eyes showed a flicker of pain. He kept looking at me. Finally he spoke.
> "Do you know?" he said, "if I weren't so busy I'd feel terrible."[24]

All the factors that distinguished the new generation of musical figures were especially salient in Gershwin and his contemporary Aaron Copland, both of whom rose to prominence in the 1920s. Each was single (Gershwin probably heterosexual, and Copland quietly homosexual)[25] and Jewish.

Each, in his own way, was drawn to jazz. And both Gershwin and Copland were based in New York, the new and thriving center of the music business, where composing, performing, recording, and broadcasting were coming together in a heated ferment.

Yet for all the characteristics that Gershwin shared with his modernist contemporaries, he was clearly not one of them. Peers such as composers Copland and Henry Cowell and critic Paul Rosenfeld were careful to distinguish their own modernism from the populist leanings of Gershwin. Carol Oja, in her recent article on Gershwin and the modernists, points out that comparative assessments between Copland and Gershwin were consistently made by modernist composers and critics, always with the conclusion that Copland was the more "advanced," true musician of the two, even in his experimentations with jazz. Those who championed modernism, Oja concludes, "saw Gershwin as a threat to the basic value system on which they had been weaned: that of European high art. Thus Gershwin's interaction with the modernists adds another chapter to a long-standing struggle in American culture, revealing a barrier beyond which American modernism was not yet prepared to go."[26]

In short, Gershwin's image played out the generalizations that the established guardians of American high culture found so disturbing. He grew up as part of a Jewish, working-class, immigrant family—an "outsider" to mainstream middle-class America, straddling volatile racial lines. And unlike others of his generation who composed concert music, Gershwin remained connected to the vital popular music of his day rather than a classical tradition that was evolving farther and farther away from a general audience. For Gershwin, the consequence of his background and choices was a subtle sense of being regarded either as an outsider or, once "inside," as associated with "lower" art. In this respect, Gershwin was not unlike rock-and-roll musicians, who have often used music to gain social visibility and viability. Gershwin's impact was less socially disturbing than that of early rock: he was white, and his music fit into the existing genres of Tin Pan Alley and show music rather than creating a new one. But his music was nonetheless discomforting to many Americans through its incorporation of stylistic elements of music such as jazz and blues from the African American community. In this blend, too, Gershwin anticipated the issues of later popular musicians, discussed later.

The second characteristic of Gershwin's career that links him with subsequent figures in popular music is that he gained great fame at a relatively young age—not only as a writer but as a performer and cultural figure. By the mid-1920s Gershwin's career in music theater was firmly established: a string of mostly successful shows and several hit songs, including "Swanee" (1919). The 1924 premiere of *Rhapsody in Blue* by Paul Whiteman's orchestra was widely heralded in both musical and general cultural circles: a celebrated event, the high profile of which would have been unthinkable for any other composer of concert music. The 20 July 1925 issue of *Time* magazine, mentioned earlier, featured Gershwin's picture on the cover and an article inside. Isaac Goldberg's 1931 biography, *George Gershwin: A Study in American Music*, was "authorized" by Gershwin, and he cooperated with Goldberg during its writing. Published when the composer was only thirty-three years old, Goldberg's biography both reflected and nurtured the growing stature of Gershwin as a "legit" figure to be recognized and honored. Through his killing schedule of concertizing as pianist and conductor—and, in particular, through his arduous celebrity tour with the Reisman orchestra early in 1934 through much of the United States and into Canada—Gershwin was "clearly the center of attention as composer and performer," underscoring his image as both.[27]

In short, early in his career Gershwin found a glamorous cultural persona, transcending specifically musical circles and moving with seeming ease among the social elite. In true American fashion, he shot to the top yet was never truly of the upper class—a contradiction that possibly underlay Gershwin's discomfort at social affairs and his regular retreat to the piano in the middle of a party. He became something of a male icon, reflected in his publicity photos: physically attractive, suave, successful. His untimely death was felt throughout society, causing shock and public grief comparable to that over John Lennon's death in 1980. Gershwin's popular stature is reflected not only in Merle Armitage's 1938 collection of essays honoring Gershwin[28] but also in the creation of the 1945 Hollywood film *Rhapsody in Blue*, which glamorized and mythologized his life and even featured people such as Paul Whiteman and Oscar Levant, who had genuinely been part of that life.[29] Yet the movie was not simply Hollywood camp, prescribing the way that Gershwin should be viewed, but also a reflection, a description of the way that Gershwin was already perceived in American culture —the high esteem in which he was held and the tremendous popular audience that he had affected.

Similarly revealing of Gershwin's cultural importance is the sheer amount of popular journalism that has taken Gershwin on—both during and after his life—including critics of popular music, show music, jazz, and classical. Topics such as the racial implications of *Porgy and Bess* or the immediate success of many of his Broadway songs have engaged both music critics and journalists. Such coverage is a tribute to the power that Gershwin had, extending far beyond the boundaries of most other popular musicians and nearly all twentieth-century classical composers. The critical prose that greeted Gershwin was rarely perfunctory, baffled, or cool, as it was in much writing about other concert composers. Writings about Gershwin reflected his proximity and accessibility to people from a wide range of musical and educational backgrounds. That the language of music lovers beyond the edges of a relatively small classical music world is heated and personal corroborates the widespread performance of his music, illustrating again the magnitude of Gershwin's power as a popular figure.

The third aspect of Gershwin's career that parallels later popular musicians is his complicated relationship with race, not only through his own Jewish background but also through his incorporation of elements of

African American music into a style that became wholly identified with him and brought him great success. Such racially charged appropriations, of course, are not unique to Gershwin in American music history. The use by white songwriters of styles or affects from African American music has a long and problematic history, from nineteenth-century minstrelsy to coon songs and cakewalks. Such borrowings also underlie the history of rock music; elements from the blues, R&B, gospel, and later reggae and rap were exploited—usually to far greater financial advantage—by white musicians.

These thorny issues are particularly evident in Gershwin's "American Folk Opera," *Porgy and Bess*. Musicologist Richard Crawford has examined the aesthetic complexities in the work as an opera, as folklore, as racial stereotype, and as cultural exploitation.[30] Crawford's first perspective, viewing *Porgy and Bess* as an opera, focuses on musical considerations such as style, or the implications of that style for Gershwin's status as a "serious" composer. Yet Crawford's subsequent three areas of discussion have more to do with the relationship of the opera, written by a white southerner and a Jew, to the African American community that it represented. Crawford concludes that *Porgy and Bess* is a work of art, but one bound forever to a complicated relationship: Gershwin's distance from the authenticity of the original material, the act of two white men manipulating the imagery and issues of African American culture for their own purposes, and the fact that the opera was "not only written but produced, directed, and staged by whites, which means that whites reaped the monetary profits of its success."[31]

These three factors—folklore, race, the validity of a mainstream art that exploits music from the African American community—are precisely those that characterize later popular musics. And Gershwin was one of the first to work with those issues in the context of the early-twentieth-century music industry. Gershwin took various musical styles, including music from the African American traditions, recrafted them and gave them his own identifiable thumbprint, and created hugely successful songs within mainstream genres, foreshadowing the amalgams of subsequent songwriters such as the teams of Jerry Leiber and Mike Stoller or Carole King and Gerry Goffin.

Fourth and finally, Gershwin anticipates twentieth-century popular music figures in his dealings with a new and immediately complicated music business that embraced both technology—whether in print, recording, or film—and attendant legalities, such as royalties. Gershwin's career was taking off just as royalties were being systematically gathered for popular music. Brand-new radio and recordings—which ultimately and exponentially expanded the power of royalty collection—were gaining momentum. The idea of royalties received for music publishing and performing was still relatively new. Copyright for the publishing of a musical work had been set up by Congress in 1831 and for its performance in 1897, but the mechanism for the collection of royalties for publication or performance was addressed only in 1914 by the newly formed ASCAP. Such collection had only begun to be worked out in practice when new technologies of sound reproduction arose—piano rolls, sound recordings, and radio—that would not only change the face of popular music in America but would also add yet another dimension to musical ownership.

A confusing tangle of publishing and performing rights for radio, recording, and performance ensued, and Gershwin was not unaffected. For instance, what were the financial ramifications of Paul Whiteman's use of *Rhapsody in Blue* as his "signature piece," given that the *Rhapsody* earned Gershwin "more than a quarter million dollars from performances, recordings, and rental fees" between 1924 and 1934?[32]

Even in the wake of the stock market crash of 1929, when the country found itself in economic depression, Gershwin continued to thrive. Concerts and tours featuring conductor or pianist Gershwin continued during the depression decade, and by the mid-1930s Gershwin was drawing as much as $2,000 per performance. The 1930s also saw George and Ira developing their relationship with the burgeoning movie business in Los Angeles. That relationship had begun in 1923, when the brothers had written the title song for the 1923 silent film *The Sunshine Trail*. In 1930, Gershwin received $50,000 for permission to use *Rhapsody in Blue* in the film about Paul Whiteman entitled *The King of Jazz*. Gershwin earned another $10,000 for performing the *Rhapsody* with Whiteman live for two weeks at the time of the film's opening at the Roxy in New York. In April 1930, George and Ira wrote the songs and lyrics for the movie *Delicious*, starring Janet Gaynor and Charles Farrell; this effort paid George $70,000 and Ira $30,000. And their 1936 contract to write songs for RKO resulted in a more permanent move to Hollywood: $55,000 for sixteen weeks' work on the Fred Astaire–Ginger Rogers movie *Watch Your Step* (renamed *Shall We Dance*), as well as an option by the studio for another film (*Damsel in Distress*) at a salary of $70,000.[33]

Gershwin also took on radio, a medium fast becoming the most important mode of popularizing songs, resulting in greater publishing and recording activity. In 1934, just after the grueling Reisman tour, he began his radio show *Music by Gershwin*, Monday and Friday evenings from 7:30 to 7:45 on the New York station WJZ (later broadcast by CBS in a single weekly half-hour format), for a reported salary of $2,000 per week. Writer Gilbert Seldes noted: "What he can play on the piano—and he can play anything—he puts down on paper, forgetting that we who listen are not gifted with his mastery of complicated rhythms. So he composes to be heard, not to be sung. He is lucky because we are becoming a nation of listeners, thanks to the radio."[34]

In an interview with the *New York Times* on 4 March 1934, Gershwin suggested that he found the radio show even more demanding than touring.[35] But the work came just as he was composing *Porgy and Bess*, and the income helped to finance the opera, as DuBose Heyward pointed out in an essay for *Stage Magazine*:

> It is the fashion in America to lament the prostitution of art by the big magazine, the radio, the moving pictures. With this I have little patience. Properly utilized, the radio and the pictures may be to the present-day writer what his prince was to Villon, the King of Bavaria was to Wagner. . . .

I decided that the silver screen should be my Maecenas, and George elected to serve radio. . . .

Statistics record the fact that there are 250,000,000 radios in America. Their contribution to the opera was indirect but important. Out of them for half an hour each week poured the glad tidings that Feenamint [the sponsor of *Music by Gershwin*] could be wheedled away from virtually any drug clerk in America for one dime—the tenth part of a dollar. And with the authentic medicine-man flair, the manufacturer distributed his information in an irresistible wrapper of Gershwin hits, with the composer at the piano.

There is, I imagine, a worse fate than that which derives from the use of a laxative gum. And, anyhow, we felt that the end justified the means.[36]

Moreover, beyond his musical activity, Gershwin was in demand as a public figure. For example, in 1936 he appeared before the House Patents Committee along with Irving Berlin, Rudy Vallee, and Gene Buck of ASCAP to protest the Duffy Bill, legislative action that would have altered the 1909 copyright act.[37]

In this particular grouping of fame, unusual talent, financial success, and activity, all within the emerging forms of musical technology, Gershwin stands apart from his predecessors and even his contemporaries. Stephen Foster, for example, was known largely as a songwriter, and even that image, as public knowledge, was limited. Foster "managed his finances badly, waiving royalty rights on many songs in order to get spot cash, then making up for the lack of royalty income by turning out potboilers."[38] His musical influences were primarily British and German folk song, despite his use of dialect that parodied African American speech patterns. Evidence about his piano-playing abilities is sketchy. And he knew too little about the new phenomenon of advertising for the arts that was beginning to take shape in the mid–nineteenth century, one of the most striking examples of which was P. T. Barnum's campaign for the singer Jenny Lind. Foster himself rode the tide of that wave with the marketing success of "Jeanie with the Light Brown Hair," but it was too little too late. In general, he rarely promoted himself and, according to musicologist William Austin, "deliberately sought to preserve some of his obscurity."[39]

Unlike Foster, pianist and composer Louis Moreau Gottschalk was well-known both as composer and performer. Moreover, Gottschalk captured the public imagination as a larger-than-life romantic figure. But he composed primarily piano music rather than songs. Even given the considerable rate of piano music publication and the popularity of the piano as a domestic instrument in the nineteenth century, piano music was a far more specialized and less popular venue than were songs. And ultimately—like Foster—Gottschalk predated twentieth-century technology and royalty fee collection.

Songwriters contemporary to Gershwin such as Kern or Porter or even Berlin were not usually known as performers or "famous" personalities and generally participated only passively in technological media by merely collecting royalties. And Kurt Weill was simply not the same kind of figure as

Gershwin. A German immigrant, he did not come to the United States until 1935, when he left Nazi Germany behind. Though Weill embraced such popular forms as the musical, he came to them from the point of view of a modernist composer and was never well-known as a performer. At the time of Gershwin's death, he was still known in America primarily for the *Three-penny Opera*. His first American musicals, *Johnny Johnson* (1936) and *Knicker-bocker Holiday* (1938), had not been popularly successful, and only in 1940 did he and Moss Hart approach Ira Gershwin about collaboration on the musical *I Am Listening*, soon retitled *Lady in the Dark*, after which Weill's Broadway and Hollywood careers gained momentum.

The career of George Gershwin was unique for his day and a harbinger of things to come in the careers of American popular musicians.

Gershwin came from a working-class background, with little formal music training, and almost immediately entered the arena of popular song, performing the music of others and eventually writing his own. He applied himself to the most vital popular venues of the day, from piano rolls and publishing to musical theater and film, and quickly gained both recognition and compensation. He was a composer who was both good *and* sought by a large popular audience, and he faced squarely the complexities of what talent and popular fame meant, dealing with sound reproduction, publishing, and media. In short, he was a fully functioning and highly visible popular musician within American culture, constantly crossing boundaries between composer and performer, talent and "star," gifted musician and compelling, sexy socialite with other popular luminaries such as Fred Astaire, Paulette Goddard, Ginger Rogers, Charlie Chaplin, and many others.

And here Gershwin broke ground in American music history. No one before had taken on such a range of technology and legality, with the attendant media attention, and arguably no contemporaries straddled the lines of performance, composition, and public imagery in quite the way he did: "By the early 1930s, his fame, his earning power, and the range of his works made Gershwin unique among American musicians."[40] Not until the rise of a new popular phenomenon—rock and roll—did American musicians such as Chuck Berry or Bob Dylan have to confront analogous factors.

Such a perspective suggests areas of further research that may enhance an understanding of Gershwin's role in American culture. First, in the popular journalism surrounding Gershwin, which kinds of writers—beyond the Virgil Thomsons and Paul Rosenfelds—addressed which topics? More systematic study of all contemporary views of Gershwin would contribute to a clearer idea of his imagery and power in the culture at large.

Second, what did Gershwin's stylistic derivations mean in his own context, particularly with regard to racial overtones? For example, William Austin's study of Stephen Foster explores the meaning of Foster's songs in their original nineteenth-century context, apart from the meanings cast backward upon them by the twentieth century.[41] Austin prefaces the study with eloquent, thoughtful insight into the problematic nature of the racial implications of Foster's songs—both in Foster's time and in the periods that have recycled them since his death. What would such a study of Gershwin's songs in their various twentieth-century contexts produce?

Third, what further information about Gershwin's career—such as royalty income from both publishing and recording, his relationship with ASCAP, and other publishg activities—should scholars explore? What songs sold best, and in what form: published or recorded? To what extent did these considerations guide Gershwin's artistic decisions?

Altogether, these factors point to a quality in Gershwin yet to be fully understood: Gershwin as a new kind of popular musical figure. Oscar Levant relates the story of Gershwin taking a taxi "uptown to see a Columbia football game. The driver wove an arabesque between the supports of the then elevated railroad. George leaned over and tapped him on the shoulder. 'For God's sake, man,' he remonstrated, 'drive carefully! You've got Gershwin in the car!'"[42] Gershwin had embraced the composite nature of American culture, and American culture had reinvented and exalted him. Like rock and roll itself, Gershwin was a genuinely and uniquely American phenomenon, more than the sum of its parts. George Gershwin had become simply Gershwin.

Notes

1. Ray Charles, "Strike Up the Band," from *Genius + Soul = Jazz*, Sandstone Music 5003, 1961; Big Joe Turner, "Summertime," from *In the Evening*, Pablo Records 2310-776, 1976.

2. Etta James, *Mystery Lady: Songs of Billie Holiday*, Private Music 82114, 1994; Booker T and the MGs, *And Now!*, Stax 711, 1966; Willie Nelson, *Stardust*, Columbia 35305, 1978 (produced by Booker T. Jones of Booker T and the MGs).

3. Aretha Franklin, "It Ain't Necessarily So," *Aretha*, Columbia 8412, 1960.

4. Sam Cooke, "Summertime"/"You Send Me," Keen 4013, 1957.

5. Billy Stewart, "Summertime," Chess 1966, 1966; Janis Joplin, "Summertime," *Cheap Thrills*, Columbia LP KCS 9700, 1968.

6. When People Were Shorter And Lived Near The Water, *Porgy*, JAF/Shimmy-Disc S044, 1991.

7. *The Glory of Gershwin*, Mercury 314522 727-4.

8. Isaac Goldberg, *George Gershwin: A Study in American Music* (New York: Simon & Schuster, 1931), 57.

9. Letter from George Gershwin to Isaac Goldberg, 30 June 1931, Harvard Theater Collection.

10. Charles Schwartz, *Gershwin: His Life and Music* (Indianapolis: Bobbs-Merrill, 1973), 56.

11. See Paul Charosh, "'Popular' and 'Classical' in the Mid–Nineteenth Century," *American Music* 10 (Summer 1992): 117–35.

12. Victor Fell Yellin, *Chadwick: Yankee Composer* (Washington, D.C.: Smithsonian Institution Press, 1990); Nicolas E. Tawa, *The Coming of Age of American Art Music* (New York: Greenwood Press, 1991); MacDonald Smith Moore, *Yankee Blues: Musical Culture and American Identity* (Bloomington: Indiana University Press, 1985).

13. Chadwick, "The Popular Music—Wherein Reform Is Necessary," *Proceedings of the Music Teachers' National Association 1877* (Delaware, Ohio: Geo. H. Thomson, Job Printer, 1877), 34–39, quoted in Yellin, *Chadwick*, 23–24.

14. Chadwick, "The Popular Music," quoted in Yellin, *Chadwick*, 24.

15. Yellin, *Chadwick*, 77–78.

16. Moore, *Yankee Blues*, 66.

17. Ibid., 80.

18. Ibid., 89.

19. Ibid., 131.

20. "Gershwin Bros.," *Time* 6 (20 July 1925): 14. A photo of Gershwin is on the cover.

21. Moore points out that Mason wondered why Gershwin got published when he did not. Further, "pointing to the prominence of Jews such as David Sarnoff in the new media, some Americans believed there existed a New York–Hollywood axis of Jewish cultural control" (Moore, *Yankee Blues*, 150).

22. John Ryan, *The Production of Culture in the Music Industry: The ASCAP-BMI Controversy* (Lanham, Md.: University Press of America, 1985), 72.

23. Schwartz, *Gershwin*, 188–93 and passim.

24. Samuel Nathaniel Behrman, *People in a Diary: A Memoir* (Boston: Little, Brown, 1972), 245, 246.

25. See K. Robert Schwartz, "Composers' Closets Open for All to See," *New York Times*, 19 June 1994, sec. 2, p. 1.

26. Carol J. Oja, "Gershwin and the American Modernists of the 1920s," *Musical Quarterly* 78 (Winter 1994): 646–68.

27. Schwartz, *Gershwin*, 256.

28. Merle Armitage, ed., *George Gershwin* (New York: Longmans, Green, 1938).

29. The 1939 movie *Swanee River*, a loose biography of Stephen Foster, was itself less a response to the actual figure of Foster than a rendering of American cultural history at a time when the nation was seeking to reinforce its own identity—a statement that applies in some degree to all Hollywood biopics of American composers. Regarding the film *Rhapsody in Blue*, see Charlotte Greenspan's essay in this collection.

30. Richard Crawford, "It Ain't Necessarily Soul": Gershwin's 'Porgy and Bess' As a Symbol," *Yearbook for Inter-American Musical Research* 8 (1972): 17–38.

31. Ibid., 23.

32. Stanley Sadie, ed., *New Grove Dictionary of Music and Musicians*, 6th ed., s.v. "Gershwin, George."

33. Schwartz, *Gershwin*, 275.

34. Gilbert Seldes, "The Gershwin Case," *Esquire* 2 (October 1934): 108, 130.

35. "Composer of a Thousand Songs Finds Radio Is Fast Pace-Maker," *New York Times*, 4 March 1934, sec. 9, p. 11.

36. DuBose Heyward, "Porgy and Bess Return on Wings of Song," *Stage Magazine* 13 (October 1935): 25–28.

37. Schwartz, *Gershwin*, 275.

38. Sadie, *New Grove Dictionary of Music and Musicians*, 6th ed., s.v. "Foster, Stephen."

39. William W. Austin, *"Susanna," "Jeanie," and "The Old Folks at Home": The Songs of Stephen C. Foster from His Time to Ours*, 2d ed. (Urbana: University of Illinois Press, 1987), 202.

40. Sadie, *New Grove Dictionary of Music and Musicians*, s.v. "Gershwin, George."

41. Austin, *"Susanna," "Jeanie," and "The Old Folks at Home."*

42. Oscar Levant, *A Smattering of Ignorance* (New York: G. P. Putnam's Sons, 1941), 150.

9 : George Gershwin and Jazz

C. ANDRÉ BARBERA

Gershwin, for all of his profound talents as a pianist and a composer of a modern classical music form, had little in common
with jazz. His was a superficial knowledge at best, acquired
chiefly from his occasional visits to Lenox avenue, uptown, and
from his acquaintances among colored musicians on Broadway.

—Dave Dexter Jr., *Jazz Cavalcade: The Inside Story of Jazz*

It is no longer possible, as it was fifteen or twenty years ago, for
an alert, reasonably well-informed person to confuse authentic
jazz with cheap dance music or pretentious pieces like *Rhapsody
in Blue*. . . .
    It is assuredly one of the great miracles of jazz that the same
harmonic humus in which Gershwin, for all his gifts, had raised
only the vapid "Embraceable You" could produce, in the hands
of Charlie Parker . . . such a marvelous melodic flower as his famous solo.

—André Hodeir, *Jazz: Its Evolution and Essence*

The estimation of music as jazz confers honor, distinction, and racial identity. Certainly Dave Dexter and André Hodeir did not consider George
Gershwin a jazz musician or composer. They made these remarks in response to writings from the 1920s and 1930s that defined jazz so broadly
as to include pieces like *Rhapsody in Blue*. Early commentators such as Paul
Whiteman, Henry Osgood, and Isaac Goldberg, writing on the *new* music,
had proclaimed Gershwin to be its leading exponent.[1] Osgood even entitled
a chapter of his book on jazz "Gershwin, the White Hope." In recent decades
the need to classify popular music and to decide whether or not Gershwin
wrote jazz may be less pressing. In summarizing Gershwin's music, Richard
Crawford noted: "Such matters of musical taxonomy no longer seem as significant today."[2] Nevertheless, as long as the label "jazz" connotes honor
and racial identity, the issue of classification is still relevant, as it was for
Dexter and Hodeir in the 1940s and 1950s.

One might address the issue of Gershwin and jazz naively by looking in jazz reference books to see if his name appears as an entry. In most recent works Gershwin is absent, but if one goes back thirty years, his name is listed. For example, Gershwin is entered in both the 1955 and 1960 editions of Leonard Feather's *Encyclopedia of Jazz*.[3] One reads in the later edition: "Gershwin's symphonic works made only superficial use of jazz devices and are now not generally considered to be an important part of jazz history; his main importance to jazzmen has been the use of the chord patterns (and frequently the melody) of many of his popular songs as the basis for jazz improvisation and orchestrations."

Proceeding less naively, one might attempt to define jazz first and then to evaluate Gershwin's music accordingly, although one discovers that the definition of jazz has changed since the 1920s, when Gershwin's music first achieved widespread popularity. Writers on jazz often flounder in their attempts to define the subject, owing in part to the uncertain status of jazz as popular, folk, or art music. Further complicating the task of definition are the characteristics of improvised performance, oral transmission, and living tradition. Thirty years ago, David Baskerville offered the following:

> Jazz is a vocal or instrumental music for solo or group performance which is sometimes written down, other times improvised; it is usually based on a regularly-flowing rhythm against which occur, from time to time, polyrhythms and syncopations; jazz improvisers and arrangers normally use popular songs and employ them in a theme-and-variations technique; until ca. 1950 jazz has been based on western European tonal harmony, to which performers often add "blue" tonality and special timbres; jazz occurs only when the music is performed in jazz style.[4]

Baskerville does not directly mention African Americans in his definition, although "blue" tonality may refer indirectly to African American folk song.

In a color-blind society a definition of jazz might be sufficient if it determined whether or not a certain uncatalogued piece or performance fell into the category of jazz. But jazz is hardly color-blind music. Recent definitions of jazz acknowledge to varying degrees the racial stance of the music. Thus, one reads that jazz is an "eclectic, expanding collection of twentieth-century styles, principally instrumental and of black American creation. Swing and improvisation are essential to several styles, but only an emphasis on characteristic timbres spans all musics called jazz, whether functional or artistic, popular or esoteric, instrumental or vocal, improvised or composed, 'hot' or 'cool.'"[5] Even here "black American creation" may refer only to the origins of jazz or to the successive changes in style, sometimes in reaction to appropriation by the mainstream, established styles. More recently jazz has been defined as "a music created mainly by black Americans in the early 20th century through an amalgamation of elements drawn from European-American and tribal African musics."[6]

Jazz is black music. It originated as music of African Americans and has been developed primarily by them. Jazz has grown up in an affluent, racist society, one that over a century ago accorded its members citizenship regardless of race. But citizenship has been no guarantee of affluence. In this decade, 44 percent of black children in the United States are living in poverty, triple the percentage for white children.[7] In such an environment, one *ought* to document the appropriation of African American culture regardless of when or how ingenuously it took place. It is only a slight exaggeration to claim that the oppressor, not being satisfied with hoarding the material goods, has attempted to steal the soul of the oppressed. In this regard, Gershwin's appropriation of African American music is hardly unique but is nevertheless troublesome, since his musical legacy has provided so much beauty and pleasure.

There exist, in fact, two facets to the identification of George Gershwin with jazz—one historical and one analytical. The first concerns the labeling of Gershwin's music as jazz during the 1920s and 1930s. The second concerns the adoption of Gershwin's songs by jazz musicians, especially in the 1930s, 1940s, and 1950s, as vehicles for improvisation. This essay addresses these two matters, further subdividing the historical issue along the lines of popular music and art music.

The 1920s witnessed widespread and lengthy discussion of jazz—what it is? is it here to stay?—because its complex rhythms, blue tonality, and idiomatic timbres had reached a large audience during that decade. Moreover, its popularity had spread like wildfire. A related and specialized aspect of this discussion concerned the search for a characteristically American school of composition. Although the search was eventually abandoned,[8] it held the attention of many composers, musicians, and writers of the time. In the minds and ears of some, no music could be more typically American than jazz. Composers and critics alike took note of the tendency for the cultivated musical traditions to draw from the vernacular. Gershwin wrote: "The great music of the past in other countries has always been built on folk-music. This is the strongest source of musical fecundity. America is no exception among the countries. The best music being written today is music which comes from folk-sources."[9] Even after rejecting the use of jazz in his own works, Aaron Copland observed in 1941: "The serious composer needs freshening occasionally from the less conscious and more naive springhead of popular or folk music. . . . The contemporary composer's use of jazz had logic and tradition behind it and was more or less to be expected."[10] Gershwin had noted earlier: "One country may prefer a peculiar rhythm or a note like the seventh. This it stresses, and it becomes identified with that nation. In America this preferred rhythm is called jazz. . . . Jazz is the result of the energy stored up in America. It is a very energetic kind of music, noisy, boisterous and even vulgar. One thing is certain. Jazz has contributed an enduring value to America in the sense that it has expressed ourselves."[11]

The matter of symphonic jazz requires, first, a consideration of the popular songs of the Jazz Age. No product of Tin Pan Alley would likely satisfy the definitions of jazz cited earlier, but definitions and categories were broader and vaguer in the 1920s. In his 1926 volume on jazz, Henry O. Osgood devoted two chapters to Gershwin in which he discussed jazz songs as well as symphonic jazz works. Special praise went to "Swanee" and "Fascinating Rhythm."[12] Books like Osgood's had a mission in addition to presenting and explaining the new music—they aimed to defend jazz against charges of musical and moral subversion. Osgood indicates scant awareness of the jazz tradition now recognized as the main line: the music of Joe Oliver, Louis Armstrong, and Jelly Roll Morton. Rather than discussing this music, Osgood sought to ward off criticism leveled against the compositions of Irving Berlin and George Gershwin.[13]

Among Jazz Age writings on jazz, the two volumes by Isaac Goldberg present the rare view that takes into account the blending of African American and European sources in America's popular music. In a book on Gershwin's music, Goldberg devoted a chapter to jazz, much of which defended the new music against charges that it was immoral, entertaining and therefore not serious, and a product of the Machine Age.[14] In an earlier work on Tin Pan Alley, Goldberg addressed the jazz nature of popular songs of the 1920s. A chapter entitled "King Jazz" begins: "Jazz is all things to all ears."[15] Later Gershwin noted similarly: "It is difficult to determine what enduring values, esthetically, jazz has contributed, because jazz is a word which has been used for at least five or six different types of music."[16] In a frank appraisal of the origins and development of jazz, Goldberg observed: "Jazz is essentially an American development of Afro-American thematic material. Its fundamental rhythm and its characteristic melody derive from the Negro; its commercialization belongs largely to the popular-song industry of the New York white."[17] Goldberg discussed the jazz rhythms of "Clap Yo' Hands" and "Fascinating Rhythm" but concluded by emphasizing the separation between origin and popular manifestation. "What began as Afro-American folksong became transformed into cosmopolitan culture. The commercialism of Gotham quickly denatured the article for white consumption."[18]

Although "jazz" could mean all things to all people in the 1920s, for some it was a disease, a dangerous infection originating in black culture and infiltrating the white mainstream.[19] In this context, the blue thirds of "How Long Has This Been Going On?" were sufficient to contaminate the entire piece in the ears of some listeners. From today's perspective, one can see and hear those blue thirds as attractive reflections of black music encapsulated within the thirty-two-measure American popular song. That they were an honest translation from one culture to another is attested to by the multitude of black jazz musicians—usually singers—who have performed and recorded this song.[20] But few thoughtful listeners over the past half century would consider "How Long Has This Been Going On?" or any other song of Gershwin to be jazz per se. These songs are musical miniatures that lack, in their original formulation, most of the identifying timbral, rhythmic, and improvisatory characteristics of jazz.

Gershwin's symphonic works, especially *Rhapsody in Blue* and the Concerto in F, have attracted wider attention and spurred far more controversy within the jazz world than his songs. Under the direction and lavish promotion of Paul Whiteman, *Rhapsody in Blue* premiered 12 February 1924 at Aeolian Hall in New York. Although this performance turned out to be one of the major musical events of this century, the *Rhapsody* was hardly the first attempt to incorporate jazz or jazz-related material into the cultivated musical tradition. Famous experiments along this line by Debussy, Stravinsky, Milhaud, and other Europeans as well as Henry Gilbert, John Carpenter, and other Americans preceded the *Rhapsody*. In New York, too, there was significant precedent for introducing jazz music into the concert hall. As early as 1912, and again in 1913 and 1914, James Reese Europe conducted his Clef Club Orchestra in a "Concert of Negro Music" at Carnegie Hall.[21] More immediate to the *Rhapsody* was a recital given at Aeolian Hall on 1 November 1923 by the singer Eva Gauthier, accompanied by pianists Max Jaffe and Gershwin. The program comprised a mixture of art songs (accompanied by Jaffe) and popular songs (accompanied by Gershwin), the latter including, among others, Berlin's "Alexander's Ragtime Band" and Gershwin's "Innocent Ingenue Baby," "Stairway to Paradise," and "Swanee."[22] Gershwin had also preceded the *Rhapsody* with *Blue Monday*, a jazz opera ("Opera Ala Afro-American") that closed after its first New York performance on 28 August 1922 at the Globe Theater. The opera was orchestrated by Gershwin's African American friend Will Vodery, who had been a member of Reese's Clef Club Orchestra.

The familiar story of the *Rhapsody*'s origin need not be retold here. The work's composition and performance, however, were the primary cause for the connection of Gershwin's name with jazz in the 1920s. With this composition, Gershwin "fired the jazz shot that was heard round the world."[23] Although other works such as the Concerto in F, Preludes for Piano, several songs, and even *Porgy and Bess* (in the 1930s) contributed to this association, it was primarily *Rhapsody in Blue* and its promotion by Whiteman that elicited comment, praise, and condemnation revolving around the notions of symphonic jazz, musical taxonomy, and the school of American classical composition. That discussion, which extends to the present, began with reviews of the work that appeared in the New York press on the day following the premiere.

Ferde Grofé orchestrated the *Rhapsody* for Whiteman's dance band, a band normally consisting of fourteen musicians but expanded to twenty-three for the Aeolian Hall concert.[24] With musicians playing more than one instrument, a total of thirty-six instruments were employed. Wind instruments predominated.[25] Thus, the very nature and sound of the band invited listeners to associate what they heard with jazz, as did the setting and the program notes.[26]

The first sound of the *Rhapsody*, the clarinet glissando, says "jazz" to audiences from 1924 to the present, but neither Gershwin nor Grofé was responsible for this special effect. Gershwin's piano score contained a seventeen-note run leading from a trill on F below middle C to high B♭. Grofé assigned this run to the clarinet. Apparently intending to be humorous, Ross Gorman, lead reed player in Whiteman's band, performed the run as a glissando during a rehearsal. Gershwin liked the sound, and thus it became the jazz—or was it klezmer?—opening statement of the piece.[27] The opening theme, with its minor seventh and both minor and major thirds, presents a notated form of the blue tonality. A subsequent theme is accompanied by the first half of the rhythmic figure associated with the Cuban *clavé* —♩. ♩. ♩—which is also found in the Charleston, one of the jazz dances of the Jazz Age. Thus, the audience's predisposition to hear the *Rhapsody* as jazz was confirmed by the music. Gershwin himself left little doubt as to his intentions in composing the work. As reported by Goldberg, Gershwin remarked: "There had been so much chatter about the limitations of jazz, not to speak of the manifest misunderstandings of its function. Jazz, they said, had to be in strict time. It had to cling to dance rhythms. I resolved, if possible, to kill that misconception with one sturdy blow. . . . The rhapsody, as you see, began as a purpose, not a plan."[28]

The *Rhapsody* received mixed reviews,[29] and some later writers on jazz were especially critical of Gershwin's attempt to move beyond "the limitations of jazz." Twenty years after the premiere, Dave Dexter inveighed against the work:

> The *Rhapsody*, of course, was and always will remain nothing more than *ersatz* jazz, equally as incompatible with the original New Orleans jazz music as Pee-Wee Russell's clarinet would appear if featured in a Ravel suite conducted by Toscanini. In one respect, the Aeolian concert (which later was followed by a repeat performance at Carnegie Hall) is to be regretted in the colorful history of jazz music, for it gave rise to a misunderstanding which still exists and which may never be eliminated completely.[30]

Thirty years after the premiere, jazz writers continued to pillory the *Rhapsody*. Hodeir's vitriol was cited earlier (p. 1). Jazz historians William Grossman and Jack Farrell condemned the entire Aeolian Hall concert. "[Whiteman's] clumsily syncopated 'jazz' was gradually replaced with ponderous pseudosymphonic harmonies played over dance rhythms, culminating in the concert rendition of Gershwin's *Rhapsody in Blue*, one of the most ludicrous of the popular attempts during the 1920s to merge jazz and 'serious' music."[31]

Not all criticism of the *Rhapsody* was negative, however. Deems Taylor, writing for the *New York World*, labeled the *Rhapsody* "genuine jazz music, not only in its scoring but in its idiom. . . . [Gershwin] may yet bring jazz out of the kitchen."[32] Subsequently Taylor had second thoughts about these observations, discussed later. Two years after the *Rhapsody's* premiere, Osgood published one of the most enthusiastic and favorable responses to the work, as well as to Gershwin's Concerto in F. Noting that Victor Herbert had died without engaging in real jazz experimentation, Osgood argued that Gershwin was uniquely suited "to take the elements of jazz and employ them with a distinct degree of success in forms of composition higher and larger than popular songs and musical comedy." With the *Rhapsody*, Gershwin had succeeded in "graft[ing] upon the great trunk of legitimate music little offshoots of that vigorous sapling which is the only really original thing America has produced in music—jazz."[33] Osgood extolled the originality of Gershwin's work by asking: "Can anybody show pages from an orchestral score that preceded the 'Rhapsody' and say, 'Here is where Gershwin got his idea.'"[34] In the 1930s, Virgil Thomson acknowledged the work as "the most successful orchestral piece ever launched by any American composer."[35] Nearly forty years after its premiere, the arguments surrounding the *Rhapsody* have narrowed from discussion of Gershwin's compositional skills and their application in the work to dialectic on the *Rhapsody*'s unique combination of jazz and the cultivated tradition. Samuel Charters wrote:

> The first extended composition in a "jazz" idiom, [the *Rhapsody in Blue*] is perhaps the only successful one. Since the twenties, most of the successful jazz orchestra leaders, especially Duke Ellington, have attempted to write long "jazz suites," but the music has usually been little more than a suite of dance melodies interspersed with unrelated orchestral bridges. Gershwin successfully worked within the melodic framework of the symphonic rhapsody while still keeping the idiomatic characteristics of the popular blues song."[36]

With a commission from conductor Walter Damrosch and the New York Symphony Orchestra, Gershwin followed the *Rhapsody in Blue* with his Concerto in F, which premiered at Carnegie Hall on 3 December 1925. Gershwin desired to put his fledgling studies of orchestration into practice as well as to demonstrate that the *Rhapsody* was not a fluke. He noted:

> Many persons had thought that the *Rhapsody* was only a happy accident. Well, I went out, for one thing, to show them that there was more where that had come from. I made up my mind to do a piece of absolute music. The *Rhapsody*, as its title implied, was a blues impression. The Concerto would be unrelated to any program. And that is exactly how I wrote it. I learned a great deal from the experience. Particularly in the handling of instruments in combination.[37]

The Concerto received a more favorable reception than the *Rhapsody*, perhaps because critics had some idea of what to expect. The Concerto also represents an advance in compositional complexity over the *Rhapsody*. Walter Damrosch, whose association with the Concerto was similar to Whiteman's with the *Rhapsody*, proclaimed:

> Various composers have been walking around jazz like a cat around a plate of hot soup, waiting for it to cool off, so that they could enjoy it without burning their tongues, hitherto accustomed only to the more tepid liquid distilled by cooks of the classical school. Lady Jazz . . . has encountered no knight who could lift her to a level that would enable her to be received as a respectable member in musical circles.
>
> George Gershwin seems to have accomplished this miracle. He has done

it boldly by dressing this extremely independent and up-to-date young lady
in the classical garb of a concerto. Yet he has not detracted one whit from her
fascinating personality.[38]

Osgood praised the Concerto as the worthy successor to the *Rhapsody*.
The Concerto carried out "the promise of the *Rhapsody* in proving the
adaptability of jazz elements to compositions in the larger form."[39] Abbe
Niles viewed the Concerto as expressing "The Spirit of Young America,"[40]
and Isaac Goldberg, in the most extensive contemporary treatment of the
work, found the Concerto "to be in more than one respect a decided advance over the *Rhapsody*."[41]

All this praise notwithstanding, Constant Lambert decried the work a
few years later:

> The composer, trying to write a Lisztian concerto in jazz style, has used only
> the non-barbaric elements in dance music, the result being neither good jazz
> nor good Liszt, and in no sense of the word a good concerto. Although other
> American composers, and even Gershwin himself, have produced works of
> greater caliber in this style, the shadow of the *Rhapsody in Blue* hangs over
> most of them and they remain the hybrid child of a hybrid. A rather know-
> ing and unpleasant child too, ashamed of its parents and boasting of its
> French lessons.[42]

In a more recent evaluation, David Baskerville observed: "As with the *Rhapsody*, the composer had trouble with the connection of ideas, but his presentation of certain material, specifically the theme at rehearsal number 4,
elevated 'the blues to unprecedented height.'"[43]

From their observations and criticisms of *Rhapsody in Blue* and Concerto
in F, the Jazz Age writers and colleagues from subsequent decades clearly
revealed that to their ears Gershwin had wedded jazz with music from the
cultivated tradition. Whether or not the marriage was a happy one remains
a matter of contention. It is sufficient here to note the basic connection of
Gershwin's name to jazz during the 1920s. Subsequent compositions such as
An American in Paris and *Cuban Overture* reinforced the basic connection.
Only with the refined and more narrow definitions of jazz formulated over
the past two decades can one categorically exclude works such as the *Rhapsody* and Concerto from the world of jazz proper.

Porgy and Bess, Gershwin's most mature and best work, presents a special
case. No critic in the 1930s and no one since has labeled the opera outright
"jazz." In fact, the label "jazz" played a smaller role in Gershwin's musical
life by the mid-1930s, although the categorical controversy over the Jazz
Age compositions persisted. While the term "jazz" had figured prominently
in Gershwin's self-perception during the 1920s, "folk music" seems to have
emerged in the 1930s and replaced the earlier label. When asked to comment on the relationship of jazz to American music, especially of the cultivated tradition, Gershwin was quick to include jazz with other folk music:
"Jazz, ragtime, Negro spirituals and blues, Southern mountain songs, coun-

try fiddling, and cowboy songs can all be employed in the creation of American art-music, and are actually used by many composers now."[44] In 1934, Gershwin exchanged his occasional sojourns to Harlem nightclubs for a summer's residence on Folly Beach, an island off the coast of Charleston, South Carolina, in order to work on *Porgy and Bess*. Adjacent to Folly Beach, James Island is inhabited by Gullahs, whose music Gershwin sought to absorb. With *Porgy and Bess*, therefore, one should seek not the opera's relationship to jazz but rather its relationship to African American folk song. With what degree of authority could a Brooklynite son of immigrants appropriate music from African Americans?

Among the various criticisms of *Porgy and Bess*, those leveled at it by Virgil Thomson were among the most severe and caustic. He railed: "One can see through *Porgy* that Gershwin has not and never did have the power of sustained musical development." But the critic could not completely suppress his enchantment with the opera or his admiration for Gershwin's compositional gifts. After noting that Gershwin "is still not a very serious composer," Thomson observed: "With a libretto that should never have been accepted on a subject that should never have been chosen, a man who should never have attempted it has written a work that has considerable power." Regarding Gershwin's use of black music in the opera, Thomson wrote: "Folklore subjects recounted by an outsider are only valid as long as the folk in question is unable to speak for itself, which is certainly not true of the American Negro in 1935."[45]

In response to criticism of the opera, especially of his appropriation of African American folk song, Gershwin wrote:

> "Porgy and Bess" is a folk tale. Its people naturally would sing folk music. When I first began work on the music I decided against the use of original folk material because I wanted the music to be all of one piece. Therefore I wrote my own spirituals and folksongs. But they are still folk music—and therefore, being in operatic form, "Porgy and Bess" becomes a folk opera.
>
> However, because "Porgy and Bess" deals with Negro life in America it brings to the operatic form elements that have never before appeared in opera and I have adapted my method to utilize the drama, the humor, the superstition, the religious fervor, the dancing and the irrepressible high spirits of the race. If, in doing this, I have created a new form, which combines opera with theatre, this new form has come quite naturally out of the material.[46]

Gershwin's remarks about folk music don't ring true, especially his claim that he has written folk songs. "I Got Plenty o' Nuttin'" was doubtless intended to be one of these folk songs, with its simple, triadic opening phrase. The abrupt modulation in the second half of the first phrase to the major submediant, however, and especially the setting of the bridge section in the relative minor of the dominant hardly seem indicative of folk song. Gershwin composed one song for the opera that has become a folk song—namely, "Summertime"—although not according to the means that he intended. Decades of performance by jazz musicians, pop singers, rock bands, and parents singing their children to sleep have transformed this opening song of *Porgy and Bess* into common parlance. The transformation has taken its toll on the original, simplifying and homogenizing a tune that already was fairly simple. For example, in vernacular performance, one rarely hears the ascending melodic minor scale that so beautifully accompanies the melody.

Gershwin wrote about his attempt to write black music in the opera:

> When I chose "Porgy and Bess," a tale of Charleston Negroes, for a subject, I made sure that it would enable me to write light as well as serious music and that it would enable me to include humor as well as tragedy—in fact, all of the elements of entertainment for the eye as well as the ear, because the Negroes, as a race, have all these qualities inherent in them. They are ideal for my purpose because they express themselves not only by the spoken word but quite naturally by song and dance.

After remarking on the good fortune to have John W. Bubbles, Todd Duncan, and Anne Brown sing leading roles in the opera, Gershwin continued: "We were able to find these people because what we wanted from them lies in their race. And thus it lies in our story of their race."[47]

These remarks objectify African American people, especially the sentence that begins: "They are ideal for my purpose . . ." Such statements are demeaning and, in their casualness, reveal the deep-seated racism that pervades our culture. Gershwin, of course, is no more culpable than the majority of us who subvert our own dignity by unconsciously participating in racist oppression. And Gershwin deserves some musical credit, because his attraction to and appropriation of African American music, ever since "Swanee" of 1919, was based on his recognition of the intrinsic merit of that music.

Gershwin concluded his defense of *Porgy and Bess* by quoting the lyrics of several songs in the opera. Ending with "There's a Boat Dat's Leavin' Soon for New York," Gershwin noted: "All of these are, I believe, lines that come naturally from the Negro. They make for folk music. Thus 'Porgy and Bess' becomes a folk opera—opera for the theatre, with drama, humor, song and dance."[48] Gershwin's conclusion is obviously sincere and well-intended. The authenticity of *Porgy and Bess* as African American music, of course, was and always will be dubious.[49] That the opera is filled with gorgeous music is clear to most listeners, although it is the music of Gershwin and no one else. The music does not speak for African Americans, but it speaks eloquently of them.

In summary, the loosely defined label of jazz in the 1920s easily included George Gershwin's ventures into art music. This already vague notion of jazz, a notion that materialized during the Jazz Age, had an evolutionary aspect that Osgood recognized in the conclusion to his study of jazz:

> Already jazz has shown itself to be the first art innovation originating in America to be accepted seriously in Europe and acknowledged as purely American. Only time will tell whether it is to become a school in serious music, an acknowledged influence in the music of the world.

Will there arise a super-Gershwin to develop it far, far away from its faults? That, to become a real note in world music, it must rid itself of certain limitations is patent. In another ten years, twenty years, we shall know its fate. And if, as is not unlikely, it withers and dies, still only the popular dance music of the day, to be succeeded by some new form that catches the popular fancy, at least the honor of having been the first and only original art that the United States of America has brought forth in a century and a half of trying can never be taken away from it.[50]

By the 1930s, Gershwin saw himself not as a jazz composer but rather as a composer who drew inspiration from jazz and African American music. Goldberg reported in his study of 1931: "Gershwin and I were once discussing the mathematical element at the bottom of the jazz rhythms and counter-rhythms. He has a very definite notion of what he is doing, always. All of a sudden, after an involved exposition, he exclaimed: 'Now, what the deuce do I care about Jazz!'" Goldberg went on to explain that the category of jazz per se was of little interest to Gershwin:

> To George, as to any genuine composer, it is Music that comes first. If jazz should threaten to become a hampering stereotype, a "tradition" in its turn, George would go forward to the next fresh impulse that arose in him. You may call him the King of jazz and associate his name with the lifting of jazz into musical artistry. Very well, and his best thanks. But not on that account is he to be thrust into a pigeonhole.
> George Gershwin did not begin as a jazzer; he will not end as one.[51]

Two years later, Henry Cowell recorded remarks by Gershwin that clarify Gershwin's thought about jazz as musical inspiration. As I reported earlier, Gershwin pointed out the tendency of many art composers to draw on the vernacular. He concluded: "Jazz I regard as an American folk-music; not the only one, but a very powerful one which is probably in the blood and feeling of the American people more than any other style of folk-music. I believe that it can be made the basis of serious symphonic works of lasting value, in the hands of a composer with talent for both jazz and symphonic music."[52] Significantly, Gershwin cited jazz as only one of many American folk musics, albeit one of the most distinctive.

Gershwin did not abandon jazz in the 1930s so much as he expanded his horizon to include black music in general. Aaron Copland was much more explicit in severing his ties with jazz. He wrote: "The whole gamut of jazz emotions consists of the 'blues' mood and the wild, hysterical, grotesque mood."[53] After noting the use of jazz in his piano concerto and *Music for the Theater*, Copland continued: "This proved to be the last of my 'experiments' with symphonic jazz. With the *Concerto* I felt I had done all I could with the idiom, considering its limited emotional scope. True, it was an easy way to be an American in musical terms, but all American music could not possibly be confined to two dominant jazz moods: the 'blues' and the snappy number."[54]

Copland's remarks about the expressive capability of jazz betray his ignorance, although to his mind these were the limitations of jazz as a well-spring for art music. Deems Taylor held similar views about so-called symphonic jazz:

> There is much talk in contemporary circles of making jazz the basis of American music. Thus far only one composer, the lamented George Gershwin, has done anything memorable in that idiom. The *Rhapsody in Blue*, the Concerto in F, and *An American in Paris* may be reckoned as genuine, if not monumental, contributions to contemporary music; but I am inclined to credit their achievement to Gershwin rather than to jazz. The trouble with jazz, to this observer at least, is twofold. First, it is, so far, extremely limited in its emotional range. The best jazz appeals, as Gilbert Seldes once put it, exclusively to the feet. It stimulates, it stirs, it cheers—even inebriates; but it opens no doors to the unseen and the inexpressible. It neither inspires nor consoles. When it does essay the tragic mood, as in the much-admired "blues," it is merely mawkish.
>
> Moreover, jazz is not a wellspring of music; it is a method of writing music, a rhythmic idiom, a formula. And formulas are pretty sterile ground upon which to grow the flower of art.[55]

Both Copland and Taylor address the matter of an American school of composition, a concern that helped strengthen the link between Gershwin's name and jazz by attaching additional importance to works such as the *Rhapsody* and Concerto in F.

Taylor's dismissal included not only jazz but also spirituals, and by extension one might infer all African American music. Regarding the use of spirituals as a basis of American music, Taylor wrote:

> They were undoubtedly created in this country, and they are a mine of magnificent musical material. But they are not American—that is, in the sense of expressing the soul of the average white American. We may be thrilled by their beauty. But beauty is not enough, at least in a folksong. What we are looking for is some common fund of music that awakens ancestral echoes within us; and so far as blood is concerned, the finale of the Ninth Symphony is more likely to do that than "Swing Low, Sweet Chariot."[56]

These lines, published in 1937, are a timely response to *Porgy and Bess*. Taylor's observations ring less true now, after an ensuing half century of popular music thoroughly permeated by African American folk music and jazz. As the distinction between cultivated and vernacular traditions becomes blurred, one wonders if African American music is not in fact the musical source that Taylor sought to deny. And particularly ironic is the fate of spirituals, which have become exactly what Taylor denied them to be—an expression of the average white American's soul—while their emotional justification among black Americans has dissipated. In this light, Gershwin's art music can be viewed not as isolated compositions resisting categorization but rather as early examples of a vaguely defined yet characteristic musical tradition of the United States.

In the 1990s, probably no thoughtful listener would identify Gershwin's art music as jazz. Many listeners would base this decision on the absence of improvisation in these compositions. Although neither necessary nor sufficient for jazz, improvisation is one of the most strongly marked characteristics of jazz. Improvisation marks jazz as a performers' art, with the composer usually standing on the sidelines. Some jazz musicians, such as Duke Ellington, are perceived as composers as well as performers or band leaders. But Ellington's fame and prestige as a jazz musician rests at least as much on his songs and shorter pieces, and on his band's performances of them, as it does on his large-scale compositions, his art works.

Had Gershwin never written *Rhapsody in Blue*, *Porgy and Bess*, or any of the other art-music compositions, his name would still be closely associated with jazz and African American music because of his songs. Like Harold Arlen and others, Gershwin relied often on blue tonality to add pungency to his songs, although this reliance is merely a superficial link to the world of jazz. A more important connection to jazz than blue notes is the widespread adoption of Gershwin's songs by jazz musicians as vehicles for improvisation. The remainder of this essay considers some of the reasons why Gershwin's songs have proven so attractive to jazz musicians, especially during the 1930s, 1940s, and 1950s.

First, some caveats and disclaimers. Gershwin's songs have received innumerable renditions on record and in performance. Ella Fitzgerald, Oscar Peterson, Miles Davis, Dave Grusin, and many others have recorded entire albums of Gershwin's music. The performances cited later are simply instances of general claims for which hundreds of other performances could be cited. And counterexamples exist for just about every generalization made in the following paragraphs. One's listening experience can account for only a small fraction of the total number of Gershwin's songs performed by jazz musicians. Moreover, this study, like most others in jazz, is limited and skewed by the nature of sound recordings. In other words, the record industry has preserved only a segment of jazz. As is the case with other oral, largely nonliterate traditions, some aspects of influence and the material itself—in this case, musical performances—are lost.

Second, two general observations. Gershwin's songs were popular among jazz musicians first of all because they were very popular in general. Since the 1920s, jazz musicians have drawn freely upon the rich store of American popular song, where they found music by Irving Berlin, Jerome Kern, Cole Porter, and, of course, George Gershwin. Thus, the affinity to jazz, although based on the intrinsic quality of Gershwin's songs, has nothing to do initially with the songs' special suitability for jazz.

A second reason for jazz's appropriation of Gershwin's songs is at least superficially musical—that is, the appearance of blue notes in the melodies. Gershwin's use of African American music goes back at least to his first hit, "Swanee," although the appropriation is minimal in that instance. Many writers of popular songs, especially in the 1920s, availed themselves of the blue tonality as well as jazz or popular dance rhythms, but few employed

EXAMPLE 9.1

blue notes to the extent that Gershwin did. Especially clear and memorable are the occurrences of blue thirds, actually well-tempered blue thirds, in "Somebody Loves Me" (m. 4)[57] and "How Long Has This Been Going On?" (See example 9.1.)

The affinity between Gershwin and jazz goes deeper. Gershwin is probably the favorite songwriter of jazz musicians. This is so not only for the general reasons stated earlier, which are not peculiar to jazz, but also because his songs contain internal musical characteristics that jazz musicians find attractive. Four such characteristics will be considered here: rhythm, melody, harmony, and phrasing or structure.

Rhythm

Of the four characteristics, rhythm in Gershwin's songs is the least important for this discussion. It may seem odd that the most prominent aspect of jazz, its rhythm, would have the slightest connection with the rhythms of Gershwin's songs. There are, for example, those superficially jazzy rhythms in "Fascinating Rhythm" (mm. 1–4) and "I Got Rhythm" (mm. 1–6). In 1926, Henry Osgood could describe "Fascinating Rhythm" as "one of the best examples in existence of jazz syncopation."[58] But those rhythms are now recognized as stilted notations of jazz syncopation, and of little interest to jazz musicians, who tend to completely ignore the rhythmic joke of "I Got Rhythm" as well as the rhythmic curlicues of "Fascinating Rhythm."[59]

The relatively common and natural syncopations of Gershwin's songs along with the conversational setting of text probably account more for the jazz association than the hard-cast rhythms of "I Got Rhythm" and "Fascinating Rhythm." Syncopation occurs characteristically at the beginning of "How Long Has This Been Going On?," "A Foggy Day," and "They Can't Take That Away from Me." (See example 9.2.) Slightly less natural but nevertheless jazzy is the approximation of swing that occurs in many songs, such as at the beginning of "The Lorelei" and in the final measure of example 9.2. Despite these jazz accouterments, the rhythmic invention bestowed on these songs by jazz musicians owes more to phrasing and rhyth-

EXAMPLE 9.2

The way you wear your hat,———   The way you sip your tea,———

The mem-'ry of all that.———   No, no! They can't take that a-way from me!

mic space (see the discussion later), available in songs like "Embraceable You," than to notated rhythms.

Melody

A stronger case can be made for the jazz-worthy nature of Gershwin's melodies. Gershwin's penchant for repeated notes in his melodies is well-known—for example, "They Can't Take That Away from Me" and "Oh, Lady, Be Good!" This device builds melodic tension while emphasizing rhythm and opening the door for harmonic ingenuity. Jazz musicians, especially Billie Holiday,[60] tend to flatten out the contour of popular melodies. In a case of less-is-more, harmonic interest and rhythmic drive are increased by reducing shapely melodies to a couple of pitches plus embellishment. One effect of this flattening process is the replacement of melody with recitation in an apparent reversal of musical sophistication. In other words, recitation and final tones, not always distinct, of hollers, moans, and shouts seem to have supplanted unique melodic contour. In the best cases, the melodic cost is more than repaid harmonically and especially rhythmically. The harmonic dividend is achieved because, in the absence of melody, the ear simply is drawn to harmonic progressions. The constituent harmonies are often enriched by the retention of the recitation pitch, forming an upper pedal point or drone. Flattening out the melody also provides the performer with rhythmic freedom and responsibility.

One of Billie Holiday's best-known and most effective uses of this technique occurs in her performance of Neil Moret's "(S)He's Funny That Way," 13 September 1937,[61] in the bridge or B section, where she replaces the ascending scale with repeated leading tones and in the second chorus, with heightened rhythmic nuance. (See examples 9.3a, 9.3b.) The leading tone is a pitch Holiday extracts from the melody of the A section and emphasizes throughout the performance. On a smaller scale, one can hear Holiday employ the same technique of flattening a melody in her recording of "Summertime," 10 July 1936,[62] one of the earliest "popular" recordings of perhaps Gershwin's most famous and popular song. A more substantial instance

EXAMPLE 9.3a

EXAMPLE 9.3b

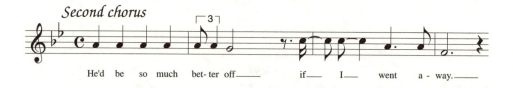

occurs in Holiday's recording of "They Can't Take That Away from Me" with Count Basie's orchestra in 1937,[63] in the second phrase of the bridge section. By reducing the arpeggios and scalar passages of Gershwin's original to repeated notes, Holiday concentrates attention on her rhythmic improvisation. (See examples 9.4a, 9.4b.) Ironically, when presented with a repeated-note melody, Holiday transforms the repeated notes into arpeggios and scales. This reverse technique is apparent in the same recording. (See example 9.2 for Gershwin's original.) The beginning of the second A section is even more embellished. (See examples 9.5a, 9.5b.)

Thelonious Monk's dismemberment and partial reconstruction of "Nice Work If You Can Get It," 24 October 1947,[64] provide a more complex example of the flattening out of melody. Here the fifth and the third, embellished respectively by the semitones below, function as recitation tones in Monk's rhythmic improvisation. (See examples 9.6a, 9.6b, 9.6c.)

The repeated-note melodies of Gershwin's songs, then, approximate the improvisatory technique of flattening melodies. One immediately thinks of the beginning of "They Can't Take That Away from Me," although other examples proved to be more attractive to jazz musicians, such as "A Foggy Day" and the bridge sections of "Oh, Lady, Be Good!,"[65] "I Got Rhythm," and "'S Wonderful." This last song may well represent the clearest intersection between Gershwin's compositional device and the jazz musician's improvising technique.

In the world of popular song, the words to "'S Wonderful" have probably generated more interest than the music. The melody and harmonies, after all, are simple, whereas the lyrics are cute. The lyrics, however, have

EXAMPLE 9.4a

We may nev-er, nev-er meet a-gain On the bump-y road to

love,— Still I'll al-ways, al-ways keep the mem 'ry of—

EXAMPLE 9.4b

We may nev-er,— nev-er— meet a-gain— On that bump-y road—

to love,— Still I'll al-ways,— al-ways— keep— the mem'ry of—

EXAMPLE 9.5a

The way you wear— your hat,— The way you sip your— tea,—

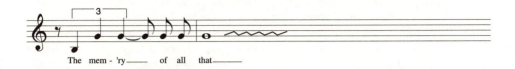

The mem-'ry— of all that—

EXAMPLE 9.5b

The way your smile— just beams—

EXAMPLE 9.6a

EXAMPLE 9.6b

EXAMPLE 9.6c

not interested jazz musicians so much as the repeated-note melody of the bridge combined with the rifflike melody of the A section. Of the eighteen notes in the bridge, fourteen of them are d, the leading tone in E♭ major— the key of the song, but not of the bridge. The fourteen ds occur in two strings: one of four and another of ten. A full six of the eight measures of the bridge are given over to repetitions of this pitch (example 9.7a).

The A section is also worthy of comment. Its melody is essentially a riff —that is, a melodic gesture whose primary function is rhythmic. The melody, therefore, is barely one stage more complex than repeated notes— here, a falling minor third, the interval with which children around the world taunt one another (example 9.7b).

A slightly more complex, embellished version of repeated-note melodies is the two-note, scalar melody. These melodies or motives can be heard as recitation tones with whole-step or half-step embellishments, either above

EXAMPLE 9.7a

EXAMPLE 9.7b

or below (cf. examples 9.6a–c). At the beginning of "The Man I Love,"
recitation on the fifth degree of the scale, in weak metric position, is embellished by the sixth scale degree. Indeed, nearly the entire A section of
this song consists of this two-note vacillation. That this kind of embellished
recitation caught jazz musicians' ears is clearly evident in Lionel Hampton's
solo when "The Man I Love" was performed and recorded at Carnegie Hall
by Benny Goodman's quartet, 16 January 1938.[66] Other examples of embellished recitation can be heard in Dick Hyman's piano introduction to the
same song, recorded with Roy Eldridge in 1950;[67] the Modern Jazz Quartet's
extended, formal introduction to "But Not for Me," 1953;[68] and Sarah
Vaughan's rendition of "How Long Has This Been Going On?," 1978.[69]

"Oh, Lady, Be Good!" provides one last example of repeated-note melodies. The repeated notes occur in the bridge, although one can easily dis-
cern the structural role of the fifth scale degree in the A section. Benny
Carter capitalizes on this recitative structure by playing a rhythmic embellishment of the recitation pitch in the first solo chorus of his performance
recorded on 22 April 1946.[70] (See examples 9.8a, 9.8b.) Here the rhythmic license afforded by recitation has coalesced into rhythmic motive. Carter repeats this three-beat embellishment throughout the A section, thereby creating a polyrhythmic effect with the basic quadruple pulse of the rhythm
section.

In addition to the principal melody in these songs, Gershwin often implied or explicitly stated a contrapuntal accompaniment. This contrapuntal tendency reaches its peak in the songs of *Porgy and Bess*, especially "Bess,
You Is My Woman Now," where the composer seems intent on filling up
much of the available space with additional melodic lines. Although not as
important here as repeated-note and vacillating melodies, this aspect of

EXAMPLE 9.8a

EXAMPLE 9.8b

Gershwin's songs caught the ears of jazz musicians in the 1930s through 1950s, providing them with a built-in alternative to the tune.

An obvious, explicitly composed example of counterpoint occurs over the first six measures of the A section of "The Man I Love." (See example 9.9.) One can hear this contrapuntal line stated by Lionel Hampton, playing with Benny Goodman in the celebrated 1943 concert at Carnegie Hall. The song's counterpoint serves a much more artistic purpose in Coleman Hawkins's solo, where the pitches g–g♭–f–e–e♭–d provide the deep struc-

EXAMPLE 9.9

EXAMPLE 9.10

ture for the explosive melodic ascents and descents that occur in each of the first six measures.[71]

Gershwin's contrapuntal tendencies are evident and even developed in the well-known collaboration between Miles Davis and Gil Evans.[72] On their recording of "Summertime," the two-note, vacillating accompaniment of the original is expanded into melodic counterpoint to the principle melody. (See example 9.10.)

One of the most dense contrapuntal passages in Gershwin's music occurs in the first four measures of "Nice Work If You Can Get It" (see example 9.6a). In addition to the tune and bass line, there are three mostly descending contrapuntal melodies. This passage argues persuasively for the linear, melodic character of chromatic harmony, a characteristic of Gershwin's music that was recently pinpointed and discussed by Dave Grusin and Keith Jarrett.

Grusin: Incidentally, my perception of Gershwin is that he already figured out what the best substitution changes were going to be.

Jarrett: I think that's true of Gershwin because, contrary to many of the standard tune writers, he's not writing vertically. He's writing how a line moves in harmony under . . .

Grusin: The "thumb lines."

Jarrett: It's all counterpoint. . . . Somehow I associate the counterpoint, the lines moving under other lines, as an awareness of the roundness of time. As so on the "flatland," Gershwin's poking up through there, which is why those things remain unable-to-be-made-better. He not only had the inspiration for the discrete components of these pieces, but he had the inspiration for the glue between those components.[73]

Harmony

Gershwin's harmonies—to the extent that harmony can be separated from melody—were as attractive to jazz musicians as his melodies, if not more so. In discussing the affinity between jazz musicians and Gershwin's songs, Charles Hamm noted: "It is even possible to come full circle and suggest that the increased harmonic sophistication of jazz in the 1920s and 1930s owed some small debt to the new chord changes black musicians learned from playing Gershwin tunes."[74] Songs such as "Nice Work If You Can Get It"

EXAMPLE 9.11a

EXAMPLE 9.11b

and Jerome Kern's "Yesterdays" exemplify this increased harmonic sophistication that is appropriated by jazz musicians. In general, however, songs
with less complex harmonies have proven to be the magnet for jazz. In ac-
counting for the jazz use of Gershwin's songs, Alec Wilder observed: "The
melody should be spare, containing a minimal number of notes, and the
harmony should be similarly uncluttered, almost skeletal. . . . And this harmony mustn't change too quickly."[75] A song whose harmonies generally
change at a rate no faster than once every half measure seems to be the
norm. Such a rate of harmonic change allows for the characteristic rhythmic
and melodic improvisations of jazz. In addition to slow-moving harmonies,
there generally occur opportunities for harmonic embellishment and substitution. Harmonic embellishment often takes the form of a chord, usually
a "dominant seventh," built on the upper chromatic neighbor of the harmonic goal. Slightly more advanced is the connection of two structural
harmonies with a series of chords descending chromatically. This technique can easily be applied to measures 23–25 of "Oh, Lady Be Good." The
original harmony (example 9.11) in measure 24, with its augmented sixth,
invites a chromatic connection between the supertonic and the tonic (examples 9.11a, 9.11b). The melodic passing tone c♯ also allows for the tonic
to be embellished by an ascending chromatic chord built on F♯ (concern
over parallel fifths be damned). The structural harmonies in measures 3–6
of the same song are tonic and dominant. Dick Hyman suggests connecting
these with a chromatic descent ending on the supertonic (cf. example 9.8a).[76]
(See example 9.12.) Even more advanced is the substitution of new for composed harmonies. Hyman's suggestion for the first two measures of "I Got
Rhythm" shows both substitution and chromatic descent.[77] (See examples
9.13a, 9.13b.)

EXAMPLE 9.12

Many of Gershwin's songs meet Wilder's criterion of slow, regular harmonic movement. Some of those most popular with jazz musicians are "Embraceable You," "I Got Rhythm," "The Man I Love," "Oh, Lady, Be Good!,"
"Somebody Loves Me," and "Summertime." Such harmonic movement may
be attractive, although it is hardly sufficient to account for the use of these
songs in jazz. Their popularity among jazz musicians rests in large measure
on the presence in the original composition of descending and ascending
chromatic harmonies, many of which are so-called substitute harmonies and
embellishments. Moreover, even as these harmonies may account for the
initial attraction, their mere presence did not dissuade jazz musicians from
supplying their own substitute harmonies.

As a subset of substitute chords, one may first consider those conventional harmonies that are enriched, such as dominants and secondary dominants appearing as major- or minor-ninth chords or augmented triads.
"Secondary dominants" take on an especially bluesy character if they occur
as subdominant harmony that does not resolve typically. Virtually identical
$IV\flat^9_7$-chords occur in "Somebody Loves Me" and "Oh, Lady, Be Good!" —
measures 4 and 2, respectively. Somewhat more pungent is the minor-ninth

EXAMPLE 9.13a

EXAMPLE 9.13b

EXAMPLE 9.14

secondary dominant in "Somebody Loves Me," measure 14. Even more complex are the dominants and secondary dominants of "A Foggy Day." (See example 9.14.) The rather common occurrence of augmented dominant and secondary dominant chords also belongs in this category ("Somebody Loves Me," m. 24, and "Soon," m. 10). A genuine substitution, an example of so-called tritone substitution, occurs in "Love Is Here to Stay," where the dominant preparation of G minor on its supertonic is replaced harmonically with a seventh chord on the flat sixth degree of G. One hears this passage in the context of the first five measures and thus expects a return to the tonic (F major) in measure 7. (See example 9.15.)

Besides enriched and substitute harmonies, jazz musicians encountered built-in descending and ascending chromatic bass lines accompanying the harmonies. One of the most famous examples occurs in "The Man I Love," where by means of inversion the harmonies of the first six measures can be rendered with a chromatically descending bass. In the other direction, there is the strident chromatically ascending bass at the beginning of "Liza," measures 1–4.

Gershwin's enriched harmonies attracted the jazz musician as long as they moved at a relatively slow and regular rate. Thus, "A Foggy Day," "How Long Has This Been Going On?," "Liza," and "Someone to Watch Over Me" have entered the standard repertory of jazz musicians and singers. Many of the harmonic gestures of jazz occur naturally in these tunes. "Nice Work If You Can Get It," on the other hand, is an exception that proves the rule. The song appears to fit the harmonic criteria established here. The first four mea-

EXAMPLE 9.15

EXAMPLE 9.16

sures present a remarkable sequence of secondary dominant thirteenths, ninths, minor ninths, and augmented chords (see example 9.6a). To appreciate the richness of this passage, consider the melody without the harmony. It is a simple matter to provide this tune with a prosaic harmonization, one that stays close to the tonic. (See example 9.16.) But Gershwin saves the harmonically tame progression for the second phrase, with its increased rhythmic activity, a combination that jolts and complements the richness of the first phrase. If jazz musicians, especially horn players, have shied away from this song to some extent, it is perhaps because the opening passage is too dense harmonically for their purposes of improvisation. In other words, the harmonic and melodic potential of the passage is already actual. Keith Jarrett noted: "[Other songwriters] gave you some very inspired things, but there's a fill-in-the-blanks process. You are not stuck with an already-existing best-possible method."[78]

Phrasing and Structure

Harmony cannot be isolated from phrase and structure. Wilder's notion of regular, slow-moving harmonies hints at the importance of larger-scale harmonic movement and repetition. Most of Gershwin's songs fit neatly into the mold of the thirty-two-measure pop song subdivided into four eight-measure phrases. The tendency of jazz musicians to reduce the occasional extended thirty-four-measure structure to thirty-two indicates the need for regularity of phrase in jazz. Thus, the ten-measure final phrase of "I Got Rhythm" is often rendered exactly as the second phrase of eight measures, especially in improvisations based on "Rhythm Changes," that is, the harmonies of the song.

Gershwin's songs adopted by jazz musicians often display remarkable economy of means achieved through repetition and sequence. The first half of "Embraceable You" is a good example of melodic and harmonic sequence. Such regularity of construction with minimal materials gives the improviser considerable freedom. The criticisms leveled against this song by Hodeir (in the second epigraph to this chapter) and Alec Wilder[79] ignore Gershwin's economical achievement. As with Irving Berlin's "White Christmas," it is hard to imagine how one could improve "Embraceable You" by rearranging or adding a few notes.

Charlie Parker's famous improvisation based on "Embraceable You" unfolds with a melodic sequence as an initial motivating force (mm. 1–5).[80] Parker's florid explosion largely ignores the notes of Gershwin's melody, but the recurrence of sequence in the improvisation must be inspired by the original tune. Parker was not the first jazz musician to give artistic expression to this song. Earlier recordings by Bobby Hackett and Charlie Shavers provide further evidence for the power of melodic sequence, the attractiveness of the original melody, and the tight construction of the song. Hackett and Shavers give exquisite, lyric paraphrases of the melody, perhaps more studied and far less effusive than Parker's solo.[81]

In many of Gershwin's songs, one finds the general economy that characterizes "Embraceable You" in the repeated four-measure phrases of bridge sections. Among Gershwin's songs popular with jazz musicians, such repeated phrases occur in "How Long Has This Been Going On?," "Somebody Loves Me," "The Man I Love," and "They Can't Take That Away from Me." Succinctness of phrase, harmony, and melody combine to make "Oh, Lady, Be Good!" especially attractive to jazz musicians. Its simple design, with the reiteration on the fifth degree of the scale that builds and then releases tension with descending arpeggios, provided the vehicle for subtle, swinging renditions by a host of musicians, including Benny Goodman, Count Basie, and Benny Carter.[82]

Of all Gershwin's songs, none is more transparent and skeletal than "'S Wonderful." Because of its rifflike melody in the A section, its repeated-note melody in the B section, and its regular phrasing, this song lends itself especially to melodic improvisation. The song may be best known for its lyrics, but it is the bare-bones tune that attracted Coleman Hawkins, Gerry Mulligan, Herbie Nichols, and others.[83] Hawkins's recordings rely heavily on call-and-response among the musicians, a performance technique that is readily accommodated by the song's riffy character.

Many of the musical characteristics that make a Gershwin song attractive for jazz musicians—repeated and two-note melodies, regular and economical phrasing, and rifflike patterns—leave musical space for improvisation. These songs, in short, are not overcomposed. Conversely, Gershwin songs with several explicit countermelodies, nonrepetitive melodies, or irregular phrasing and structure offer fewer possibilities for the jazz musician's musical imagination. So although "Bess, You Is My Woman Now" exhibits many of the harmonic progressions and melodic gestures that have been identified here, its complex structure has made it less inviting to jazz instrumentalists.

Armed with the foregoing musical analysis, can one determine which songs of Gershwin were the most popular among jazz musicians? The answer to the question differs from the 1930s to the 1950s, and from singers to instrumentalists. In addition, total number of recordings is not an accurate measure of popularity and influence. In some cases, a single recording of a song—for example, Parker's "Embraceable You"—has been more influential, or at least more highly esteemed, than several recordings of other songs. For example, in his 1993 recording of this song, Joey DeFrancesco quotes—consciously or unconsciously—the beginning of Parker's solo at the beginning of his own solo.[84] Moreover, a recording is not the only way in which a song enters the musical world of jazz. Among Gershwin's songs, "Summertime" is probably performed most often, although it appears less frequently on records than other Gershwin songs.

Dividing the jazz world into singers and instrumentalists, one finds that "A Foggy Day," "How Long Has This Been Going On?," and "Nice Work If You Can Get It" are usually sung. "Embraceable You," "I Got Rhythm," "Oh, Lady, Be Good!," "Liza," and "Somebody Loves Me" are more likely to be performed instrumentally. During the 1930s, "The Man I Love" and "Oh, Lady, Be Good!" were among the Gershwin songs most favored by jazz musicians. In the 1940s and thereafter, later Gershwin compositions such as "A Foggy Day" and "Summertime" replaced earlier songs in popularity.[85]

Among jazz instrumentalists, "I Got Rhythm" is hands-down the most common Gershwin song. Adopted no doubt because of its considerable popularity and its simplicity of design, this song undermines to some extent the usefulness of musical analysis as a guide to determining a song's suitability for jazz. Repeated-note or vacillating-note melodies, pungent harmony, and clear, tight phrasing all appeal to the jazz musician who chooses to play a Gershwin song, but what is so attractive about "I Got Rhythm"? What melodic, harmonic, or rhythmic aspect of "I Got Rhythm" is the hook that snags the jazz musician? Hardly anyone retains the rhythmic joke of the A section. Melodically, the pentatonic motive in the A section and the repeated notes in the B section provide some freedom and built-in tension for the jazz musician, but these features—the repeated notes in particular—do not distinguish "I Got Rhythm" from many other songs by Gershwin. Harmonically, the song is remarkably tame and regular.[86] Regularity and simplicity, of course, are exactly what attracted the jazz musician, because they afford so much space for invention. The predictability of harmony and phrasing provided the security for harmonic invention (substitute chords) and large-scale rhythmic daring (irregular phrasing) on the part of the jazz musician. Since this song is clearly the favorite, and seems to be so largely for what it lacks, the analyst should be reluctant to attach too much importance to correspondences between improvisations and composed aspects of the same songs. Finally, "I Got Rhythm" was published in the jazz-friendly key of B♭ major. Who could ask for anything more?

The Jazz Age understood jazz to refer to a large, loosely defined body of music that featured an approximation of the blue tonality and various popular dance rhythms. Gershwin's artistic endeavors possess both of these characteristics and were thus heard in the 1920s and 1930s as jazz or jazz-related. Subsequent, more narrow understandings of jazz exclude all of Gershwin's music, including his songs and such art-music compositions as *Rhapsody in Blue*, Concerto in F, and *Porgy and Bess*.

Gershwin's songs are intrinsically suited for jazz improvisation because of their melodic, harmonic, and structural makeup. This potential, coupled with the actual merit and popularity of the songs *as songs*, accounts for their adoption by jazz musicians throughout the century. For these two reasons, George Gershwin's name was and always will be connected with jazz.

To make evaluations of Gershwin's music in general and of his historical location in American culture are more difficult. When we listen to his music, we probably do not hear the oppressor appropriating the soul of the oppressed. Seven years have intervened since the appropriation; we are the very audience for whom the appropriation was made; and Gershwin is not unique in his dependence upon the music of African Americans. Many Tin Pan Alley composers drew from the wellspring of African American music, although few did so as consistently and overtly as Gershwin, and perhaps none with as much musical success.

The issue of musical appropriation must await another study,[87] although a general observation can be made here. The cultivation of music by African Americans is the most important musical development of the twentieth century. Virtually every genre of Western music, as well as the popular music of the world, including Africa, has imitated African American music. With Gershwin's music we have an early but beautiful instance of what the twentieth century has shown to be an historical fact—that the music of African Americans is hegemonist, primarily because of its intrinsic musical merit.

Notes

In citations of recordings of Gershwin's music, especially jazz performances, only the original release is given. All but the most recent recordings have been reissued.

1. Paul Whiteman and Mary Margaret McBride, *Jazz* (New York: J. H. Sears, 1926), especially chap. 4; Henry O. Osgood, *So This Is Jazz* (Boston: Little, Brown, 1926), chaps. 16, 17; Isaac Goldberg, *Tin Pan Alley: A Chronicle of the American Popular Music Racket* (New York: Frederick Ungar, 1930), chap. 10; and Isaac Goldberg, *George Gershwin: A Study in American Music* (New York: Simon & Schuster, 1931; reprint with supplement, New York: Frederick Ungar, 1958), especially chap. 9.

2. H. Wiley Hitchcock and Stanley Sadie, eds., *The New Grove Dictionary of American Music* (London: Macmillan, 1986), s.v. "Gershwin, George."

3. Leonard Feather, *Encyclopedia of Jazz* (New York: Horizon, 1955; rev. 1960; reprint, New York: Da Capo, 1984), s.v. "Gershwin, George."

4. David Ross Baskerville, "Jazz Influence on Art Music to Mid-Century" (Ph.D. diss., University of California, Los Angeles, 1965), 97–98.

5. Barry Kernfeld, "Jazz," *The New Harvard Dictionary of Music*, ed. Don Michael Randel (Cambridge: Harvard University Press, 1986).

6. James Lincoln Collier, "Jazz (i)," *The New Grove Dictionary of Jazz*, ed. Barry Kernfeld (London: Macmillan, 1988).

7. Statistics for 1990 from the U.S. Census Bureau, *Current Population Reports*, ser. P-60. no. 175.

8. See Henry Cowell's denunciation of the very notion in his introduction to the 1962 edition of Henry Cowell, ed., *American Composers on American Music: A Symposium* (Stanford: Stanford University Press, 1933; reprint, New York: Frederick Ungar, 1962), vii–x.

9. George Gershwin, "The Relation of Jazz to American Music," in Cowell, *American Composers on American Music*, 186.

10. Aaron Copland, *Our New Music: Leading Composers in Europe and America* (New York: Whittlesey House, McGraw-Hill, 1941), 87.

11. George Gershwin, "The Composer in the Machine Age," in *Revolt in the Arts*, ed. Oliver M. Saylor (New York: Brentano's, 1930), 264–69.

12. Osgood, *So This Is Jazz*, 177.

13. Ibid., 246–50.

14. Goldberg, *George Gershwin*, 277–93.

15. Goldberg, *Tin Pan Alley*, 259.

16. Gershwin, "The Composer in the Machine Age," 266.

17. Goldberg, *Tin Pan Alley*, 267–68.

18. Ibid., 295.

19. Regarding the general perception and reception of jazz during the 1920s, see Kathy J. Ogren, *The Jazz Revolution: Twenties America and the Meaning of Jazz* (New York: Oxford University Press, 1989), especially chap. 5.

20. A fairly recent, widely disseminated example is Lonette McKee's performance of this song in Bertrand Tavernier's film *'Round Midnight* (1986).

21. Dan Morgenstern, "The Night Ragtime Came to Carnegie Hall," *New York Times*, 9 July 1989, sec. 2, pp. 25, 32.

22. Abbe Niles, "The Ewe Lamb of Widow Jazz," *New Republic* 49 (29 December 1926): 164–66.

23. Goldberg, *George Gershwin*, 292.

24. Whiteman and McBride, *Jazz*, 97.

25. A few months after its premiere, Whiteman recorded the *Rhapsody* with Gershwin, in New York, 10 June 1924: Victor 55225 (matrix: 30173-2, part 2; 30174-1, part 1). Not until 1942 did Grofé reorchestrate the *Rhapsody* for symphonic orchestra, but this is the version that until recently was commonly known. See, for example, the recording of the *Rhapsody* by the Columbia Jazz Band, Michael Tilson Thomas conducting, which uses a piano roll cut by Gershwin himself for the solo part: CBS MGT 39488.

26. The authors of the program notes for Whiteman's "Experiment in Modern Music," Hugh C. Ernst and Gilbert Seldes, explicitly associated the music of the program, including *Rhapsody in Blue*, with jazz. Two years later, Whiteman noted that "Livery Stable Blues" and the *Rhapsody* "are so many millions of miles apart, that to speak of them both as jazz needlessly confuses the person who is trying to understand modern American music. At the same time, in the course of a recent tour of the United States, I have become convinced that people as a whole like the word 'jazz.' At least they will have none of the numerous substitutes that smart wordologists are continually offering. So I say, let's call the new music 'jazz'" (Whiteman and McBride, *Jazz*, 99–100).

27. Charles Schwartz, *Gershwin: His Life and Music* (Indianapolis: Bobbs-Merrill, 1973), 81–83.

28. Quoted in Goldberg, *George Gershwin*, 138–39.

29. For example, Olin Downes was pro whereas Lawrence Gilman was con. See Olin Downes, "A Concert of Jazz," *New York Times*, 13 February 1924, p. 16; and Lawrence Gilman, "Paul Whiteman and the Palais Royalists Extend Their Kingdom; Jazz at Aeolian Hall," *New York Tribune*, 17 February 1924, p. 9.

30. Dave Dexter Jr., *Jazz Cavalcade: The Inside Story of Jazz* (New York: Criterion, 1946), 47.

31. William L. Hartman and Jack W. Farrell, *The Heart of Jazz* (New York: New York University Press, 1956), 211–12.

32. Deems Taylor, "Words and Music," *New York World*, 17 February 1924, p. 2-M. Other critical observations on the premiere of *Rhapsody in Blue* can be found in the biographies of Gershwin. See, for example, Schwartz, *Gershwin*, 87–89.

33. Osgood, *So This Is Jazz*, 180–81. Abbe Niles makes a similar argument about Gershwin being uniquely suited among contemporary composers (1926) to serve "Lady Jazz" in "The Ewe Lamb and Widow Jazz." *The Rite of Spring* premiered in New York eleven days before the premiere of *Rhapsody in Blue*, and Osgood decided that Gershwin's work was superior to both the *Rite* and *Pacific 231*. This comparison now seems to be only half correct.

34. Osgood, *So This Is Jazz*, 186, 194.

35. Virgil Thomson, "George Gershwin," *Modern Music* 13 (November–December 1935): 13.

36. Samuel Charters, *Jazz: A History of the New York Scene* (Garden City, N.Y.: Doubleday, 1962; reprint, New York: Da Capo, 1981), 142.

37. Quoted in Goldberg, *George Gershwin*, 205.

38. Ibid., 206.

39. Osgood, *So This Is Jazz*, 217.

40. Niles, "The Ewe Lamb of Widow Jazz," 166.

41. Goldberg, *George Gershwin*, 214.

42. Quoted in Barry Ulanov, *A History of Jazz in America* (New York: Viking, 1952; reprint, New York: Da Capo, 1972), 113.

43. Baskerville, "Jazz Influence on Art Music to Mid-Century," 470–71.

44. Gershwin, "The Relation of Jazz to American Music," 186.

45. Thomson, "George Gershwin," 13–19. Thomson mollified his criticism of *Porgy and Bess* in later writings on the opera.

Duke Ellington found the music of *Porgy and Bess* to be "grand," although he questioned its "Negro musical idiom," remarking: "The times are here to debunk Gershwin's lampblack Negroisms" (quoted in Hollis Alpert, *The Life and Times of "Porgy and Bess": The Story of an American Classic* [New York: Knopf, 1990], 121–22). The release in 1959 of Samuel Goldwyn's film version of *Porgy and Bess* elicited another round of criticism of the opera, with one reviewer noting that the film "continues to prick at the sensitive underbelly of the country's number one underdog" (Era Bell Thompson, "Why Negroes Don't Like 'Porgy and Bess,'" *Ebony* 14 [October 1959]: 51).

46. George Gershwin, "Rhapsody in Catfish Row: Mr. Gershwin Tells the Origin and Scheme for His Music in That New Folk Opera Called 'Porgy and Bess,'" *New York Times*, 20 October 1935, sec. 10, pp. 1–2.

47. Ibid.

48. Ibid.

49. But Anne Brown, who originally sang the role of Bess in the opera, said in an interview: "Well, I'd like to know: what is a black man's opera, in the first place? I mean, he wrote an opera about black people. But that's Gershwin's idea of black people, and it's perfectly valid. So, I don't know about this idea of a black man's opera. I think that he captured a Negro idiom very, very well in *Porgy and Bess*." In "George Gershwin Remembered" (Program Development Company, Inc., and BBC-TV, 1987).

50. Osgood, *So This Is Jazz*, 250.

51. Goldberg, *George Gershwin*, 289.

52. Cowell, *American Composers on American Music*, 187.

53. Copland, *Our New Music*, 88.

54. Ibid., 227.

55. Deems Taylor, *Of Men and Music* (New York: Simon & Schuster, 1937), 125–26.

56. Ibid., 124.

57. Measure numbers of songs refer to the refrain only.

58. Osgood, *So This Is Jazz*, 177.

59. Of course, exceptions leap to mind, such as Oscar Peterson's treatment of this song, and recently Dave Grusin's. Peterson (pno.), Barney Kessel (gt.), Ray Brown (bass); Los Angeles: December 1952, Verve. Grusin (pno.), Gary Burton (vib.), John Patitucci (bass), Dave Wecki (dr.); New York: GRP Records, GRD-2005, 1991.

60. The model for Holiday, however, is Louis Armstrong. See especially his recording of "Star Dust"—Chicago: 4 November 1931, Okeh 41530 (matrix: 405061-1)—on which Armstrong sings the first three measures of the piece all on the tonic. His lyrics are "Sometimes I wonder why I spend such lonely nights, oh baby."

61. Billie Holiday (voc.), Buck Clayton (tr.), Buster Bailey (cl.), Lester Young (t. sax), Claude Thornhill (pno.), Freddy Greene (gt.), Walter Page (bass), Jo Jones (dr.); New York: Vocalion 748 (matrix: 21689-1).

62. Billie Holiday (voc.), Bunny Berigan (tr.), Artie Shaw (cl.), Joe Bushkin (pno.), Dick McDonough (gt.), Pete Peterson (bass), Cozy Cole (dr.); New York: Vocalion 3288 (matrix: 19537-1).

63. Count Basie and His Orchestra; New York, Savoy Ballroom: 30 June 1937, Columbia CL1759 (matrix: unknown).

64. Thelonious Monk (pno.), Gene Ramsay (bass), Art Blakey (dr.); New York: Blue Note 1575 (matrix: BN312-1). Example 6a comes from the second chorus, mm. 5–8, and 6b from the third chorus, mm. 1–4.

65. During Lester Young's first solo chorus of "Oh, Lady Be Good!" (recorded with Count Basie, 9 November 1936), he plays no repeated notes in the bridge section but more than makes up for this lack by reiterating the fifth degree of the scale—now below rather than above the tonic—in the final A section. Count Basie (pno.), Carl Smith (tr.), Lester Young (t. sax), Walter Page (bass), Jo Jones (dr.); Chicago: Vocalion 3459 (matrix: C.1660-1).

66. Benny Goodman (cl.), Teddy Wilson (pno.), Lionel Hampton (vib.), Gene Krupa (dr.); New York: 16 January 1938, Columbia CL 815 (matrix: FXLP 3602-1a).

67. Roy Eldridge (tr.), Zoot Sims (t. sax), Dick Hyman (pno.), Pierre Michelot (bass), Ed Shaughnessy (dr.); Paris: 9 June 1950, Vogue (French) 5041 (matrix: VG 4005).

68. Milt Jackson (vib.), John Lewis (pno.), Percy Heath (bass), Kenny Clarke (dr.); New York: 25 June 1953, Prestige 873 (matrix: 502).

69. Sarah Vaughan (voc.), Oscar Peterson (pno.), Joe Pass (gt.), Ray Brown (bass), Louis Bellson (dr.); Hollywood: 25 April 1978, Pablo 2310-821. It is evidently unnecessary to preserve the composed sequence of pitches of the motive. Vaughan begins the opening phrase on the sixth scale degree rather than the fifth and also inverts the fifth and sixth degrees at the beginning of the next line: "Where have I been all these years." She treats these two pitches with considerable freedom throughout her performance, thereby achieving rhythmic flexibility. Her recitative treatment of the theme eventually spills over to the second singing of the bridge, where the first four measures are rendered, with microtonal inflection, on the third scale degree of the piece, but the leading tone of the passage: "Dear, when in your arms I creep, / That divine rendezvous."

70. Benny Carter (a. sax), Sonny White (pno.), unknown (gt., bass, dr.); Los Angeles: 22 April 1946, Keynote (matrix: HL 155-3).

71. Coleman Hawkins (t. sax), Eddie Heywood (pno.), Oscar Pettiford (bass), Shelly Manne (dr.); New York: 23 December 1943, Signature 9001 (matrix T19005). Art Tatum develops a similar contrapuntal line of chromatic descent in the second chorus of his recording of "Someone to Watch Over Me." Los Angeles: 13 July 1949, Capitol 15519 (matrix: 5042-1D1).

72. *Porgy and Bess.* New York: 18 August 1958, Columbia CL 1274 (matrix: CO1421).

73. Becca Pulliam, "Maintaining Standards: Keith Jarrett and Dave Grusin," *Down Beat* 59 (May 1992): 20.

74. Charles Hamm, *Yesterdays: Popular Song in America* (New York: W. W. Norton, 1979), 352.

75. Alec Wilder, *American Popular Song: The Great Innovators, 1900–1950* (New York: Oxford University Press, 1972), 128.

76. *Dick Hyman's Professional Chord Changes and Substitutions for 100 Tunes Every Musician Should Know* (Katonah: Ekay Music, 1986). Of these one hundred tunes, fourteen are by Gershwin; Cole Porter, in second place, is represented by nine songs.

77. Ibid.

78. Pulliam, "Maintaining Standards," 20.

79. Wilder, *American Popular Song,* 149–51.

80. Charlie Parker (a. sax), Duke Jordan (pno.), Tommy Potter (bass), Max Roach (dr.); New York: 28 October 1947, Dial 1024 (matrix: D1106B).

81. Bobby Hackett and His Orchestra; New York: 13 April 1939, Vocalion 4877 (matrix: WM-1020-A). Charlie Shavers (tr.), Coleman Hawkins (t. sax), Teddy Wilson (pno.), Billy Taylor (bass), Denzil Best (dr.); New York: 18 October 1944, Keynote, EmA MGE 26011 (matrix: HL70-1). Shaver's solo may in fact build on the earlier one by Hackett, which stands in artistic relief to its sticky-sweet surroundings.

82. Benny Goodman (cl.), Teddy Wilson (pno.), Gene Krupa (dr.); Chicago: 27 April 1936, Victor 25333 (matrix: BS 100500-1). For Count Basie, see n. 65; for Benny Carter, see n. 70.

83. Coleman Hawkins (t. sax), Roy Eldridge (tr.), Teddy Wilson (pno.), Billy Taylor (bass), Cozy Cole (dr.); New York: 31 January 1944, Keynote K609 (matrix: KHL 10-1) and alternate (matrix: KHL 10-2). Gerry Mulligan (bar. sax), Red Mitchell (bass), Chico Hamilton (dr.); Los Angeles: 10 June 1952, Pacific Jazz, not released (available on Santa Monica: Mosaic Records, 1983). Herbie Nichols (pno.), unknown (gt.), Chocolate Williams (bass), Shadow Wilson (dr.); New York: April 1952, Hi-Lo 1403 (matrix: HL314).

84. *Joey DeFrancesco: Live at the 5 Spot* (New York: Columbia Records, CK 53805, 1993). DeFrancesco (organ), Illinois Jacquet (t. sax), Byron Landham (dr.), Paul Bollenback (gt.).

85. Of the thirteen new performances contained on Dave Grusin's recent recording *The Gershwin Connection* (New York: GRP Records, GRD-2005, 1991), five are drawn from *Porgy and Bess.*

86. Alec Wilder did not think much of it. See Wilder, *American Popular Song,* 151.

87. Barbera, "The Musical Property of African Americans," lecture delivered at St. John's College, 28 October 1994.

Performance Practice

10 : *Tracing Gershwin's Piano Rolls*

ARTIS WODEHOUSE

1915 to 1925 was the decade during which George Gershwin successfully negotiated the increasingly challenging hurdles of the music industry to become a commercially successful songwriter and achieve worldwide recognition as an American composer. During that time, too, Gershwin made 140 piano roll arrangements of popular sheet music, participating in an industry created to meet the huge demand for home entertainment music in America.

Before radio, before movies could talk, before the 1925 electric recording process greatly improved the phonograph, the piano was the entertainment center of homes and places of social gathering. A piano in the parlor instantly conferred prestige on its owner and encouraged music-making from performers of all abilities. Moreover, the piano was a gateway into the world of popular music, allowing ordinary citizens to tune in on the seismic social changes reflected in the gaudy covers, racy lyrics, and engaging tunes and rhythms of popular sheet music.

By the first decade of the twentieth century, Tin Pan Alley publishing of American popular sheet music had become a multi-million-dollar industry. According to Isaac Goldberg, as many as 5,000 copies of a new song were printed for free distribution among singers, pianists, organists, and band leaders. A subsequent 1,000 copies were then distributed to others in the publishing trade, and if sales seemed promising the publisher would push the song by advertising it on the backs or inside margins of other profitable sheets. Moreover, a sheet might be marketed by granting certain star performers, such as vaudevillians Al Jolson or Sophie Tucker, a portion of royalties for plugging or promoting a song.[1]

But most Americans in this era learned their popular music by playing it or hearing it played on the piano. Unfortunately, many households with a piano did not have a pianist with sufficient playing skill to tackle even simple music. Just at the moment of the explosion in the sheet music business, however, the complementary industry of the player piano was reaching its peak, and the two easily fostered a relationship to mass-market and promote each other's wares. Sales of piano roll arrangements and player pianos perfectly reciprocated sales of sheet music, and the two industries were thus linked in lucrative tandem for at least a quarter of a century. While roll artists received only a flat fee for their arrangements and did not receive royalties, the roll companies—beginning in 1909—always paid the song publisher for rights to its tune. And the sale of piano rolls encouraged the sale of sheets of Tin Pan Alley songs into "average American homes" across the country.

George Gershwin was active in both songwriting and roll-arranging in the heyday of these two industries. Gershwin overcame his initial reluctance to take up so "feminine" an instrument as the piano—despite his early and deep attraction to it—when he saw the prestige and financial potential that success could bring in the burgeoning popular-music industry. Like so many musically gifted children of immigrant Jewish parents, Gershwin quickly grasped that the popular-music business would be one avenue from which he would not be barred. His formal piano studies began late, at age twelve, and while he applied himself well enough to them he never neglected his passion for popular idioms. His most important piano teacher, Charles Hambitzer, observed: "I have a pupil who will make his mark in music if anybody will. The boy is a genius, without a doubt; he's just crazy about music and can't wait until it's time to take his lesson. No watching the clock for this boy! He wants to go in for this modern stuff, jazz and what not. But I'm not going to let him for a while. I'll see that he gets a firm foundation in the standard music first."[2]

Gershwin proved to be an omnivorous learner, a quick study, a dexterous, accommodating, and enormously energetic young musician. His first musical job was that of a song plugger for the Tin Pan Alley publishing firm Remick. Vaudevillians and performers visiting the publisher would be sent down to Gershwin's little piano cubicle in order to hear and sing through new Remick music for possible inclusion in their performances. Gershwin's well-chronicled compulsion for self-improvement must have already been in high gear in these early years, for soon he had established a reputation as one of the best pluggers in the Alley. The great ragtime pianist-composer Eubie Blake noted: "James P. Johnson and Lucky Roberts told me of this very talented ofay [white] piano player at Remick's. They said he was good enough to learn some of those terribly difficult tricks that only a few of us could master."[3]

Gershwin's ability to learn tunes quickly, embellish, transpose, and otherwise trick them up led quite naturally to roll making, beginning in late 1915. Artists who made rolls of popular songs during these decades were either staff arrangers, and paid a salary, or freelancers, like Gershwin, and paid by the roll. Ira Gershwin reported that his brother was paid $5 per roll, or six rolls for $35.[4] Considering that the average salary in the United States in 1916 was roughly $15 a week,[5] the money to be made from piano rolls was impressive indeed for a musically gifted teenager.

Apparently, Gershwin never wrote about or publicly discussed his experiences as a roll artist. Quite possibly Gershwin and other musicians and music journalists of the time did not consider roll-making as significant as other musical activities. Piano rolls were seen as promoters of sheet music and player piano sales rather than artistic documents. Moreover, by the time Gershwin's star had risen, technology in the music business was changing fast. Phonograph records, greatly improved by electric recording, and radio, which had an enormous impact and which some feared would destroy the phonograph industry, engaged and enthralled musicians and listeners and easily overshadowed the roll industry, which by 1930 was moribund.

Unfortunately for Gershwin scholars, interest in player pianos was revived only in the 1960s, long after Gershwin's death. Unfortunately, too, the recording equipment Gershwin used for making his rolls was scrapped before it could have been studied. So scholars are limited today to two principal sources of information regarding the creation of Gershwin's rolls: statements made by his contemporaries in the roll industry, and the evidence provided by the rolls and extant player pianos themselves.

Gershwin's piano rolls reflect the changes in the roll industry from 1915 to 1925. In the earliest days of roll-making, the published song sheets were mechanically perforated by editors onto the roll masters "as is"; this process simply transferred the printed musical score to roll. Hand-played rolls were introduced in 1912, when a device was invented for capturing the rudiments of live performance in a player roll. The device consisted of an acoustic piano that had been variously fitted up with carbon-tipped rods— one for each of the eighty-eight keys, plus one for the sustaining pedal. When the pianist depressed a key, the carbon tip inscribed the depression as a line on a long sheet of paper traveling underneath the rods at a constant speed. Thus, a map of the performance was preserved on a long scroll of paper indicating when keys and pedal were depressed (note-on) and released (note-off) during the performance. However, performance data so gathered was not simply punched out as the final product; rather, the pianist's rendition served as a rough draft, subject to considerable manipulation by the editors before final production. Editors corrected mis-struck notes and frequently added notes beyond those played by the pianist.

Most significantly, in the case of nearly all the popular rolls of Gershwin's day (including nearly all those he made), editors also quantized the beats.[6] Quantizing insured that the distance between the beats of the music was made spatially (i.e., temporally) equal on the paper piano roll. In other words, after editors had quantized the beats, when played back on the player piano at a constant speed the roll would produce music precisely synchronized to a metronome's click even if some note entries were staggered. Since the energy driving roll playback was subject to the vagaries of foot-pumping,[7] an industrywide decision to quantize popular rolls was made to ensure a constant tempo within the system. To compensate for the consequent temporal rigidity of quantization, the pianolist (the person foot-pumping the roll) could deliberately introduce tempo flexibility by manipulating a roll-speed lever normally installed in player pianos.

Gershwin's earliest rolls reflect the mechanically arranged rolls of the earliest years of roll production. Some are almost literal readings of sheet music (e.g., "It's a Cute Little Way of My Own" of 1917), the only embellishments consisting of octave doublings to reinforce texture, so-called rhythm beats (single quarter notes changed to pairs in long-short patterns; also called "swung" or "shuffle"), and some mordents and turns. In arrangements of this sort one cannot easily determine what, if anything, Gershwin contributed in creating the roll, even though the performance is labeled "played by Gershwin."

Fortunately for the sake of scholarly interest (and probably the interest of the original roll-buyers), most of Gershwin's arrangements go beyond the production-line quality of these early mechanically arranged but attributed-to-Gershwin roll performances. In his later and better rolls, Gershwin interjects original ideas in the introductions, breaks, and riffs; enriches or alters harmonizations; and fleshes out bass lines beyond the published sheets. Such interjections seem to fall in areas where the industry permitted a little creative ingenuity in arrangements. As long as the purpose of the roll was not undermined—that of delivering a recognizable if occasionally fanciful rendition of the published tune—the arranger's ingenuity probably was allowed and even encouraged, especially if it might increase marketability.

Most of Gershwin's early rolls and even some from the 1920s consist of literally repeated verses and choruses, alternating typically thus: VCVCC. Gershwin's later rolls show more expanded and varied designs, probably as a result of new buyer sophistication, competition, and perhaps Gershwin's urge to experiment. Then, too, by the early 1920s, Gershwin had achieved a measure of importance that possibly gave him greater artistic control over his roll-arranging. Moreover, the structure of popular tunes was changing in the 1920s—for example, the new emphasis on the chorus may have influenced the more inventive structures of Gershwin's later rolls (e.g., "Make Believe" of 1920: C-transition-V-C'-V-C'-coda).

Some of Gershwin's most appealing rolls are those that could not have been executed by his ten fingers alone. Whether by trial and error or by calculation, Gershwin or his editors exploited the mechanical sound of the player in arrangements featuring superhumanly active, fancifully enriched textures. Apparently these note-enhanced rolls appealed to listeners, for many of his rolls are of this type. On the other hand, Gershwin's rolls of "Swanee" and "On My Mind the Whole Night Long"—both rolls pretty strictly based in playing—are among the most provocative and Gersh-winesque of the entire series.

Not until style analyses of the roll work of Gershwin's many colleagues are complete will scholars have the proper basis for evaluating Gershwin's approach to arranging over the ten years he worked in the industry. If one considers that Gershwin's roll oeuvre is large, but not unusually so (for instance, Zez Confrey made approximately 170 rolls), the magnitude of such research becomes apparent. During the Gershwin era, furthermore, the New York music scene was a hotbed of intricate professional relationships and musical cross-fertilizations. Even with more information, separating style originators from imitators and determining whether forethought or accident drove the success of a certain roll-arranging approach will doubtless always be difficult.

The Perfection Rolls, 1916–1917

Gershwin made his first rolls for the Standard Music Roll Company on its Perfection label in late 1915, soon after he had begun working for Remick as a song plugger. Standard, like many other roll manufacturers, was located not in New York City but across the Hudson River near Newark, New Jersey—a convenient location for freelancers from the city to come and cut rolls. Of the twenty-seven rolls Gershwin made on Perfection, none of his own tunes.

Surprisingly, Gershwin's Perfection rolls are not all arrangements of tried-and-true titles from the catalogue of his employer, Remick. Apparently, Standard paid Gershwin to knock out arrangements of best-selling or likely-to-sell tunes, regardless of publisher. Examples include songs inspired by World War I ("The Letter That Never Reached Home," published by Kalmar, Puck, and Abrahams; "Good-bye, Good-luck, God Bless You," published by Witmark) and Southern nostalgia ("Down Where the Swanee River Flows," published by Von Tilzer; "And They Called It Dixieland," published by Remick), and novelty songs (the animal dance number "Walkin' the Dog," published by Rossiter and written by African American composer Shelton Brooks).

But why did Gershwin make arrangements of non-hit tunes? In the selections he recorded for Standard and later for Aeolian and Welte-Mignon, Gershwin himself may have suggested some titles, based on his interest in the tune, its composer, or its publisher, or because he was professionally performing the song in the many venues through which he passed as a player before the 1920s. The rolls drawn from two Jerome Kern musicals for which Gershwin served as rehearsal pianist and the rolls of two Yiddish theater tunes during the time Gershwin considered a career as a composer for the Yiddish theater are clear examples.[8] Or why, for instance, did Gershwin record so many songs published by Von Tilzer for Perfection? Was he attempting to forge an alliance with Von Tilzer similar to the one he created a few years later with Harms? In short, the reasons that prompted Gershwin to make rolls of this or that tune are not always explained by a tune's popularity and suggest areas of further research.

Perfection was a budget label, and its rolls were created for the least expensive, technologically most primitive player pianos. Gershwin's Perfection rolls required the pianolist to add dynamics and tempo by means of tempo and dynamics levers. To guide the interpretation, a suggested roll speed and a line of dynamics ranging from *pp* to *FF* was printed on the roll, visible to the pianolist as he foot-pumped.[9] Moreover, Perfection adopted the industry's common practice of using fictitious names for its arranger-players. In this way, companies would appear to have a large roster of artists from which the roll purchaser could choose. The young unknown George Gershwin appeared in Perfection's catalogue not only under his own name but also under the pseudonyms Baker, Murtha, and Wynn.

Still, Gershwin's Perfection rolls cannot be dismissed as without merit. In fact, some rolls—particularly those of less popular instrumental numbers such as "Kangaroo Hop," "Bantam Step," "Chinese Blues," and Artie Matthews's "Pastime Rag No. 3"—are excellent. These four are multisectional dances (in contradistinction to songs' standard VCVCC looping), and Gershwin felicitously embellishes them well beyond the published sheets. Among the most striking of all Gershwin's rolls is his Perfection rendition of "Pastime Rag No. 3." His performance (all but the final strain is based on his hand-playing) is an idiosyncratic reading of the Matthews sheet, replete with tasteful but ingenious harmonic, rhythmic, and textural variants.

The Aeolian Rolls, 1916–1918

In early 1916 Felix Arndt, composer of the novelty piano solo *Nola* and a prolific roll artist, brought Gershwin to the prestigious Aeolian Company to make piano rolls. The Aeolian Company was the giant of the American player piano and piano roll industry. In addition to manufacturing pianos under its own brand name, the company installed roll playback mechanisms from the simplest to the most advanced in some of the finest American pianos, including Steck, Weber, Steinway, and many others. Aeolian's enormous roll catalogue listed popular, ethnic, educational, and classical selections and featured some of the greatest pianists of the day. Aeolian produced rolls of varying technological sophistication—ranging from those without automatic expression (Universal and Mel-O-Dee),[10] through those with rudimentary automatic expression (Metro Art and, indirectly via a licensed subsidiary, Artrio-Angelus), to the most expensive top-of-the-line product with completely automatic expression (Duo-Art, intended specifically for Duo-Art reproducing pianos).[11]

Even though his move to Aeolian was a step up in his profession, Gershwin continued to make roll arrangements primarily of the popular tunes of the day. Examples include the nostalgic "Mammy's Little Coal Black

Rose," "Where the Black-Eyed Susans Grow," and "Southern Gals"; the patriotic "For Your Country and My Country"; the novelty "Huckleberry Finn"; and the Swedish dialect tune "Hello, Wisconsin."

Many of Gershwin's roll arrangements around 1917–18 at Aeolian are piano duets in collaboration with Aeolian staffers Erlebach and Wilson. The piano duet format easily legitimized the prevailing thick textures that characterize piano rolls. However, Gershwin's Aeolian duets go beyond simple textural fattening and illustrate a scoring style that takes advantage of the nearly limitless note-playing capacity of the player piano. The typical Gershwin duet roll scoring consists of a filigree obbligato (often fistfuls of chords alternating with single notes in rhythm beats high in the treble), and a ragtime-stride bass that weaves around the melody set either as a tremolo or as repeated notes in the tenor. This "wall of sound" probably astonished buyers on first hearing and effectively substituted for the full sonority of an orchestra. Gershwin, his collaborators, and his editors used the duet scoring frequently and continued to refine it: "Whispering" and "Singin' the Blues," two 1920 Gershwin duet rolls misleadingly credited as solos, reveal duet scoring as nothing less than a minor art form.

In 1917, the new jazz music began to take America's white middle class by storm through recordings by the Original Dixieland Jazz Band and other white bands. Roll companies were eager to capitalize on the fad. But despite the titles printed on his roll boxes—"Storybook Ball, a Jass–Fox Trot" or "When It's All Over, a Jass–One Step"—one hears little evidence that jazz had become part of Gershwin's roll-arranging vocabulary. In fact, most of Gershwin's rolls until 1920 are based on ragtime.

Gershwin continued, as he had done at Standard, to make excellent rolls for Aeolian of instrumentals based on ragtime. Doubtless Gershwin and his editors realized that ragtime-based instrumentals translated well to the player medium and that, more pragmatically, a profit was to be made from them. Standouts from his Aeolian days include several deserving but little-known ragtime-based rolls: "Havanola," "Buzzin' the Bee," "Ruby Fox Trot," and "Jazamine." Gershwin's roll of *Rialto Ripples* (1917; roll issued 1916), one of his first rolls of his own music (written in collaboration with Will Donaldson), shows Gershwin's mastery of ragtime style and more fully developed inner voices compared to the printed score.

Two wonderful anomalies, "Hesitation Blues" and "Mele Hula," appear in Gershwin's rollography in 1917. The melody of "Hesitation Blues" is supported by a blues pattern, and Gershwin responds with bluesy riffs and breaks—unusual for this period in his roll oeuvre—throughout the arrangement. "Mele Hula," written by the important African American composer Will Tyers (sometime music director for Vernon and Irene Castle), may sport a Hawaiian title (Hawaiian nostalgia being a minor craze of the time), but the composition—at least, in Gershwin's arrangement—showcases Spanish and Cuban rhythms in one of Gershwin's finest rolls.

In March 1917, after Gershwin had been employed by Aeolian for less than a year and had finally left Standard (apparently he worked for both companies for a brief period), he quit his job as a Remick song plugger. Gershwin had apparently had enough of this aspect of the "music racket" and was eager to concentrate on songwriting. After quitting Remick he aggressively pursued prospects for live performance and was hired on as rehearsal pianist for two Jerome Kern musicals, *Miss 1917* and *Rock-a-Bye Baby* (1917). Gershwin made three roll arrangements of songs from these shows, issued in 1918. Two selections from *Miss 1917* are typical of vividly contrasting arranging styles: "The Picture I Want to See" is very close to the published sheet and based on Gershwin's hand-playing, whereas "The Land Where the Good Songs Go" is standard-issue duet arranging (with Erlebach).

A large group of piano rolls, released in April 1919, from the 1918 Hirsch show *Oh, My Dear!* dates from Gershwin's period as a freelance performer and new staff composer at Harms. *Oh, My Dear!* was not an unusually popular musical comedy of the 1918–19 season, yet Gershwin produced six single-tune rolls plus an extended medley from the show—a comprehensive coverage unique in Gershwin's rollography. Was Gershwin the rehearsal pianist for this production? Gershwin is certainly linked to Hirsch via the *Ziegfeld Follies of 1918*, which featured music by Hirsch and for which Gershwin was indeed rehearsal pianist. Moreover, Hirsch was a Harms composer. Perhaps Gershwin in 1918–19 was cultivating a contact for writing for the *Follies* through Hirsch—an enterprising plan that never came to fruition; instead Gershwin approached George White in 1920 to write for his new revue competing with the *Follies*. Again, the relationship between Gershwin's rollography and biography poses interesting questions and connections.

How arranging styles were chosen for particular tunes during the Aeolian years is not clear. When Gershwin began to make Duo-Art rolls in 1917–18, all the titles issued on Duo-Art rolls were duet arrangements. However, not all Gershwin Aeolian duets were issued as Duo-Art rolls. Apparently, of those songs for which Gershwin made rolls during 1917–18, the most popular were treated to duet arranging and were likely to be issued as Duo-Art rolls. There are exceptions. Gershwin played the popular "Huckleberry Finn" as a duet with Wilson, but the roll was not issued as a Duo-Art. In any case, duet arrangements fade from Gershwin's rollography by the end of 1918, although duet-arranging style remains—albeit on rolls attributed to Gershwin as a solo performer.

The Welte-Mignon and Aeolian Rolls, 1919–1921

Around 1920 Gershwin's rollography changed dramatically. First, he began to make more roll arrangements of his own tunes. Most of the tunes for which he made rolls in 1920 are taken from his first successful musical comedy, *La, La, Lucille* (1919). One of his best roll arrangements from 1920 is of "Swanee," from *Capitol Revue* (1919), his first hit and most commercially successful song. This brief roll arrangement (less than two minutes; most of his rolls average around three) shows that the composer obviously took special pains in its preparation. Based on his hand-playing with but a few note elongations in the coda,[12] the arrangement percolates with sophisticated harmonies, skillful manipulation of tessitura, and inventive rhythmic and melodic counterpoint. The charming coda quotes "Listen to the Mockingbird"—an allusion to Al Jolson's whistled trademark ending.

The second change in Gershwin's rollography reflects the fact that he had begun around 1919 to make rolls for another company, the Welte-Mignon Corporation. Welte-Mignon, at its new plant in the Bronx, apparently tried to represent Gershwin as he actually hand-played rather than supplementing arrangements with extra notes, as Aeolian frequently did.[13] Unfortunately, the Welte-Mignon attempt to represent Gershwin accurately led to rolls that were rhythmically jerky compared to Aeolian's more rhythmically polished but thick-textured rolls of the same period. Such rhythmic unevenness probably stems from Welte-Mignon's different editing aesthetic and level of technical expertise rather than flaws in Gershwin's playing. In fact, Gershwin's rolls for Welte-Mignon are valuable because they are clearly based on his hand-playing. In these rolls one hears riffs and breaks of the live Gershwin ca. 1919, and furthermore, they show just how "harmony-conscious" he had become.[14] Of the thirteen rolls Gershwin is known to have made for Welte-Mignon, five are arrangements of his own tunes; one is his original salon piano solo, *Novelette in Fourths*; and the rest are arrangements of some of the most popular lyric, even operetta-like, tunes of the day by other composers.

Gershwin's singularly uncharacteristic *Novelette in Fourths* has only recently been published.[15] The composer's manuscript is in the Gershwin Collection at the Library of Congress. Gershwin worked out his Welte-Mignon rendition much more fully than the written version, including an additional strain not notated in the manuscript.[16] The roll shows that Gershwin by 1919 had assimilated one of the prevalent popular piano tricks, decorative parallel fourths and fifths, and used them as the basis for an entire composition. In this era parallel fourths and fifths evoked the mysterious East, an exotic locale that became a fad in settings of Broadway musical comedies and revues during the 1910s and early 1920s. James P. Johnson, the great stride pianist, first took note of Gershwin in the context of this style: "It was at Aeolian . . . in 1920 that I met George Gershwin who was cutting 'oriental' numbers there when I was making blues rolls which were popular then. He had written 'Swanee' and was interested in rhythm and blues."[17] The "orientals" to which Johnson refers were probably "Idle Dreams," "Just Snap Your Fingers at Care," and "Limehouse Nights"—all from 1920.

During 1919–20 Gershwin passed some significant professional and artistic milestones. Not only did he have a successful show (*La, La, Lucille*) and hit song ("Swanee") to his credit; in 1920 he had also landed a contract with George White to write for his *Scandals*. White set a distinctive tone in his fledgling endeavor by emphasizing the new jazzy hot-and-dirty dances and musical styles instead of the genteel, operetta-oriented music that his principal rival, Ziegfeld, favored. Whether Gershwin was the musical cart or the horse in this situation is unknown, but his assimilation of African American musical idioms became a noticeable stylistic feature in his music after he began to write for the *Scandals*.

Gershwin's heightened status as a songwriter undoubtedly positively affected his relationship with Aeolian. The year 1920, in fact, brought a bumper crop of wonderfully inventive piano roll arrangements. One of the best arrangements of his own tunes is "On My Mind the Whole Night Long," an early Gershwin blues tune from the 1920 *Scandals*. His roll demonstrates how well Gershwin had learned the blues piano style from James P. Johnson and others. Noteworthy roll arrangements of other composers' tunes include the mad pastiche of novelty, oriental, and Spanish rhythms applied to Schonberger's hit "Whispering"; "If a Wish Could Make It So," in which duet textures integrate with sophisticated call-and-response patterns; the kaleidoscopic juxtapositions of styles and textures in "Darling"; the allusions to jazz and the witty interpolation of Foster's "Old Black Joe" in "Waitin' for Me"; and, finally, the darkly evocative "Singin' the Blues," featuring Gershwin's own hand-played jazzlike riffs and breaks.

The Late Aeolian Rolls, 1925–1927

In the decade or so in which Gershwin made piano rolls, his production steadily declined through 1920: 1916, forty rolls; 1917, forty rolls; 1918, six rolls; 1919, seventeen rolls; and 1920, twenty-three rolls. The drop in 1918 may be explained by Gershwin's intense performing schedule on tour with Louise Dresser and Nora Bayes and as rehearsal accompanist for the *Follies* and Kern's *Rock-a-Bye Baby*, and his preoccupation with mounting his first (and disastrous) musical comedy, *Half Past Eight*.

No easy explanations can be made for the precipitous drop in Gershwin's roll output in 1921—only seven rolls—or his silence in the medium until May 1925 with the issue of part II of *Rhapsody in Blue*. Perhaps during the early 1920s, as Gershwin became famous but had yet to achieve renown, Aeolian offered him neither the money nor sufficient artistic freedom to have made the production of rolls worth his time. Or perhaps Gershwin's schedule simply did not permit such freelancing. In any case, all the piano rolls Gershwin made from 1925 on are arrangements of his own music, and all were issued on the upscale Duo-Art label.[18]

Gershwin's rolls from the mid-1920s are very different in arranging style from his previous Aeolian efforts. All of these rolls show Aeolian's attempt to re-create the now famous Gershwin performance style as accurately as possible for playback on the Duo-Art reproducing piano. The person responsible for this new approach was Frank Milne. By the mid-1920s Milne had emerged as head editor of Aeolian's popular-music piano roll division. A superb arranger, Milne had made scores of roll arrangements himself by the time he worked with Gershwin. Not only did Milne contribute strictly musical suggestions for these roll arrangements; he was also responsible for the Duo-Art expression coding that triggered the roll's dynamics.

Despite advertisements to the contrary, Aeolian had not developed a technology for capturing the pianist's note velocities—how loud or soft a note plays as measured by the speed the hammer travels to the string. In order to re-create expression, Duo-Art editors resorted to creative techniques. One such technique involved the use of an expression-marking machine that operated as the pianist recorded. While the pianist played, an editor manipulated a dial in response to the dynamics he heard; this dial inscribed a rudimentary dynamic line on a roll of paper moving in tandem with the note-on, note-off information being recorded by the carbon rods.[19] The expression-marking machine also had buttons that the roll editor pushed when he heard strongly accented chords or individual notes.[20] Coding this interpretative information onto a single roll (four holes on both end margins of the roll triggered the "expressive" note velocities) together with the note-on, note-off data probably occurred later.[21] Another technique required the editor simply to remember the pianist's performance and subsequently develop the expression coding. Clearly, the editors' memory, musical recall, coding skill, and aesthetic bias played large roles in either coding technique. Moreover, usually no score existed of the arrangements performed by pianists such as Gershwin and the documentation of expression was necessarily an interpretive, remembered response.[22] When a master was completed, it was often—though not always—played back in consultation with the pianist for suggestions and corrections before release.[23]

In addition to the challenges Aeolian editors faced in collecting accurate expression information to code the rolls for playback, they were also confronted with the problem of manipulating the Duo-Art system's technical capability to simulate more subtle aspects of the way pianists actually play. In a certain fashion, the Duo-Art piano could reproduce, at least grossly, dynamic variation among the notes of chords. The system was limited by its inability to precisely replicate the subtle but telling differences among individual note velocities within simultaneously struck chords—that is, chord balances—but the Duo-Art could be manipulated to create a facsimile of chord balance. To manufacture this facsimile, editors ever so slightly shifted attack points of notes on the roll spatially (that is, temporally). Needless to say, after these shifts had been accomplished, attack points of notes on the roll in playback rarely corresponded to the way the pianist had first positioned them in time while recording. Since minute shadings of note velocities and note placements are as unique as a fingerprint to a given artist's performance, and since the roll editor had to find ways to manipulate the limitations of the Duo-Art system in order to code equivalents of the detailed characteristics of a live performance, the editor's musicianship, technical skill, taste, and integrity were critical.

In his own arrangements, Milne had assimilated the early 1920s popular piano performance hallmarks of jazz rhythm beats and striding left-hand tenths with their frequent upper- and lower-note anticipations. To suggest hand-playing, Milne thinned out player roll textures without sacrificing full-bodied sound, and he staggered note entrances to resemble live performance. Most important, Milne masterfully re-created the extraordinary variety of accents that made 1920s jazz and dance music tick. His splendid coding of accents gives his rolls a rhythmic drive that suggests human performance.

One can gauge how closely Milne came to re-creating the Gershwin style by comparing his roll collaborations with Gershwin to Gershwin's own phonograph recordings of the same tunes—"Sweet and Low-Down" and "That Certain Feeling"—the phonograph recordings made for Columbia just a few months after the rolls. The musical arrangements are very similar for both tunes in the two media—roll and disc—although the placement of verses and refrains differs. Gershwin clearly is responsible for the shared arrangements, but Milne's hand (quite literally) may be discerned in the texturally expanded final chorus of "That Certain Feeling" and the crossed-hands effects of "Sweet and Low-Down"—both stock devices in Milne's arranging repertory. And there are other subtle differences in performance style. Gershwin's phonograph discs are never as metronomic as his quantized rolls, even when Milne cleverly disguises quantization through staggered note placement and wonderfully sophisticated accentuation coding. Gershwin's tempi on the phonograph discs are visceral, ebbing and flowing, and always accelerating as he drives to conclusion. Not so in the rolls, where the steady performances always have a slicker, more relaxed quality. Still, while Milne failed to capture that exciting but rough and hard-driving edge in Gershwin's playing, within the limits of Duo-Art he managed a satisfying copy. Moreover, Milne's polished, refined versions of the real thing may have been an aesthetic that was commercially necessary: if high-end Duo-Art dance rolls had called too much attention to themselves in a rough way, they may not have sold, Gershwin's name notwithstanding.

Among the most fascinating and controversial of the late Gershwin rolls is his slow ballad arrangement of "So Am I." The roll was evidently not quantized and convincingly represents the give-and-take of a live performance. Some roll collectors question whether "So Am I" is a genuine Gershwin performance. Doubts center on the facts that Gershwin was never recorded on phonograph discs playing in a slow tempo, that "So Am I" is performed up-tempo in the original cast recording, and that the amount of sustaining pedal on the "So Am I" roll is inconsistent with his use of it on phonograph recordings. Robert Armbruster, head of light classical rolls at Aeolian when Gershwin made his last rolls, has been suggested as the actual performer—a claim Armbruster denied when I interviewed him in 1990. To view Gershwin as a performer who could play only in an up-tempo dance style belies his extensive professional experience as accompanist to noted singers and as rehearsal pianist to important shows. Assigning a ballad character to "So Am I" probably made good marketing sense, since that lone ballad gave variety (and appeal to the salon market) within what proved to be the final group of Gershwin roll arrangements. Moreover, the performance itself suggests the rubato of a dance accompanist, such as Gershwin surely was. While effective, the ritardandos and accelerandos on the roll performance are less curvilinear than those one might expect from a classical pianist—which Gershwin most certainly was not. Finally, the nearly excessive use of the sustaining pedal may have been his editor's way of giving a bit more legato to the roll performance.

Gershwin's roll recording of *Rhapsody in Blue* was issued on two rolls: part II, released in May 1925, and part I, released in January 1927. Part II begins with the famous slow theme through the bravura conclusion of the composition; part I includes nearly three-quarters of the composition, up to the slow theme, on a single, unusually large roll. By 1927 Aeolian was already on a financial downslide, so the release of part I was probably delayed for commercial reasons: the company probably chose to release part II, with the famous theme, first, and then, when that proved financially successful, the longer part I.

In order to pack such an unusually large amount of performance data on the single roll of part I, the data from the master was telescoped down, and the roll stipulates that it must be run at slow speed. These cost-saving measures clearly compromised the data's resolution, and the roll has rhythmic distortion—a jerkiness—that is not present on either of Gershwin's phonograph recordings of *Rhapsody in Blue* with the Whiteman orchestra. Part II is rhythmically more acceptable, running at more normal roll speed—80 (eight feet per minute) versus 65 (six and a half feet per minute) of part I.

Technical problems aside, overall the roll rendition of the *Rhapsody* disappoints. To have re-created the expression and dynamics of both the piece and Gershwin's idiosyncratic playing would probably have been too expensive for Aeolian in its financially troubled condition. Still, the editor(s)[24] did a passable job, and occasional sections clearly reflect Gershwin's actual note field (relative positions of the notes in time, as spatially represented on the roll), as, for instance, in the limping G-major theme. But the rolls should be regarded with caution as bona fide representations of Gershwin's playing style. Much more authoritative are his phonograph recordings of abridged versions of the *Rhapsody* with Whiteman, particularly the earlier of the two, although even here one senses that the performers scrambled to cram as much music as possible on two sides of a twelve-inch disc.

Threading one's way through the performance documents of rolls and discs of *Rhapsody in Blue*, one is hard-pressed to say which rendition most represents a live, unfettered Gershwin performance. However, all of Gershwin's recordings and especially his rolls reinforce the impression that the composer's approach to playing his songs and the *Rhapsody* have little to do with later, more romanticized readings. His was surely an aggressively confident and livelier way, based in the raggier dance performance style of the era and completely devoid of sentimentality. Of course, it could not have been otherwise: as a tracing of his piano rolls makes clear, Gershwin cut his teeth on the exhilarating popular music of the late 1910s and early 1920s. He flowered in that rich and frenetic time when ragtime and the syncopated dance craze peaked and when jazz and the blues would change America's musical landscape forever.

Notes

Special thanks to Michael Montgomery, John Joyce, Bruce Raeburn, Horace Van Norman, and the National Endowment for the Humanities.

1. See the chapter entitled "Ballyhoo: Or the Ungentle Art of Plugging," in Isaac Goldberg, *Tin Pan Alley: A Chronicle of American Popular Music* (New York: Frederick Ungar, 1930), 197–233.

2. Charles Hambitzer, letter to his sister, Mrs. E. Reel. Quoted in Edward Jablonski, *Gershwin Remembered* (New York: Amadeus, 1992), 8.

3. John S. Wilson, "Introduction," in Robert Kimball and Alfred Simon, *The Gershwins* (New York: Atheneum, 1973), xxiii.

4. Ira Gershwin, "George Gershwin's First Scrapbook," typescript introduction dated 20 April 1962, Gershwin Scrapbooks, Gershwin Collection, Library of Congress. See also Kimball and Simon, *The Gershwins*, 12.

5. Scott Derks, ed., *The Value of a Dollar: Prices and Incomes in the United States, 1860–1989* (Detroit: Gale Research), 149.

6. "Quantization" is a term used in computer music referring to rhythmic correction. The term Aeolian editors used for the process is unknown. See Christopher Yavelow, "Music and Microprocessors: MIDI and the State of the Art," in *The Music Machine: Selected Readings from the Computer Music Journal*, ed. Curtis Roads (Cambridge: MIT Press, 1989), 210.

7. Electric motors controlling roll speed were installed only in the later years of player piano manufacture.

8. Unfortunately, these rolls have not been located.

9. Whether these ideas were Gershwin's or those of his editor is unclear.

10. The first player pianos required human intervention to add expression. But eventually player piano companies sought ways for the player mechanisms to automatically play not only notes and rhythms but also dynamics. The devices' design was modified so that hammer speed (louder = faster, softer = slower) could be triggered by certain holes perforated in the roll.

11. Reproducing pianos were fitted with the most advanced roll playback systems for duplicating human performance: a reproducing piano was said to "reproduce" the playing of a Josef Hofmann or Percy Grainger or George Gershwin. Duo-Art was one of three major reproducing systems vying for supremacy during the Gershwin era; the other two were Welte-Mignon and Ampico. Since each had its own unique technology, a Welte-Mignon roll would not play properly on a Duo-Art reproducing piano, and so on.

12. Note elongations are notes editorially lengthened on the roll beyond the physical ability of the pianist to sustain them. Such elongations were a common editing practice, and presumably they gave the roll performance a more desirable linear quality.

13. Not all of the Welte-Mignon rolls have been found.

14. Gershwin noted that his teacher Charles Hambitzer "made me harmony-conscious." Quoted in Isaac Goldberg, *George Gershwin: A Study in American Music* (New York: Simon & Schuster, 1931), 62.

15. Ed. Alicia Zizzo, New York: Warner, 1997. *Novelette in Fourths* is the only Gershwin composition played by Gershwin among the Welte-Mignon rolls to have been found.

16. Roll scholars note that the principal strain of *Novelette* bears a resemblance to the

second strain of Zez Confrey's *Kitten on the Keys*, performed often by Confrey before it was published in 1921.

17. Tom Davin, "Conversations with James P. Johnson," in *Ragtime, Its History, Composers and Music*, ed. John E. Hasse (New York: Schirmer Books, 1985), 177.

18. All the late song arrangements—but not the *Rhapsody in Blue*—were issued also on Aeolian's Mel-O-Dee label.

19. Perhaps all this information was collated on a single scroll of paper. The process is still unknown.

20. See Jim Elfers, "Recording, Coding and Re-coding: Armbruster on Duo-Art," *AMICA News Bulletin* 7 (July 1970): 16.

21. Some roll collectors believe high-speed perforators accomplished the entire coding process while the pianist recorded.

22. Perhaps scores were used occasionally. In my interview with Robert Armbruster, June 1990, he suggested that he had made sketch-scores of some of his arrangements.

23. Such a review was particularly necessary when the performer was famous or fastidious or perhaps simply of a technological bent. Barbara Milne Shaak, Frank Milne's daughter, in an interview with me, August 1990, recalled that her father told her of frequently consulting Gershwin on the preparation of the later Duo-Art rolls.

24. W. Creary Woods, head of the Aeolian Classical division in the 1920s, was most likely the supervising editor for *Rhapsody in Blue*.

11 : George Gershwin's
   : Piano Rollography

MICHAEL MONTGOMERY

A "rollography" is an annotated and classified list of an artist's piano roll recordings. George Gershwin's piano rollography, which follows, lists the 140 (perhaps 141) known piano rolls he recorded, according to roll label credits.

The earliest Gershwin rollography was a list of Ampico and Duo-Art rolls (as well as Brunswick, Columbia, and Victor phonograph recordings) then currently available, printed as an appendix in the *George Gershwin's Song Book* (1932).[1] Duo-Art rolls of Gershwin compositions played by Gershwin were listed along with Duo-Art rolls of Gershwin songs played by Gershwin's contemporaries: Phil Ohman, Cliff Hess, Muriel Pollock, Henry Lange, Freddie Rich, and Frank Milne. Ampico rolls of Gershwin songs were also listed, again played by Gershwin's contemporaries: Victor Arden, Adam Carroll, Zez Confrey, Ferde Grofé, and the Original Piano Trio.

The first attempt to list every roll Gershwin recorded (regardless of the composer) was a rollography I prepared for *Record Research* in 1962.[2] Ten years later, at Robert Kimball's request, I updated and improved that 1962 effort, and Kimball subsequently included the revised version in his 1973 book (with Alfred Simon), *The Gershwins*.[3] Now, decades later, definitive details about Gershwin's thirteen known Welte-Mignon rolls from 1919, plus one possible new listing—a Mel-O-Dee roll from September 1921 bearing his name—can be added.

As Artis Wodehouse discusses in her essay, a "hand-played" piano roll differs from a hand-played phonograph record in one critical aspect: a roll always sustained some editing and manipulation, while a phonograph record was issued "as is." The editing of phonograph records was not possible in the early days of that industry; consequently, a record represented the pianist as he or she sounded in real life and in real time. (Record companies usually made several "takes" to get at least one usable master from which to press discs. The piano roll companies had no such constraints.) Comparing discs to rolls is similar to comparing a candid photo taken with a hand-held camera to a posed studio portrait where the photographer seats the subject, professionally lights the set, and then retouches the photo print until all the wrinkles are minimized and the moles disappear. Both photos are still of your Aunt Winnie, but the professional photograph is the one you'll frame and hang up. The candid is the one you'll leave in the photo album.

In this rollography, the months and years shown above the roll titles are the dates the rolls were released for public sale. A roll was probably recorded two or three months prior to its release. Neither the order of release nor the numerical order of the rolls is an infallible indication of the order in which the rolls were recorded. The information presented here has been drawn from many sources—notably, the roll labels, company catalogues and bulletins, and trade journals. The name in parentheses under a roll title is usually the name of the composer, although sometimes the lyricist's name is also included. Some roll labels give the title of the show, revue, or musical comedy in which the tune was featured, and these references have been included here.

George Gershwin is a recording artist on all of these rolls, but he is not the sole artist on all of the rolls. Occasionally, he recorded with other roll artists, among them Rudolph O. Erlebach (fifteen duets), Edwin E. Wilson (six duets), and Cliff Hess (one duet). (One source also lists Muriel Pollock on a duet.) Gershwin's solo rolls number 118.

In his early years as a roll artist for the Standard Music Roll Company, Gershwin recorded Perfection rolls under three pseudonyms—James Baker, Fred Murtha, and Bert Wynn—in addition to the recordings under his own name. It is not known whether all rolls bearing the names of James Baker, Fred Murtha, and Bert Wynn were recorded by George Gershwin; nevertheless, all such known rolls are listed here.

Gershwin began to make piano rolls in late 1915, and his earliest rolls were hand-played rolls on the Perfection label of the Standard Music Roll Company. These rolls retailed from 24 to 30 cents. With the help of Felix Arndt, composer of *Nola* and a leading roll artist, Gershwin began to record for the Aeolian Company, the giant of the American piano roll business, in early 1916. Of his 141 rolls, 101 were made under Aeolian's aegis.

Metro-Art, Universal Uni-Record, Universal Song Roll, Mel-O-Dee, Universal, and Duo-Art are all Aeolian brand names. The Universal rolls could be played on any player piano, while the others all had special features that attempted a more faithfully reproduced piano sound with expressive subtleties and nuances.

Aeolian also leased its rolls to the Wilcox & White Company of Meriden, Connecticut, which brought out many Gershwin rolls, after their original Aeolian release, under such labels as Angelus-Voltem, Artrio-Angelus, and Angelus. Gershwin rolls also appeared in Great Britain, made from Aeolian masters. Where known, these are shown next to the U.S. issues. In addition, two late rolls have been found on the British Meloto label, indicated as such in the following rollography.

In some instances, the retail prices of rolls are shown after the catalogue numbers. Significantly, roll customers had to pay 75 cents for one song, while record customers could pay about the same and get a song on each side of a disc. Some Aeolian rolls gave the key of the music as part of the label data, and this information is included as well. Some rolls are "song rolls," where the lyrics are printed in stencil vertically along the right edge of the roll for singing along as the roll played. Some catalogues and monthly bulletins included puff descriptions to convince customers to buy: these advertising phrases are given in quotes in the following entries. An asterisk (*) appears before the titles of the twenty-three Gershwin rolls not yet in my collection.[4]

1916

January 1916

Bring Along Your Dancing Shoes
    (Kahn and Le Boy) Fox Trot Arrangement
    Played by George Gershwin
    Perfection 86585
Kangaroo Hop
    (Morris) Fox Trot
    Played by George Gershwin
    Perfection 86595

March 1916

"Latest Popular Songs—Some Being Adapted for Both Singing and Dancing"
Give a Little Credit to Your Dad
    (Vincent) One and Two Step Arrangement
    Played by Bert Wynn
    Perfection 86625
You Can't Get Along When You're with 'Em or without 'Em
    (Fischer) Fox Trot Song
    Played by Fred Murtha
    Perfection 86626
*The Letter That Never Reached Home
    (Gottler) March Song
    Played by Bert Wynn
    Perfection 86629

At the Fountain of Youth
    (Jentes) One and Two Step Arrangement
    Played by George Gershwin
    Perfection 86630
"Dance Music"
*Bantam Step
    (Jentes) A Raggy Fox Trot
    Played by George Gershwin
    Perfection 86632
"Latest Popular Songs"
When You're Dancing the Old Fashioned Waltz
    (Von Tilzer)
    Played by George Gershwin
    Perfection 86634
Good-Bye, Good-Luck, God Bless You
    (Ball) Waltz Ballad
    Played by James Baker
    Perfection 86637
I Gave My Heart and Hand to Someone in Dixieland
    (Lange)
    Played by Fred Murtha
    Perfection 86641

April 1916

"Latest Popular Songs"
Siam, How Lonesome I Am
    (Fischer)
    Played by Fred Murtha
    Perfection 86656
Down Where the Swanee River Flows
    (Von Tilzer) Fox Trot Arrangement
    Played by George Gershwin
    Perfection 86663
Wake Up America
    (Glogau) March Song
    Played by Fred Murtha
    Perfection 86667
"Dance Music"
Honky Tonky (Down in Honky Tonky Town)
    (McCarron) One Step
    Played by George Gershwin
    Perfection 86671

May 1916

Oh Joe with Your Fiddle and Bow
    (Donaldson) Fox Trot

Played by George Gershwin
Perfection 86703

International Fox Trot—A Novelty Medley of Familiar Melodies
(Platzmann)
Played by Fred Murtha
Perfection 86705

Nat'an! Nat'an! Tell Me for What Are You Waitin', Nat'an?
(Kendis) Fox Trot Arrangement
Played by Bert Wynn
Perfection 86711

Some Girls Do and Some Girls Don't
(Jentes) Fox Trot Arrangement
Played by George Gershwin
Perfection 86712

Arrah Go On I'm Gonna Go Back to Oregon
(Grant) One Step Arrangement
Played by George Gershwin
Perfection 86713

"Dances and Marches"

Chinese Blues
(Gardner) Fox Trot
Played by Bert Wynn
Perfection 86717

When You're Dancing the Old Fashioned Waltz
(Albert Von Tilzer)
Played by George Gershwin
Metro-Art 202668 $.45
Universal Uni-Record 202669 $.45

You Can't Get Along with 'Em or without 'Em
(Fred Fischer) Fox Trot
Played by George Gershwin
Metro-Art 202676 $.40
Universal Uni-Record 202677 $.40

*Bantam Step
(Harry Jentes) Fox Trot
Played by George Gershwin
Metro-Art 202684 $.50
Universal Uni-Record 202685 $.50

June 1916

"Latest Popular Songs"
*I Was Never Nearer Heaven in My Life
(Snyder) Ballad
Played by Fred Murtha
Perfection 86727

And They Called It Dixieland
(Whiting) One Step Arrangement
Played by George Gershwin

Perfection 86736
Sing-A Word Roll 5390
"Latest Dances"
Pastime Rag
    (Matthews) A Slow Drag
    Played by Fred Murtha
    Perfection 86738
    Note: This is Matthews's "Pastime Rag No. 3."
"Hebrew Music" ("Standard Rolls for June")
*Das Pintele Yud
    (Perlmutter and Wohl)
    Played by Georoge [sic] Gershwin
    Perfection (number not shown)
*Gott un Sein Mishpet Is Gerecht
    (Meyerowitz)
    Played by Geoorge [sic] Gershwin
    Perfection (number not shown)
    Note: The preceding two titles are also included in Arto Roll No. 86378—"Hebrew
    Popular Songs—Medley"—a roll that retailed for $1.10 and is shown in Arto cata-
    logues of this period as "Played by Baltuck." In the medley they comprise selections
    5 and 4, respectively.
*When Verdi Plays the Hurdy-Gurdy
    (Walter Donaldson)
    Played by George Gershwin
    Metro-Art 202712 $.45
    Universal Uni-Record 202713 $.45
*Oh! Promise Me That You'll Come Back to Alabam'
    (George W. Meyer)
    Played by George Gershwin
    Metro-Art 202714 $.40
    Universal Uni-Record 202715 $.40
*Sail On to Ceylon
    (Herman Paley)
    Played by George Gershwin
    Metro-Art 202718 $.50
    Universal Uni-Record 202719 $.50

July 1916

"Latest Dances"
Walkin' the Dog
    (Brooks) Dance, New Dance Fox Trot Arrangement
    Played by George Gershwin
    Perfection 86753

August 1916

Come On to Nashville Tennessee
    (Walter Donaldson) Fox Trot

Played by George Gershwin
"One of the latest vaudeville hits. A sure winner."
Metro-Art 202852 $.40
Universal Uni-Record 202853 $.40
You're a Dog-Gone Dangerous Girl
(Clark & Monaco) Fox Trot
Played by George Gershwin
"One of the big successes featured by Al Jolson in his latest Winter Garden produc-
tion."
Metro-Art 202854 $.40
Universal Uni-Record 202855 $.40

September 1916

*When You Want 'Em You Can't Get 'Em
(George Gershwin) Fox Trot
Played by George Gershwin
Metro-Art 202864
Universal Uni-Record 202865
Honolulu Blues
(James V. Monaco) Fox Trot
Played by George Gershwin
Metro-Art 202872
Universal Uni-Record 202873
I Was Never Nearer Heaven in My Life
(Ted Snyder)
Played by George Gershwin
Metro-Art 202902
Universal Uni-Record 202903
Rialto Ripples
(George Gershwin) Fox Trot
Played by George Gershwin
Metro-Art 202934
Universal Uni-Record 202935

December 1916

Tiddle-de-Winks
(Melville Morris) Fox Trot
Played by George Gershwin
Metro-Art 203052
Universal Uni-Record 203053
I'm Down in Honolulu Looking Them Over
(Irving Berlin)
Played by George Gershwin
Metro-Art 203054 $.40
Universal Uni-Record 203055

1917

January 1917

Note: Aeolian Song Rolls were first introduced in January 1917. All ended in odd catalogue numbers, and George Gershwin played the entire first month's output.

Somewhere There's a Little Cottage Standing
  (Music—Marshall, Lyric—Sunshine) Saxophone Arrangement
  Played by George Gershwin (Assisted by R. O. Erlebach)
  "A great song with a wonderful melody and a master lyric. One that leaves a lingering impression that guarantees applause and enchore [*sic*]."
  Universal Song Roll 2001 $.60
Mammy's Little Coal Black Rose
  (Music—Whiting, Lyric—Egan)
  Played by George Gershwin
  "A wonderful song by the writers of 'And They Called It Dixieland.' It has a delightful melody and an appealing lyric."
  Universal Song Roll 2005 $.60
  Later issued on Mel-O-Dee 2005
Just a Word of Sympathy
  (Music—Alstyne, Lyric—Kahn)
  Played by George Gershwin
  "A brand new ballad hit by the writer of 'Memories.'"
  Universal Song Roll 2007 $.60
  Later issued on Mel-O-Dee 2007
If You'll Come Back to My Garden of Love
  (Music—Gumble, Lyric—Murphy)
  Played by George Gershwin
  "This beautiful song is just commencing to reach the height of popularity. Both the words and the music are bound to please."
  Universal Song Roll 2009 $.60
  Later issued on Mel-O-Dee 2009
How Is Every Little Thing in Dixie?
  (Music—Gumbel [*sic*], Lyric—Yellen)
  Played by George Gershwin
  "A great fast song by the writers of numerous hits. A splendid roll for dancing."
  Universal Song Roll 2013 $.60
  Later issued on Mel-O-Dee 2013

February 1917

Note: The two George Gershwin song rolls issued in February 1917 have catalogue numbers that fit in numerically among the five rolls issued in January.

Whose Pretty Baby Are You Now?
  (Music—Egbert Van Alstyne, Lyric—Gus Kahn) Saxophone Arrangement
  Played by George Gershwin (Assisted by R. O. E.)
  "The answer song to the popular 'Pretty Baby' is here offered in Saxophone arrange-

ment. The lyric is a humorous one, and the roll is also arranged for dancing purposes."
Universal Song Roll 2003 $.75
Later issued on Mel-O-Dee 2003 and Angelus 6001

It's a Cute Little Way of My Own (from *Follow Me*)
(Music—Harry Tierney, Lyric—Held & Bryan)
Played by George Gershwin
"The individual song success from Anna Held's latest musical comedy offering, *Follow Me*."
Universal Song Roll 2011 $.75
Later issued on Mel-O-Dee 2011

March 1917

'Way Down in Iowa I'm Going to Hide Away
(George Meyer)
Played by George Gershwin
"One of the popular song hits of the day which is meeting with great favor."
Metro-Art 203072 $.40
Universal 203073
Angelus Voltem 1535

Hesitation Blues
(Middleton and Smythe) Fox Trot
Played by George Gershwin
"One of the best known blues ever written, here played with much swing and pep."
Metro-Art 203074 $.40
Universal Uni-Record 203075
Angelus Voltem 1525
Artrio-Angelus 7695 $1.75

April 1917

Where the Black-Eyed Susans Grow
(Whiting and Radford)
Played by George Gershwin
Universal Song Roll 2079 $.80
Later issued on Mel-O-Dee 2079

*Because You're Irish
(Van Alstyne and Kahn)
Played by George Gershwin
Universal Song Roll 2081 $.75
Angelus 6011

She's Dixie All the Time
(Tierney and Bryan)
Played by George Gershwin
Universal Song Roll 2083 $.75
Angelus 6017

May 1917

*I Wonder Why (from *Love o' Mike*)
  (Kern) Fox Trot
  Played by George Gershwin
  Metro-Art 201208 $.50
  Universal 201209
Havanola (Have Another)
  (Frey) Fox Trot
  Played by George Gershwin
  Metro-Art 203098 $.50
  Universal 203099
Buzzin' the Bee
  (Wendling and Wells) Fox Trot
  Played by George Gershwin
  Metro-Art 203184 $.50
  Universal 203185

July 1917

Ain't You Comin' Back to Dixieland?
  (Richard Whiting) Jass–Fox Trot
  Played by Erlebach & Gershwin
  Universal Song Roll 2205
  Duo-Art 1545 $1.25
  Artrio-Angelus 7745 $1.75
*Rolling in His Little Rolling Chair
  (Halsey K. Mohr) Jass–Fox Trot E-Flat
  Played by Gershwin & Erlebach
  Universal Song Roll 2257 $.80

August 1917

Lily of the Valley
  (Anatol Friedland) Jass–Fox Trot
  Played by Gershwin & Erlebach
  Universal Song Roll 2293 $.80
  Later issued on Mel-O-Dee 2293
  Angelus Voltem 6051 (9/17)
  Duo-Art 1547 (9/17) $1.25
For Your Country and My Country
  (Irving Berlin) Jass–One Step
  Played by Gershwin & Erlebach
  Universal Song Roll 2307 $1.00
  Angelus Voltem 6051 (9/17)
  Duo-Art 1543 $1.25
*Mele Hula
  (William H. Tyers) Fox-Trot
  Played by George Gershwin

Metro-Art 203198
Universal 203199

September 1917

*You're a Great Big Lonesome Baby
    (Richard Whiting) Fox Trot
    Played by George Gershwin
    Universal Song Roll 2329 $.80
Sweetest Little Girl in Tennessee
    (Harry Carroll) Jass–Fox Trot
    Played by Gershwin & Wilson
    Universal Song Roll 2333 $.80
Story Book Ball
    (George Perry) Jass–Fox Trot
    Played by Gershwin & Erlebach
    Universal Song Roll 2337 $.75
    Later issued on Mel-O-Dee 2337
Huckleberry Finn
    (Joe Young) Jass–Fox Trot
    Played by Wilson & Gershwin
    Metro-Art 203224 $.50
    Universal 203225
Some Sweet Day
    (Abe Olman) Jass–Fox Trot
    Played by Gershwin & Erlebach
    Metro-Art 203232 $.50
    Universal 203233
    Artrio-Angelus 7768
Chu-Chin-Chow (from *Follies 1917*)
    (Dave Stamper) Jass–Fox Trot
    Played by Gershwin & Wilson
    Metro-Art 203238 $.50
    Universal 203239
    Artrio-Angelus 7769 $2.00
    Note: The Artrio-Angelus issue of this roll appears in a medley as follows:
Chinese Medley
    (Berlin, Smith, & Stamper) Fox Trot
    Introducing: (1) From Here to Shanghai; (2) While the Incense Is Burning; (3) Chu-Chin-
    Chow. Jazz Arrangements
    Played by Youmans, Erlebach, Wilson, Nelson, & Gershwin

October 1917

I've Got the Nicest Little Home in Dixie
    (Walter Donaldson) Jass–Fox Trot
    Played by Gershwin & Wilson
    Universal Song Roll 2383 $.80
    Angelus 6082

When It's All Over
    (Kerry Mills) Jass—One Step
    Played by Erlebach & Gershwin
    Universal Song Roll 2393 $.80
    Angelus 6088
Whose Little Heart Are You Breaking Now
    (Irving Berlin) Fox Trot
    Played by Gershwin & Wilson
    Universal Song Roll 2411 $.80
Some Sunday Morning
    (Richard Whiting) Saxophone Drag
    Played by Gershwin & Erlebach
    Universal Song Roll 2413 $1.00
    Later issued on Mel-O-Dee 2413
    Duo-Art 1566 (1/18) $1.25
    Note: On this roll, the Duo-Art catalogue calls the song a "Fox Trot."
Southern Gals
    (Albert Gumble) Fox Trot
    Played by Gershwin & Wilson
    Universal Song Roll 2417 $.80
*My Faultless Pajama Girl
    (Louis H. Fischer) Fox Trot
    Played by Gershwin & Erlebach
    Metro-Art 203248 $.50
    Universal 203249
Ruby Fox Trot
    (Harry Ruby) Fox Trot
    Played by Gershwin & Erlebach
    Metro-Art 203256 $.50
    Universal 203257
Jazamine
    (Harry Akst) Fox Trot
    Played by George Gershwin
    Metro-Art 203262 $.50
    Universal 203263

November 1917

Mr. Jazz Himself
    (Irving Berlin) Jass—Fox Trot
    Played by Gershwin & Erlebach
    "Irving Berlin's latest effort. The jazziest of all jazz songs."
    Universal Song Roll 2529 $.80
    Later issued on Mel-O-Dee 2529
Hello Wisconsin
    (Harry Ruby) Fox Trot
    Played by George Gershwin
    "The prize-winning novelty song of the season."
    Universal Song Roll 2543 $.80

So Long Sammy
    (Albert Gumble) One Step
    Played by George Gershwin
    "The latest of war songs has made a hit with the boys in 'Khaki.'"
    Universal Song Roll 2553 $.80
    Angelus 6098

December 1917

My Sweetie
    (Irving Berlin)
    Played by George Gershwin
    Universal Song Roll 2567 $.80
    Angelus 6107
*The Bravest Heart of All
    (Whiting) Fox Trot—Key of E-flat
    Played by Wynn
    Sing A Word Roll 53 (full number unknown)
    Perfection 87113
    Note: This roll is listed as having been "Played by Bert Wynn," but whether it is
    Gershwin may never be determined, even if a copy of the roll is discovered. Though
    he was an exclusive Aeolian artist by this time, Gershwin may have returned to Stan-
    dard to visit and cut a roll for them for old times' sake; or this might have been a
    number he recorded the previous year that wasn't issued until December 1917; or
    some other Standard pianist might have recorded it at this time and used Gershwin's
    old pseudonym. The roll is listed here because it seems to be the only "Bert Wynn"
    roll issued by Standard after Gershwin left in mid-1916. It is very likely a genuine
    Gershwin item.

1918

January 1918

The Picture I Want to See (from *Miss 1917*)
    (Kern) Fox Trot
    Played by George Gershwin
    Metro-Art 203334 $.55
    Universal 203335
    Artrio-Angelus 7807 $1.50
The Land Where the Good Songs Go (from *Miss 1917*)
    (Kern) Jass—Fox Trot
    Played by Gershwin & Erlebach
    Metro-Art 203336 $.55
    Universal 203337
    Angelus Voltem (number unknown)
    Duo-Art 1590 (7/18) $1.25

February 1918

Some Sweet Day
    (Abe Olman) Jass–Fox Trot
    Played by Gershwin & Erlebach
    Universal Song Roll 2683 $.85
    Angelus 6150
    Artrio-Angelus 7768 $1.75
    Note: This roll was first released in September 1917 as an instrumental roll, at a price
    of $.50.

September 1918

Garden of My Dreams (from *Follies 1918*)
    (Dave Stamper) E-flat
    Played by George Gershwin
    Universal Song Roll 3085 $1.00
Little Tune, Go Away (from *Rock-a-Bye Baby*)
    (Jerome D. Kern) Fox Trot Key D
    Played by George Gershwin
    Universal Song Roll 3087 $1.00
When I Hear a Syncopated Tune (from *Follies 1918*)
    (Louis A. Hirsch) Fox Trot Key G
    Played by George Gershwin
    Universal Song Roll 3091
    Angelus 6259

1919

April 1919

I'd Ask No More (from *Oh, My Dear!*)
    (Louis A. Hirsch) Key C
    Played by George Gershwin
    Universal Song Roll 3259 $1.00
    Later issued on Mel-O-Dee 3259
You Never Know (from *Oh, My Dear!*)
    (Louis A. Hirsch) E-flat
    Played by George Gershwin
    Universal Song Roll 3261 $1.00
    Later issued on Mel-O-Dee 3261
    Angelus 6365
City of Dreams (from *Oh, My Dear!*)
    (Louis A. Hirsch) E-flat
    Played by George Gershwin
    Universal Song Roll 3263 $1.00
    Later issued on Mel-O-Dee 3263
I Wonder Whether (from *Oh, My Dear!*)

(Louis A. Hirsch) E-flat
Played by George Gershwin
Universal Song Roll 3265 $1.00
Later issued on Mel-O-Dee 3265
Angelus 6359
Girl of My Heart (from *Somebody's Sweetheart*)
(Buffano) E-flat
Played by George Gershwin
Universal Song Roll 3267 $1.00
Later issued on Mel-O-Dee 3267
Angelus 6355
Land Where Journeys End (from *Oh, My Dear!*)
(Louis A. Hirsch) A-flat
Played by George Gershwin
Universal Song Roll 3271
Later issued on Mel-O-Dee 3271
Oh, My Dear—Fox Trot Medley (from *Oh, My Dear!*)
(Louis A. Hirsch)
Introducing: (1) I Wonder Whether; (2) You Never Know; (3) I'd Ask No More; (4) The
Land Where Journeys End; (5) City of Dreams; (6) I Wonder Whether
Played by George Gershwin
Metro-Art 203518 $1.00
Universal 203519
Angelus Voltem 1602
Artrio-Angelus 7958 $1.75

July, August, or September 1919 (Estimated)

Note: Since 1905, the German firm M. Welte and Sons, Inc., had been making quality pianos, player/reproducing pianos, and special oversized Red T-100 rolls that could only be played on Welte-Mignon instruments. The company established its U.S. factory in Poughkeepsie, New York, and was consequently in competition with Ampico and Duo-Art for customers of reproducing pianos. In 1918, however, Welte's Poughkeepsie plant was seized by the U.S. government as "alien" property, as ordered under federal law.

In March 1919 the U.S. subsidiary of the company was sold at auction, and in mid-1919 the new owners relocated the firm to the Bronx, where the Welte-Mignon Corporation continued to record and produce its unique Red T-100 rolls (the paper for which measured 12⅞" in width). A new roster of recording pianists was hired to make the Bronx rolls, the earliest known issue being 3962 (the highest known number— 4062— came out a year later, in mid-1920). After these 101 titles, Welte-Mignon stopped making new Red T-100 rolls and began reissuing its previous best-sellers, scaling them down to the 11¼" width that almost all American players and reproducers were using.

George Gershwin was the first of the new crop of New York area pianists to start making the Bronx Red T-100 rolls, and his recordings represent the first thirteen of these 101 numbers (3962 through 3974) to be issued.

Although Gershwin made his Welte-Mignon rolls during the same year he was recording for Aeolian, the apparent conflict of loyalty can be explained by the fact that only owners of Welte-Mignon Red T-100 pianos could play these odd-sized rolls. One supposes that Aeolian officials felt not at all threatened or betrayed by Gershwin's Welte-Mignon caper as long as he continued to make rolls for them. On the other hand, if the

Aeolian people *were* upset at Gershwin's Welte-Mignon rolls, he may have replied that he made the Bronx rolls in a hurry, over a one- or two-day period (probably the case), and that he planned to make no more Welte-Mignon rolls (and he did not). Indeed, the rolls sold so poorly that only seven of the thirteen have been located today. American Welte-Mignon dealers were probably in short supply, and the marketing effort was obviously unsuccessful. Those few who could afford the expense of the special Welte-Mignon instruments and the fairly expensive rolls may have realized that they had a better choice of popular music with Ampico and Duo-Art pianos and rolls. Welte-Mignon sales may also have been hampered by patriotic hostility against anything German during and just after World War I. Welte-Mignon Corporation could have reissued the Gershwin Red T-100 rolls in a 11¼" format (on its Purple Seal Label) but did not, possibly because such popular-music rolls were not expected to be as steady a seller as classical rolls.

These Welte-Mignon rolls as a group are so rare that even the listing of them was not possible until the 1994 publication of Charles Davis Smith and Richard James Howe's book *The Welte-Mignon: Its Music and Musicians*.[5] Smith and Howe's reconstruction of the complete catalogue of Welte-Mignon reproducing piano recordings from 1905 through 1932 was a labor that took eight years to complete.

Each of the seven Gershwin rolls that has been found (and probably the other six also) credits Gershwin as follows: "Played by George Gershwin, composer of La, La, Lucille." This plug linking him to his first successful musical comedy appears even on rolls of tunes that have no connection to *La, La, Lucille* Since the show opened 26 May 1919 and closed 19 August 1919, Gershwin probably recorded the Welte rolls during that period and arranged to have the *La, La, Lucille* label credit on each of the rolls while the show was running. Welte-Mignon would have released them gradually during the next few months, however.

Three of the Welte-Mignon titles also appeared as Aeolian rolls played by Gershwin: "Tee-Oodle-Um-Bum-Bo," "Nobody But You," and "I Was So Young, You Were So Beautiful."

The Gershwin Welte-Mignon rolls may well have been recorded in the order in which they are listed—numerically. An asterisk appears to the left of the six titles that are still missing.

*There's More to a Kiss Than X-X-X (from *Good Morning Judge* and *La, La Lucille*)
   (George Gershwin) Novelty
   Played by George Gershwin, composer of La, La, Lucille
   Welte-Mignon 3962
*Nobody But You (from *La, La, Lucille*)
   (George Gershwin)
   Played by George Gershwin, composer of La, La, Lucille
   Welte-Mignon 3963A
*Tee-Oodle-Un-Bam-Bo [sic] (from *La, La, Lucille*)
   (George Gershwin)
   Played by George Gershwin, composer of La, La, Lucille
   Welte-Mignon 3964
Yearning
   (Neil Moret) Fox-Trot
   Played by George Gershwin, composer of La, La, Lucille
   Welte-Mignon 3965
The First Rose of Summer (from *She's a Good Fellow*)

(Jerome Kern) Fox Trot
Played by George Gershwin, composer of La, La, Lucille
Welte-Mignon 3966A
*I Was So Young (You Were So Beautiful) (from *Good Morning Judge*)
(George Gershwin)
Played by George Gershwin, composer of La, La, Lucille
Welte-Mignon 3967
Novelette in Fourths—Salon Selection
Composed and played by George Gershwin, composer of La, La, Lucille
Welte-Mignon 3968
Chinese Lullaby (from *East Is West*)
(Robert Hood Bowers) Chinese Waltz
Played by George Gershwin, composer of La, La, Lucille
Welte-Mignon 3969
I'm Forever Blowing Bubbles (from *The Passing Show of 1919*)
(Kenbrovin and Kellette) Waltz
Played by George Gershwin, composer of La, La, Lucille
Welte-Mignon 3970
Sometime (from *Sometime*)
(Rudolf Friml) Waltz
Played by George Gershwin, composer of La, La, Lucille
Welte-Mignon 3971
*Till We Meet Again
(Richard Whiting)
Played by George Gershwin, composer of La, La, Lucille
Welte-Mignon 3972
Tulip Time (from *Ziegfeld Follies 1919*)
(Dave Stamper) Fox Trot
Played by George Gershwin, composer of La, La, Lucille
Welte-Mignon 3973
*Mandy (from *Yip Yip Yaphank* and *Ziegfeld Follies 1919*)
(Irving Berlin)
Played by George Gershwin, composer of La, La, Lucille
Welte-Mignon 3974

September 1919

Tee-Oodle-Um-Bum-Bo (from *La, La, Lucille*)
(Gershwin) One Step
Played by George Gershwin
Universal Song Roll 3517
Later issued on Mel-O-Dee 3517
Duo-Art Song Roll 10023
Artrio-Angelus 8033 $1.50

October 1919

From Now On (from *La, La, Lucille*)
(George Gershwin) Fox Trot Key G

Played by George Gershwin
Universal Song Roll 3543 $1.25
Artrio-Angelus 8044 $1.50
Nobody But You (from *La, La, Lucille*)
(George Gershwin) One Step E-flat
Played by George Gershwin
Universal Song Roll 3549 $1.25
Later issued on Mel-O-Dee 3549
Artrio-Angelus 8045 $1.50
I Was So Young, You Were So Beautiful (from *Good Morning, Judge*)
(George Gershwin) Ballad Key G
Played by George Gershwin
Universal Song Roll 3557 $1.25
Later issued on Mel-O-Dee 3557
Duo-Art Song Roll 10033
Artrio-Angelus 8047 $1.50
Note: In January 1920 Aeolian introduced its new Mel-O-Dee label for its song rolls, and the company quietly dropped its Universal Song Roll series. The Mel-O-Dee rolls continued the Universal Song Roll catalogue numbers. As I mentioned earlier, some of the pre-1920 rolls were kept in the catalogue and sold as Mel-O-Dee rolls during the 1920s.

1920

February 1920

Come to the Moon
(Gershwin) Fox Trot
Played by George Gershwin
Mel-O-Dee 3701
Swanee
(Gershwin) One Step
Played by George Gershwin
Mel-O-Dee 3707
Duo-Art 1649; British Duo-Art 0502

March 1920

Limehouse Nights (from *Century Whirl*)
(Gershwin) One Step
Played by George Gershwin
Mel-O-Dee 3739
Duo-Art 1654; British Duo-Art 0541
Artrio-Angelus 8105 $1.50
Note: The show was retitled *Morris Gest Midnight Whirl*.
Poppy Land (from *Century Whirl*)
(Gershwin)
Played by George Gershwin

Mel-O-Dee 3741
Artrio-Angelus 8108 $1.50

June 1920

Left All Alone Again Blues (from *Night Boat*)
(Kern) Fox Trot
Played by George Gershwin
Mel-O-Dee 3845
Duo-Art 1664 (5/20); British Duo-Art 0536
Artrio-Angelus 8139 $1.50
Whose Baby Are You? (from *Night Boat*)
(Kern) One Step
Played by George Gershwin
Mel-O-Dee 3853
Duo-Art 1667 (5/20); British Duo-Art 0522

Note: The 19 June 1920 *Music Trade Indicator*, included the following article (pp. 34–35), entitled "A GRAND, A ROLL—AND PENNINGTON—Dancer Cavorts Atop a Weber Grand to Tune of Mel-O-Dee Roll—LISTEN!—New York, June 16":

Perhaps—no unquestionably—the liveliest bit of tabasco in that whole saucepan of jazz and Mel-O-Dee, the scandals [*sic*] of 1920 is Miss Ann Pennington.

From her feet up Ann is "tres bien" but no small part of her success in the *Scandals of 1920* is her "dancing piano." No! The piano doesn't really dance. Ann dances on the roof of a Weber Grand to the tune of a Mel-O-Dee Roll in the cleverest stunt of this year's Scandals.

Dancing on a piano may be a common stunt, but—you don't know the half of it. This piano is an orchestra and dance floor both. And some orchestra!!

When Ann gets anything in her head you can't stop it—it goes right to her feet and George White knows enough not to stop Ann's feet; what is more Ann always insists on the best.

Cause: Ann's idea—

Result: George White went to the Aeolian Company and told them his story. They took a Weber Grand Electric Player Piano and made a special dancing top.

Then they called in George Gershwin, that ever ready, ever tuneful pianist who makes Mel-O-Dee rolls exclusively for the Aeolian Company. George just ran his fingers up and down the keys and turned out a real, regular, Pennington Mel-O-Dee Special.

All you need do is to see Scandals of 1920 to realize that the best dance team this year is Ann Pennington, the dancing piano, and her Mel-O-Dee orchestra. They are the hit of the Scandals and Ann says, "Don't thank me, thank Aeolian and George and Mel-O-Dee!"

Possibly the roll mentioned here was a special roll made for Ann Pennington's use in the show, as described, and not one of the three regular-issue rolls listed next. Also possible is that the roll referred to is "Scandal Walk," released August 1920.

August 1920

On My Mind the Whole Night Long (from *Scandals of 1920*)
(Gershwin) Blues—Fox Trot
Played by George Gershwin
Metro-Art 203576
Universal 203577
Artrio-Angelus 8167 $1.50

Idol [*sic*] Dreams (from *Scandals of 1920*)
(Gershwin) Fox Trot
Played by George Gershwin
Mel-O-Dee 203579
Artrio-Angelus 8168 $1.50
Note: The correct spelling of this title is "Idle Dreams." The first edition of sheet music also reads "Idol," but a later printing corrects the error. Apparently that correction never influenced piano roll labels, all of which read "Idol."

Scandal Walk (from *Scandals of 1920*)
(Gershwin) Fox Trot
Played by George Gershwin
Mel-O-Dee 203583
Artrio-Angelus 8169 $1.50

September 1920

Whispering
(Schonberger) Fox Trot, Key E-flat
Played by George Gershwin
"A splendid arrangement of this latest Pacific Coast hit."
Mel-O-Dee 4007 $1.25
Artrio-Angelus 2013 (Song Roll, with Words) $1.75

October 1920

Sweetheart Shop Selection
Comprising: (1) Waiting for the Sun to Come Out; (2) Didn't You?; (3) Is There Any Little Thing I Can Do?; (4) My Caravan
(Felix and Gershwin)
Played by George Gershwin
"This new musical comedy which has met with great success in Chicago and is soon due for a New York run."
Mel-O-Dee 203733 $1.25
Note: The labels on some rolls list tune (2) as (4) and vice versa.

Note: The 14 August 1920 *Music Trade Indicator*, p. 33, carried this article entitled "MEL-O-DEE'S LATEST HIT": "The song hit from the Musical Show, 'The Sweetheart Shop,' now playing at the Illinois Theater in Chicago, is 'Waiting for the Sun to Come Out,' written by George Gershwin, star pianist of the Mel-O-Dee Company. This number has proved so popular in Chicago that the Mel-O-Dee Company are bringing out a special roll from the 'Sweetheart Shop' because of the unusual call. Mr. Gershwin is also responsible for the music in 'George White's Scandals of 1920.' "

A Young Man's Fancy (The music box number from *What's in a Name*)
    (Music by Milton Ager) Fox Trot, Key E-flat
    Played by George Gershwin
    "Mr. Gershwin has played a music box effect in this roll that is somewhat startling. It makes a wonderful fox-trot and is used by dance orchestras from coast to coast."
    Mel-O-Dee 203737 (Instrumental) $.85
    Mel-O-Dee 4083 (Song Roll) (11/20)
    Artrio-Angelus 8025 (Instrumental) $1.50

December 1920

*When the Right Little Girl Comes Along (from *Jim-Jam-Jems*)
    (Hanley) One-Step, Key of E-flat
    Played by George Gershwin
    Mel-O-Dee 3985 $1.25
Darling
    (Schonberg) (*sic*) Fox-Trot
    Played by Gershwin & Hess
    Mel-O-Dee 4109 $1.25
    Note: Although the Mel-O-Dee bulletin gives Schonberger as the composer of this roll, the roll label reads "Schonberg."
If a Wish Could Make It So (from *Tickle Me*)
    (Stothart) Fox-Trot, Key of E-flat
    Played by George Gershwin
    Mel-O-Dee 4117 $1.25
Singing the Blues
    (Conrad & Robinson) Fox-Trot, Key of E-flat
    Played by George Gershwin
    Mel-O-Dee 4133 $1.25
    Artrio-Angelus 2027 (Song Roll with Words) $1.75
Sweet Little Stranger (from *Jim-Jam-Jems*)
    (Hanley) Fox-Trot, Key of E-flat
    Played by George Gershwin
    Mel-O-Dee 4135 $1.25
Waitin' for Me
    (Pinkard) Fox-Trot, Key of E-flat
    Played by George Gershwin
    Mel-O-Dee 4139 $1.25

1921

January 1921

Just Snap Your Fingers at Care (from *Greenwich Village Follies*, 1920)
    (Silvers) Fox-Trot, Key G

Played by George Gershwin
Mel-O-Dee 4151 $1.25
Rock-a-Bye, Lullabye Mammy
(Donaldson) Fox-Trot, Key G
Played by George Gershwin
Mel-O-Dee 4165 $1.25
Duo-Art 1705
Grieving for You
(Gold) Fox-Trot, Key F
Played by George Gershwin
Mel-O-Dee 4167 $1.25
Duo-Art 1702
Artrio-Angelus 2030 (Song Roll, with Words) $1.75
I'm a Lonesome Little Raindrop
(Hanley) Fox-Trot, Key E-flat
Played by George Gershwin
Mel-O-Dee 4179 $1.25
Artrio-Angelus 2031 (Song Roll, with Words) $1.75

March 1921

Make Believe
(Shilkret) Fox-Trot, E-flat
Played by George Gershwin
Mel-O-Dee 4267 $1.25
Duo-Art 1718 (George Gershwin "Assisted by Muriel Pollock")
Whip-Poor-Will
(Kern) Fox Trot, B-flat
Played by George Gershwin
Mel-O-Dee 4275 $1.25
Duo-Art 1719

August 1921

In a Boat (For Two)
(Lange) Fox Trot, Key of G
"Played by George Gershwin" (Mel-O-Dee roll label); "Played by Frank Banta" (Aeolian catalogues)
Mel-O-Dee 4471 (9/21)
Duo-Art 17305 (8/21)
Note: A copy of Mel-O-Dee 4471 surfaced in 1979 showing the roll credit as "Played by George Gershwin." Aeolian rarely made errors of credit. Banta was a regular Mel-O-Dee staff artist during this period and is credited with playing (either solo or on duets with Cliff Hess or Henry Lange) a total of six of the nineteen Mel-O-Dee rolls released in September (including "In a Boat"). The roll does not sound particularly like Gershwin. If it is he, he played the number fairly straight and added nothing to it that would be characteristic of his musical thinking at this time. The last Gershwin roll for 1921 appeared only on Duo-Art as an October 1921 release. Gershwin would not record further until 1925.

October 1921

Drifting Along with the Tide (from *George White's Scandals of 1921*)
(George Gershwin) Fox Trot and Song Roll
Played by George Gershwin
Duo-Art 17445 $1.25

1925

Note: The 7 March 1925 issues of two major trade weekly magazines, *Music Trade Review* and *Music Trade Indicator*, carried an Aeolian press release indicating that Gershwin was now recording exclusively for Duo-Art and that he has recorded *Rhapsody in Blue* for that firm. Neither mentions that the *Rhapsody in Blue* rolls would not be available until May 1925. The cover of *Duo-Art Monthly* carries a photo of Gershwin sitting at a grand piano and looking at the cover of the published score of *Rhapsody in Blue*. If the actual recording of the *Rhapsody* occurred in late February or early March, the release in May of the finished product gives some indication of the time required to edit, master, and mass-produce any given recording from start to finish.

May 1925

Rhapsody in Blue. Part II; Andantino and Finale
(George Gershwin)
Played by George Gershwin
Duo-Art 68787 $1.75
"Beyond question George Gershwin's 'Rhapsody in Blue' is the most imposing and most important composition thus far achieved by anybody in the jazz idiom. Its title is particularly appropriate, for it is freely rhapsodic in form and it makes plentiful and effective use of the contrasting discords which the jazz artists call 'blue notes.' It is really a Concerto in Fantasia Form for Piano and Jazz Orchestra (the first of its kind ever written). It was commissioned by Paul Whiteman, and had its first performance at Mr. Whiteman's now historic concert, in Aeolian Hall, New York, on February 12, 1924, with the composer at the piano.
"Everybody who takes any interest at all in American music will want to hear this Rhapsody. It is a remarkable work, from every point of view. It has a throbbing, pulsating vitality, and a glamour of great popular appeal. It discloses a genuine melodic gift —novel, individualistic and fine; an astonishing skill in handling the new harmonies produced by American jazz bands; a still more noteworthy ability in the invention and manipulation of striking rhythms; and a happy facility in the arrangement of form. It is a free development of Mr. Gershwin's outstanding characteristics of crispness, sense of variation in rhythm, of shifting accents, of emphasis and color; and it at once places him in the forefront of the young American composers who are bent on breaking away from banality and transforming the popular jazz music of the day into something worth while and interest-compelling.
"It has been said that delicacy, even dreaminess, is a quality that Gershwin alone brings into jazz music. Something of this phase of his talent is shown in the impressively beautiful theme of the *Andantino*, beginning the Second Part of the Rhapsody incorporated in the present Duo-Art Record of the composer's own brilliant and masterly per-

formance. And this finely expressive theme itself demonstrates his command of melodic ideas quite as convincingly as the Finale shows his ability to pile up a powerful and thrilling climax.

"George Gershwin, who now records his piano playing exclusively for the Duo-Art, was born in Brooklyn, N.Y., on September 26, 1898. When he was thirteen years old his mother bought a piano and decided that young George must learn how to play it. A new and hitherto undreamt of world was opened to him. He learned rapidly and well, the best of his early teachers being Charles Hambitzer, who gave him his first lessons in harmony and his first real reverence for music, but who died before his pupil had gone very far. Later he studied harmony with Eduard Kilenyi, and after that took some work in composition with Rubin Goldmark, for early in his piano lessons he had begun to dabble at writing. When sixteen he went to work as a 'song plugger' for a music publisher, often playing piano all day for vaudeville acts and far into the night at cafés. This led to his engagement to play for the chorus rehearsals of various musical shows. Meanwhile he kept trying his hand at composition, until, in 1918, with 'I Was So Young and You Were So Beautiful,' he found himself launched as the author of a popular song hit. Since that successful start his work has shown a steady advance" (*Duo-Art Monthly*, May 1925).

Note: Almost certainly Gershwin recorded both parts I and II of *Rhapsody in Blue* in early 1925, but the company decided to issue only the second part in May. Also certain is that the Duo-Art number immediately preceding 68787 (68777) was reserved for part I. By the time part II finally came out, however, in January 1927, it carried a "new" number: 70947. The unused number was never assigned to another roll.

June 1925

Note: Aeolian printed the following in its June 1925 *Duo-Art Monthly* bulletin, even though no Duo-Art rolls of Gershwin's music or his playing were released that month:

George Gershwin, following his recording of "Rhapsody in Blue" for the Duo-Art piano, has gone to Europe, bearing with him a commission to compose an orchestral work for the New York Symphony Society. He will write a "New York Concerto" in three movements. It is to reflect the spirit of the American Metropolis, but he says "this will not be done in any obvious way." He will compose the work in London and will play the piano part at the New York Symphony's concerts in Carnegie Hall, on December 3 and 4, and also on tour.

July 1925

Kickin' the Clouds Away (from *Tell Me More*)
(George Gershwin)
Played by George Gershwin
Mel-O-Dee 47014 $1.00
Duo-Art 713122 $1.25; British Duo-Art 0686
Brisith Meloto 31081
"George Gershwin himself has here recorded one of his newest popular hits—one of the numbers that have made *Tell Me More* a great musical comedy success. This is a snappy Fox-Trot with a great dance tune and an abundance of real Gershwin harmonies" (*Duo-Art Monthly*, July 1925).

September 1925

So Am I (from *Lady, Be Good!*)
  (George Gershwin) Ballad B-flat
  Played by George Gershwin
  Mel-O-Dee 47056 $1.00
  Duo-Art 102625 (With Words) $1.25
  "One of the popular hits of one of Broadway's outstanding musical-comedy successes of the year, *Lady, Be Good!* This is a ballad setting in George Gershwin's best style of a clever and pretty little duet, the words of which are by Ira Gershwin" (*Duo-Art Monthly*, September 1925).

October 1925

"George Gershwin is said to be at work on a jazz opera in answer to the invitation of Otto H. Kahn to American composers. Gershwin seems to have hesitated between a red Indian and a negro subject, but decided upon the latter. The opera will be in three acts and rumor says that it is going to be extremely fantastic" (*Duo-Art Monthly*, October 1925).

1926

February 1926

"In December George Gershwin's Piano Concerto was produced by Walter Damrosch and the New York Symphony Orchestra, with the composer at the piano; his '135th Street' was played for the first time by Paul Whiteman's Orchestra; and his latest musical comedy 'Tip-Toes' was staged at the Liberty Theater, New York. Isn't this pretty nearly a record for one month?" (*Duo-Art Monthly*, February 1926).

April 1926

Sweet and Low-Down (from *Tip-Toes*)
  (George Gershwin) Fox-Trot
  Arranged and Played by George Gershwin
  Duo-Art 713214 $1.25
  Mel-O-Dee 47175 $1.00
That Certain Feeling (from *Tip-Toes*)
  (George Gershwin) Fox-Trot
  Arranged and Played by George Gershwin
  Duo-Art 713216 $1.25
  Mel-O-Dee 47178 $1.00; British Meloto 31225
  Note: These are almost certainly the last piano rolls recorded by George Gershwin. The April 1926 *Duo-Art Monthly* bulletin describes them as follows: "In 'Sweet and Low-Down' and 'That Certain Feeling' George Gershwin himself has recorded in his individualistic and inimitable style the two big Fox-Trot hits from his very successful new musical comedy, *Tip-Toes*. These are special arrangements made by Mr. Gershwin exclusively for the Duo-Art Piano—and they are winners."

1927

January 1927

Rhapsody in Blue, Part I
(George Gershwin)
Arranged and Played by George Gershwin
Duo-Art 70947 $1.75

"Most celebrated of all the compositions thus far written for the Jazz Orchestra, Gershwin's 'Rhapsody in Blue' deserves both this distinction and its great popular vogue, for it is the most remarkable work yet created in the jazz idiom. Its title is appropriate. It is freely rhapsodic in form and it makes plentiful and effective use of the contrasting discords which the jazz artists call 'blue notes.' It is really a Concerto in Fantasia Form for Piano and Jazz Orchestra (the first of its kind ever composed). It was commissioned by Paul Whiteman, and had its first performance at Mr. Whiteman's now historic concert, in Aeolian Hall, New York, on February 12, 1924, with the composer at the piano.

"Here is a piece of American music, throbbing with vitality, energy, the zest of life; and unmistakably typifying the spirit of Young America of today. It is jazzy, yes; but there is a deal more than jazz in this extraordinary work. It is a rhapsodical fantasia of glamorous popular appeal, and it discloses a gift for creating new and original melodies, a real talent for the invention and manipulation of striking rhythms, a felicity in the arrangement of form, and an astonishing skill in handling for artistic ends the new harmonies produced by American jazz bands. Mr. Gershwin himself has arranged it for piano solo, and has recorded exclusively for the Duo-Art Piano a brilliant and masterly performance of it. Because the work is too long for a single music roll, it has been recorded in two parts. The second part has already been issued, so that now the whole work is available for the Duo-Art" (*Duo-Art Monthly*, January 1927).

April 1927

The April 1927 *Duo-Art Monthly* carried the following article entitled "Longo Features Duo-Art Piano with Orchestra in Seattle":

> Francesco Longo, conductor of the Columbia All-Artist Orchestra of Seattle, Washington, recently featured the Duo-Art Piano as soloist with that orchestra in several performances of Gershwin's "Rhapsody in Blue." These performances were highly successful and were hailed by the local newspapers as "a tonic—a novel musical experience." Mr. Longo writes: "We certainly put the 'Rhapsody in Blue' over big. I would like to try something else if you can suggest anything similar to this. The Seattle public was simply thrilled with the presentation of the Duo-Art."

The use of reproducing rolls and reproducing pianos in live public concerts was widespread during the 1920s. The same issue of the *Duo-Art Monthly* quoted here prints a letter from Ethel Leginska, conductor of the Boston Philharmonic Orchestra. Ms. Leginska announced her intention to perform with, and conduct, the orchestra on 10 April 1927. Her idea was to conduct Beethoven's C Minor Concerto for piano and orchestra. For the first movement a Duo-Art piano would play her recording of the piece. "The second and third movements I will play personally in addition to leading the orchestra."

April 1928

From the April 1928 *Duo-Art Music*, an article entitled "Gershwin to Write New Rhapsody": "George Gershwin, jazz composer of 'Rhapsody in Blue' and other successes, hopes to complete a second rhapsody and an orchestral ballet, 'An American in Paris,' before the end of the coming summer. Mr. Gershwin will be on his way to Europe when this note appears in print. After visiting London and Paris, he plans to take a house in Southern France, where he will work and study until mid-summer."

During Gershwin's four-year hiatus from making rolls (1921–25), and throughout the 1920s, a great number of his compositions were brought out by Aeolian played by other artists. Clearly Gershwin's impact on American music, as preserved on Duo-Art piano rolls, kept growing even though he himself had stopped making rolls in the mid-1920s. These rolls of Gershwin songs performed by other artists are listed here by date of release, song title, and performer. Publicity releases from Duo-Art bulletins are also included.

January 1922: "South Sea Isles," played by Henry Lange
June 1922: "Do It Again," played by Cliff Hess
November 1922: "I Found a Four Leaf Clover," played by Phil Ohman
December 1922: "Yankee Doodle Blues," played by Henry Lange
January 1923: "Where Is the Man of My Dreams?," played by Erlebach & Milne
February 1923: "I'll Build a Stairway to Paradise," played by Irving Bradley
June 1924: "Virginia," played by Ray Perkins, assisted by Bud Earl
"George Gershwin's 'Virginia' is the great fox-trot hit of another successful musical comedy, 'Sweet Little Devil,' which has been playing to crowded houses in New York since last January" (*Duo-Art Monthly*, June 1924).
October 1924: "Somebody Loves Me," played by Freddie Rich and Jack Denny
"'Somebody Loves Me,' here presented in a wonderfully full, rich orchestral record-roll produced by the efficient collaboration of Jack Denny and Freddie Rich, is a corker—a jazzy and compelling fox-trot and the best thing in 'Scandals,' which has already scored as the biggest musical comedy hit of the year" (*Duo-Art Monthly*, October 1924).
February 1925: "Oh, Lady Be Good!," played by Freddie Rich
"The inimitable Freddie Rich has recorded a captivating performance of 'Oh, Lady Be Good,' another great musical comedy hit, from 'Lady Be Good' which has been running for two months at the Liberty Theater, New York" (*Duo-Art Monthly*, February 1925).
March 1925: "Fascinating Rhythm," played by Freddie Rich
"George Gershwin's 'Fascinating Rhythm' is another great dance number and a best seller. This catchy Fox-Trot is the particular hit of the musical comedy 'Lady Be Good,' one of the great successes of the New York season. It is well-named, for its rhythm is fascinating" (*Duo-Art Monthly*, March 1925).
July 1925 "Tell Me More," played by Phil Ohman.
"Phil Ohman at his best is flawlessly represented by this superb Duo-Art Record of another of George Gershwin's great popular hits from the smashing musical comedy success 'Tell Me More.' This is an irresistible Fox-Trot and inimitable in its individuality—a wonderful dance tune with a rich harmonic setting in which some beautiful chime effects give a piquant element of novelty" (*Duo-Art Monthly*, July 1925).
March 1926 "Looking for a Boy," arranged and played by Phil Ohman
"'Looking For a Boy' is the outstanding popular hit of 'Tip-Toes,' one of the most suc-

cessful musical comedies on the New York stage today. It has a nice, catchy lyric, and musically is George Gershwin at his best—a great Fox-Trot. And here it is inimitably recorded by Phil Ohman, whose playing is one of the most applauded features of the show, 'Tip-Toes'" (*Duo-Art Monthly*, March 1926).

April 1926 "Song of the Flame," arranged and played by Rube Bloom and Frank Milne

"'Song of the Flame,' from the romantic operetta of the same name, is a Fox-Trot with a Russian flavor, a strikingly new and different kind of melody, and other novel features that give it distinction and a sure popular appeal" (*Duo-Art Monthly*, April 1926).

January 1927 "Someone to Watch Over Me," played by Phil Ohman

"The musical comedy 'Oh, Kay!' is Broadway's newest big sensation in a season of unprecedented lavishness in musical shows; and one of the outstanding popular hits of the show is George Gershwin's snappy new ballad, 'Someone To Watch Over Me,' of which Phil Ohman has made another of his inimitable Duo-Art Song Rolls. Ira Gershwin wrote the words of the song" (*Duo-Art Monthly*, January 1927).

January 1927 "Clap Yo' Hands," played by Phil Ohman

January 1927 "Do-Do-Do," played by Phil Ohman

"Here are two marvelous Fox-Trots from George Gershwin's new musical comedy 'Oh, Kay!,' just about the biggest popular hit of the season on Broadway. 'Do-Do-Do' is a real sensation—a great dance number with everything that a great dance number should have. It's *the* hit of a hit show and the talk of New York. 'Clap Yo' Hands' is also a most fascinating dance tune, with a new idea in rhythm. Phil Ohman knows this novel new music inside out and upside down, for he is in the cast of 'Oh, Kay!' and his playing is one of the outstanding features of the show" (*Duo-Art Monthly*, January 1927).

February 1927 "Maybe," played by Phil Ohman

"This is the second of Phil Ohman's inimitable song rolls of the great song hits from George Gershwin's new musical comedy, 'Oh, Kay!,' which is the sensational success of the current season on Broadway. The piano playing of Phil Ohman is one of the outstanding features of this remarkable 'show,' and both Gershwin and Ohman record their playing exclusively for the Duo-Art piano. Like 'Someone to Watch Over Me' which was issued in a Duo-Art Song Roll last month, 'Maybe' is in Gershwin's best vein—characteristically snappy and melodious and singable. The words of the song are by Ira Gershwin" (*Duo-Art Monthly*, February 1927).

February 1928 "Funny Face Medley"—"Funny Face," "He Loves and She Loves," "Let's Kiss and Make Up," "'S Wonderful," "Funny Face," arranged and played by Phil Ohman

"Here is a musical comedy medley that is different—a group of the hits from George Gershwin's new musical comedy sensation, 'Funny Face'—inimitably played by Phil Ohman who is one of the stars of the show. Ohman has made a wonderful arrangement of this music and has played some parts of it in ballad tempo and other parts in Fox Trot tempo, just as he plays it on the stage. Every number included is a sure-fire hit, and the whole medley is one of the most attractive ever made—George Gershwin's music and Phil Ohman's playing make an unbeatable combination" (*Duo-Art Music*, February 1928).

February 1928 "The Man I Love," arranged and played by Alan Moran

"A great Fox Trot that is making a sensation wherever it is heard, for it is George Gershwin at his best—abounding in typical Gershwin harmonic changes as well as tunefulness. It's a zippy dance number, and Alan Moran has recorded a zippy performance of it" (*Duo-Art Music*, February 1928).

February 1928 "'S Wonderful," arranged and played by Phil Ohman

"The big hit number from Gershwin's gay and tuneful musical comedy sensation 'Funny Face.' As here played as a Fox Trot by the redoubtable Phil Ohman, it's a corker" (*Duo-Art Music*, February 1928).

May 1928 "Musical Comedy Medley," including "The Man I Love," arranged and played by Phil Ohman

May 1928 "Oh, Gee! Oh, Joy!," arranged and played by Phil Ohman

"Here's a new Gershwin number and a great one—a great Fox Trot with a real tune to it and lots of pep and swing and go. It's the big popular hit number of his newest 'show'—'Rosalie'—and is simply great for dancing. And Phil Ohman has played it in his own inimitable way" (*Duo-Art Music*, May 1928).

May 1930 "Strike Up the Band," played by Frank Milne

"In 'Strike Up the Band' George Gershwin has given us a stirring and enthralling marching song which holds the listener spellbound with its martial strain and succession of majestic chords in harmonies that are typically Gershwin-ian. The recording by Frank Milne starts with novel and realistic drum effects which make a very fitting introduction to a performance that gives to this Fox Trot a rhythm that is replete with military precision" (*Duo-Art Music*, May 1930).

December 1930 "Musical Comedy Medley," including "Embraceable You" and "I Got Rhythm," played by Muriel Pollock

"Five fine and varied numbers comprise this medley selected and played by Muriel Pollock. The best of the Musical Comedy season's hits, recorded in an entertaining manner" (*Duo-Art Music*, December 1930).

December 1930 "Embraceable You," played by Phil Ohman

"George Gershwin's beautiful fox-trot Ballad, 'Embraceable You,' as recorded by Phil Ohman sparkles with rhythm and color. The hit number from the new Gershwin Musical Comedy 'Girl Crazy'" (*Duo-Art Music*, December 1930).

Notes

Special thanks to the many people who helped me prepare the 1973 rollography and this 1998 revision: the late Jack Edwards, who loaned me his vast collection of original roll catalogues; Agatha Kalkanis, director of the Music and Performing Arts Division, Detroit Public Library, who provided the library's collection of original Duo-Art bulletins, which pinned down release dates from 1923 forward; and other collectors, including Bill Burkhardt, Trebor Tichenor, George Blau, Alvin Johnson, Mark Reinhardt, Jerry Biasella, Bob Berkman, and especially Dick Howe and Charles Davis Smith, whose remarkable Welte-Mignon scholarship will be described later on.

1. *George Gershwin's Song-Book* (New York: Simon & Schuster, 1932).

2. Michael Montgomery, "George Gershwin Piano-Rollography," *Record Research* 42 (March–April 1962): 3–4.

3. Robert Kimball and Alfred Simon, *The Gershwins* (New York: Atheneum, 1973), 286–90.

4. Information on the existence and possible availability of any of these rolls would be greatly appreciated. Please contact me at 17601 Cornell Road, Southfield, MI 48075. Telephone: (248) 559-8885.

5. Charles Davis Smith and Richard James Howe, *The Welte-Mignon: Its Music and Musicians* (Vestal, N.Y.: Vestal Press for the Automatic Musical Instrument Collectors' Association, 1994). I am greatly indebted to this extraordinary work and to its authors.

12 : *What about Ira?*

EDWARD JABLONSKI

When George Gershwin died in July 1937 at the age of thirty-eight, Hollywood gossip rumored that the career of his lyricist and older brother (by twenty-two months), Ira, would perish too. Theirs had been a unique fraternal collaboration, but, the word went, Ira Gershwin had been riding on his brother's elegant coattails and had lived in his shadow. With George gone, Ira would fade into obscurity and inactivity.

The only enduring truth in all this prattle is that Ira was indeed almost two years George's senior.

The shock of his brother's death from an unsuspected brain tumor crushed Ira with despair and guilt. Like his friends—and especially his wife, Leonore—Ira initially attributed George's abnormal behavior during the last weeks of his life to a psychosomatic reaction to an unappreciative Hollywood. Since he first complained of "composer's stomach" in the early 1920s, Gershwin had been humored by family and friends as a hypochondriac, not to be taken seriously. Leonore Gershwin's opinion was that he needed a psychiatrist, not a physician.

That she was wrong and that he had not realized it sooner would haunt Ira Gershwin for years. When he did realize that his brother was ill, Ira secured their release from contract for the film *The Goldwyn Follies* (1938), leaving the score incomplete. He did not believe that George could be fatally ill, nor did he want to believe it. To that degree he agreed with his wife, who was upset by matters that, in hindsight, were obviously symptoms of an organic disorder. She complained about George's behavior at the table—dribbling as he drank, dropping his knife, leaving food on his chin. In one temper tantrum, she ordered him away from the table. Ira accompanied George up the stairs to his bedroom. He later told his old friend and George's, Mabel Schirmer, that he would never forget the look in his brother's eyes as he entered the room.

At this time, E. Y. Harburg, who lived nearby, was about to leave for New York to work on a musical with Harold Arlen. To bring peace to the Gershwin home, he offered his own home to George. Gershwin moved in with his man of all work—Paul Mueller—and a male nurse. Gershwin lived in Harburg's house, in near isolation, for a few days before falling into a coma and dying two days after what had proved to be hopeless surgery.

Almost immediately after George's death, the myths began to flourish. After his brother's funeral in New York on 15 July 1937, Ira returned to the tuneless house on Roxbury Drive. A believer in the sanctity of contracts—once when asked which came first, the words or the music, Ira replied, "The contract"—he chose composer Vernon Duke to finish the *Goldwyn Follies* score.

On completion of two final songs for the film, Ira took time off—an entire weekend!—as he and Leonore took a motor tour (unusual for the stay-at-home lyricist) through parts of California and Nevada.

Back in Beverly Hills Ira returned to song. He remembered a song he and George had written for Fred Astaire that he felt would fit nicely into the score of their last completed film, *A Damsel in Distress* (1937), then in production. True to form, the studio did not use it. Entitled "Heigh-ho, the Merrio," the song was recycled almost twenty years later as "The Back Bay Polka" for the film *The Shocking Miss Pilgrim* (1946), about which I will say more later.

In 1939, longtime friend and composer Kay Swift, recently appointed Chairman [*sic*] of Music for the New York World's Fair, approached Ira with the idea of creating the fair's theme song, with music by George and lyrics by Ira. Ira obliged by dipping into his brother's store of unused melodies, tune fragments, and other compositional snippets, notated in what George called "Tune Books." With Swift's help he stitched together three of these to fabricate "The Dawn of a New Day."[1] The song effectively expressed the fair's theme, in the years before World War II, of America's optimistic anticipation of "the world of tomorrow."

This unusual collaboration would have a bountiful sequel. For ten weeks in the spring of 1946, Ira, again working with Kay Swift, compiled a score from the soon-to-be organized Gershwin Archive of unpublished melodies by George for the film *The Shocking Miss Pilgrim*, starring an anomalously fully clothed Betty Grable in an 1870s Boston setting. "Kay," Ira noted in his *Lyrics on Several Occasions*, "a composer-musician in her own right, a close friend of George's and mine, was ideal for the job. She knew almost everything George had written, had frequently taken down sketches as he composed in his New York apartment, and had total musical recall. (At one time she could play from memory the entire *Porgy and Bess* vocal score of 559 pages.)"[2]

They began, Ira Gershwin recalled, by "going carefully through all my brother's notebooks and manuscripts; from them she played and then copied for me well over a hundred possibilities—forty or fifty complete tunes (several of which, such as 'Aren't You Kind of Glad We Did?,' I had started setting lyrics to in George's lifetime), plus verses, plus themes for arias, openings, &c . . ."[3]

This effort yielded not only the songs for a quite lackluster Betty Grable musical but also prompted Ira to continue sorting and organizing his brother's papers, musical notebooks, letters, clippings, photographs, and scrapbooks. These efforts, with the aid of Kay Swift and later Lawrence D. Stewart, preserved a unique collection of Gershwiniana in the Gershwin Archive (now stored at the Library of Congress).[4]

Probably the richest, most intriguing portion of the archive is the "Gershwin Melody Collection," a group of songs and thematic ideas garnered from the early Tune Books, manuscripts, and Kay Swift's vivid memory. Inexplicably, the Melody Collection begins with number 17. (Lawrence D. Stewart, who worked closely with Ira Gershwin during the years of the collection's compilation and annotation, believes the numbering takes up after the final songs written for *Shall We Dance*, *A Damsel in Distress*, and *The Goldwyn Follies*—the three Gershwin films of 1936–37.)

Gershwin Melody number 17 is entitled "Sleepless Night"; the designation and title are in Ira Gershwin's hand. At the top of the page Kay Swift has written "Prelude." This was one of the six preludes Gershwin played at recitals in concert with contralto Marguerite d'Alvarez late in 1926. He apparently performed a different program at different locations (New York, Buffalo, and Boston in January 1927). He played five in New York and six in Boston and chose to publish three. In the 1940s Ira Gershwin answered a query about the preludes with this statement: "There is an actual 4th prelude, however unpublished. Since it is in 32 bar song form I'm going to put a lyric to it some day." This was the form that Kay Swift set down in the Melody Collection, slightly adjusting the song to make it more singable. This version differs from Gershwin's prelude form as notated in three fragments in his Prelude notebook dating from 1925. Possibly the Gershwins were planning "Sleepless Night" as a song for one of their final films. But Ira never wrote the lyric.

Other titles in the collection include the evocative *Fifty-second Floor* (no. 24), *Violin Piece* (no. 40), "Ask Me Again" (no. 50), "Verse" (no. 105), and "You Started It" (no. 125, written for the Gershwins' first film score, *Delicious*, ca. 1931). Stewart recalls that Ira had planned to publish a piano folio of a dozen of these pieces without words, to be entitled *Gershwin in New York*, in the 1970s. The first piece in the set was to have been *Siren (Puerto Rico)* (no number), followed by "Sleepless Night," *Sutton Place* (no. 59), *Three-Note Waltz* (no. 42), and others. Though this project never came off, some of the pieces from the collection were published individually—*Irish*

Waltz (no. 32) as *Three-Quarter Blues* and *Comedy Dance* (no. 43) as *Merry Andrew*—for solo piano.

The stickler for neat chronology will have a problem with the Gershwin Melody Collection. Its order is haphazard, and some numbers are untitled. Moreover, all numbers following number 50 ("Ask Me Again") may be incomplete, and several unpublished pieces—all have since been published —were not included at all: "The Real American Folk Song," "Just Another Rhumba," "Harlem River Chanty," and "Hi-Ho! At Last!" As to chronology, number 38, "Thanks to You," was written for *Delicious* (1931); number 44, "Ain't It Romantic?," was written for *Oh, Kay!* (1926); and number 100, "Put Me to the Test," was heard only instrumentally in *A Damsel in Distress* (early 1937).[5]

In the period between the assembly of "The Dawn of a New Day" and the compilation of the Gershwin Melody archive, roughly between the spring of 1938 and the summer of 1946, Ira Gershwin's career without George blossomed. In that first year he collaborated with his neighbor Jerome Kern on at least eight songs—virtually half a score for a musical and more than sufficient for a film. Whether or not these were intended for any special work is not known, though three were eventually published in 1968. Typically Ira are the two songs designed to be sung sequentially, "Once There Were Two of Us" and "Now That We Are One." The first concludes with

> Always one,
> Never two
> Always one—
> Thanks to you!

The second begins

> Now that we are one,
> Which one shall we be?
> Shall we be you?
> Shall we be me?

and concludes:

> Always one,
> Never two,
> But which one
> Is up to you!

Such twinkling lines flow from the same guying lyricist who could write such tongue-in-cheek ballads as "Blah, Blah, Blah," "The Half of it, Dearie, Blues," and "I Don't Think I'll Fall in Love Today" (with George), as well as "What Can You Say in a Love Song?" and "Let's Take a Walk around the Block" (with E. Y. Harburg and Harold Arlen, from *Life Begins at 8:40*, 1934) and "I Can't Get Started" (with Vernon Duke, from *Ziegfeld Follies of 1936*).

During this same period of "retirement" after his brother's death, Ira Gershwin also collaborated with Johnny Green ("Baby, You're News," with

E. Y. Harburg, 1939), and Harold Arlen ("I'll Supply the Title [You Supply the Tune]," around 1939, and "If That's Propaganda," 1941). He also wrote a song for *China Relief*, "Honorable Moon," with Harburg, music by Arthur Schwartz, in 1941, by which time his retirement had ended dramatically.

Retirement had officially ended on New Year's Day 1940, when another longtime friend, playwright Moss Hart, called from New York with an idea for an unusual musical. The composer for the prospective show was a distinguished refugee from Nazi Germany, Kurt Weill. Would Ira consider writing the lyrics? To the astonishment of Hart (and others in Ira's circle), the reply was yes.

Burton Lane, who had known the Gershwins since he was fifteen and would eventually collaborate with Ira, expressed the consensus when he said, "For years I had heard it said of Ira Gershwin that if you should ask him what his plans were for the coming year, he would answer, 'I have a show to get out of doing with so and so, and such and such a studio wants me to do a film, but I want to get out of that too.'"[6] Columnist Leonard Lyons had a favorite anecdote in which someone asked Ira what he was up to that day. The reply was, "I have a full day's work ahead of me." "Really? What are you doing?" "I have to change the typewriter ribbon."[7] Ira's occasional avoidance of work and his meticulous (and time-consuming) attention to every minute detail of a lyric were probably the sole sources of irritation in the fraternal collaboration, George being the hare to Ira's tortoise. However, a dip into the substantial *Complete Lyrics of Ira Gershwin*, edited and intelligently annotated by Robert Kimball, is impressive proof that there was a great deal he did not "get out of."[8]

Moss Hart's telephone call generated *Lady in the Dark*, Kurt Weill's first major American success and a landmark in our musical theater, not only because it marked the return of Ira Gershwin to Broadway but also for the show's sophisticated, contemporary libretto (the eponymous protagonist undergoes analysis—a Broadway musical first). Composer Weill was especially proud of what he called the "one-act operas" he and Gershwin had devised for the analysis sessions—the patient's Freudian dreams—all three of which employ music. (The workaday sequences use dialogue without music.) In fact, these mini-operas underscored and illuminated the plot with "integrated" songs (a term not yet in vogue in the theater) a full two years before *Oklahoma!*'s celebrated integrated songs and "dream ballets" interpreted the psychological disposition of that show's female protagonist, Laurey.

Working within the show's singular structure, Ira Gershwin reveled in his favorite form, the patter song (a tribute to his spiritual mentor, W. S. Gilbert), though he managed to squeeze out a mere two ballads (a form he preferred to skip, if possible). These were the sinuous "This Is New" and the haunting ritornello "My Ship," the "elusive tune" (according to the script) not heard in its entirety until the final psychiatric session that solves all the anxieties of protagonist Liza.

Ira's verbal dexterity and his flair for the offbeat were showcased in *Lady in the Dark* in the tongue twister "Tchaikowsky," introduced by emerging star Danny Kaye with breathtakingly speedy articulation. In fact, the lyric had been written by one "Arthur Francis" (Ira's early pseudonym, used at a time when he did not want to be accused of slipping into songwriting on his brother's already established name). As "The Music Hour," the lyric had been published in the 12 June 1924 issue of *Life*, back when *Life* was not a pictorial publication but a humor magazine. Of this effort, Ira wrote, a little wistfully, "I have waited hopefully—but in vain—these many years for someone to accuse me of plagiarism."[9] The lyric consists entirely of the names, forty-nine in all, of Russian composers "compiled from advertisements on the back covers of piano music and orchestral scores in my brother's collection."[10] The song, and Danny Kaye, stopped the show. To mollify the star Gertrude Lawrence, Gershwin and Weill created an equally smashing audience-pleaser in the rambunctious "The Saga of Jenny," a compilation of the willful ways of a strong-minded, if destructive, young woman:

> Jenny made her mind up when she was twelve
> That into foreign languages she would delve;
> But at seventeen to Vassar it was quite a blow
> That in twenty-seven languages she couldn't say no.

(The plot of *Lady in the Dark* turns on Liza's inability to choose between two men in her life and which cover should be selected for the next issue of the fashion magazine she edits. "Jenny" is her subconscious rationalization for doing neither.)

Ira demonstrated another kind of wordplay in *Lady in the Dark* in what he called a "Fairy Tale from Left Field": a story, in the tradition of the classic English ballad, that solves a riddle ("What word of five letters is never spelled right?"—an idea that came to him while engaged in word games with Richard Rodgers). The song is "The Princess of Pure Delight," in which a minstrel wins the hand, plus whatever came with it (for he already had her heart), of the title damsel. In competition with "the Prince in Orange and the Prince in Blue / And the Prince whose raiment was of Lavender hue," the minstrel wins with Ira's answer to Rodgers's conundrum: "W-r-o-n-g."

Typical Gershwinesque verbal whimsy occurs in *The Circus Dream*, the mini-opera/analyst's session that includes "The Saga of Jenny" and "Tchaikowsky." In this sequence, Liza finally decides to abandon her married lover and is ordered to stand trial in a most fitting setting, a circus. The prosecutor is the Ringmaster, who sums up the predicament:

> The mister who was once the master of two
> Would make of his mistress his Mrs.
> But he's missed out on Mrs. for the mistress is through—
> What a mess of a mish mash this is!

After the triumphs of *Lady in the Dark*, Ira's Broadway experiences were disheartening: the sadly neglected *The Firebrand of Florence* (with Weill, 1945) and the single-joke (marital complications among the affluent) *Park*

Avenue (with Arthur Schwartz, 1946). Neither libretto even approached the deft, well-crafted work of Moss Hart. *The Firebrand*, on whose book Ira worked with playwright Edwin Justus Mayer to convert Mayer's 1924 play of that title into an operetta, was a curious vehicle for him. The story was set in Florence in the time of Cellini—a "costumer"—and was intended to be a parody of operetta, not a revival. Because of the musical's time, place, and elaborate sets and costumes, Ira admitted that writing the book and lyrics had taken a great deal of effort but finally had been "a lot of fun, as being in period, I could do a lot of things in form that I'd hesitate to experiment with if the show were placed in modern times." Moreover, he considered Weill's score "the best job he's ever done."[11]

Ira was quite proud of his *Firebrand* lyrics, especially "The Cozy Nook Trio," with its exercise in spoonerisms (Duke: "I know where there's a nozy cook" / Angela: "My lord, you mean a cozy nook"), and the ode "A Rhyme for Angela," in which the hapless poet (the duke) can come up with rhymes for sixteen previous mistresses but none for Angela. Ira even prepared an additional five, should the song inspire an encore.

But there were no encores and *The Firebrand of Florence* was extinguished after only forty-three investment-forfeiting performances, the victim of a book whose theme eluded the audience, poor casting (including a very miscast Lotte Lenya), as well as the ponderous period sets and fussy costumes that smothered the Weill-Gershwin lightheartedness.

Park Avenue, which came next, despite a book by such masters of comedy as George S. Kaufman and Nunnally Johnson, was not the very contemporary, "smart" show its creators, including Ira, projected—a brittle, bright new musical on the Broadway scene after the Americana folksiness of *Oklahoma!*, *Carousel*, *Up in Central Park*, and *Annie Get Your Gun*. Unfortunately, they were wrong. The critics mauled the book, with its two acts of variations on a joke about divorce and multiple marriages among, as Ira called the show's protagonists, "the upper-bracket-income-and-black-tie-set."[12] The music, by Arthur Schwartz, was also poorly received, though many of the truly smart songs (that is, those with intricately rhymed and pointed lyrics) were noted. Among the highlights were the before-its-time "Don't Be a Woman If You Can," the perceptive "There's Nothing Like Marriage for People," and the caustic calypso "The Land of Opportunitee." But, as Ira wrote to a friend a few weeks after the opening, "there were no longer any audiences," and no chance to overcome the poor reviews. Ruefully, he added, "Heigh ho—guess I can't afford to do any more flops—two in a row is about six too many."[13] These experiences cured him of the stage; he never ventured there again.

Hollywood proved to be a bit more gratifying, but to a degree. The major attractions were the climate and being able to work at home (most of the time) on the magnificent "Gershwin Plantation," as Harold Arlen called the house on North Roxbury Drive. There would be no out-of-town tryouts, no hotels, no rehearsals, no back-stage infighting—and the inevitable cold he brought back from the East.

Following his return to Hollywood after the warmth and pride of *Lady in the Dark*, Ira's first collaborator was Aaron Copland. Copland wrote the bulk of the score for *The North Star* (1943), a pro-Russian film glorifying America's then ally pitted against the Nazi invasion of the Soviet Union. The sentiments expressed in Lillian Hellman's screenplay would lead to accusations and investigations by the McCarthy-like Tenney Committee five years later. The songs written for the film *are* patriotic and reasonably ethnic, but they are hardly un-American (no more, in fact, than was the script). When Ira appeared later before the Tenney Committee because he had opened his home for a meeting of the Committee for the First Amendment—a committee whose members included John Huston, Lauren Bacall, Humphrey Bogart, and others —he responded to the inquiry by laughing. The committee dismissed him.

More a documentary than musical, *The North Star* featured peasanty songs (in several, Copland drew upon existing Russian songs) about village, wagons, and work. All were sung by the most un-peasant-like cast assembled this side of the Ukraine: Farley Granger, Ann Baxter, Dana Andrews, and others. Their costumes might recently have been bought at Macy's.

Ira Gershwin's versatility was evident in the range of song for the film, from a gently defiant children's song to a farmer's work song—with appropriately folkish settings by Copland. The first is entitled "The Younger Generation":

> If I eat too much jam,
> Mother, look how young I am;
> Father dear, please recall
> That at one time you were small.
> If I'm hard on my clothes
> And I do not wipe my nose,
> Parents dear, please recall
> That at one time you were small.

And the most pointed quatrain:

> Parents dear, use your tact
> If you don't like how we act,
> Do not fret, do not mourn—
> Is it our fault we were born?

These seem perceptive lines for a man with minimal experience with children. Nor was Ira familiar with farm life, but "Wagon Song" (which was not used in the film) revealed his rustic side:

> Wheels fall off and axles break—
> It's not all honey and cake.
> When I'm in my wagon, jogging along.
>
> Roads go bad, and, then, of course,
> A horse can eat like a horse
> When I'm on my wagon, jogging along.

Ira returned to a more traditional film musical in the wartime *Cover Girl* (1944), collaborating with Jerome Kern. The film's best-remembered song was "Long Ago and Far Away," one of his least favorite lyrics. He deemed it merely "adequate," attributing the song's long stay on *Your Hit Parade* to Kern's stately melody. "The other lyrics are better," he felt.

He even took a liking to the film's other ballad, "Sure Thing," cast in Kern's favorite song form. The tune was one he remembered from his and Kern's earliest collaborations in the year after George Gershwin's death. Unfortunately, Kern had failed to write it down. With the aid of Kern's daughter, Elizabeth, who had also liked the melody, they recalled it for the composer.[14] Ira's affection for the song can be attributed to the allusions to the race track and its terminology—a tribute to one of his own favorite recreations.

Especially timely in the film was the song "Who's Complaining?," as patriotic submission to wartime rationing. Ira considered it one of his better lyrics, with lines like:

> Because of Axis trickery
> My coffee now is chicory,
> And I can rarely purloin
> A sirloin.

Or:

> I go to work by bicycle
> My house is like an icicle,
> And oh, my lack of butter
> Is utter.

And:

> My vanity may wonder where
> To get new clothes and underwear;
> My legs may be forgotten
> In cotton.

However, such sacrifices were bearable if, as the lyric concludes, "So long as they don't ration my passion for you." *Cover Girl*, like *Lady in the Dark* was very successful, and the popularity of "Long Ago and Far Away" via radio and recordings was especially gratifying to Gershwin.

For his next film, Ira was reunited with Kurt Weill for another war-inspired effort, *Where Do We Go from Here?* (1945). Its protagonist Bill (portrayed by Fred MacMurray), who has been classified 4-F in the draft (i.e., ineligible for the military) is desperate to get into uniform. Doing his part by collecting scrap metal, he one day rubs a lamp and a genie appears prepared to grant Bill three wishes. Patriotically, he has only one—to join the army. The genie, however—rusty, perhaps—turns out to be a bumbler. Bill finds himself marching in the army, only it's George Washington's. He then requests naval service and ends up on the deck of Columbus's *Santa Maria*.

The final fantasy sequence takes place on Manhattan Island, or New Amsterdam, around 1660 or so. All is eventually resolved when the genie arrives on a magic carpet, rescues Bill, and deposits him in the marine corps of 1944.

"A lot of effort and imagination has gone into the film," Ira wrote to a military friend. "It's the first movie musical I know that has some of the flavor of 'Of Thee I Sing' in the writing and the music."[15] The screenplay was written by Morrie Ryskind, who had co-written all three Gershwin political operettas. Ryskind's script gave Gershwin and Weill the opportunity to fashion a Broadway musical for a film. Ira took special pride in a twelve-minute little opera, for which he wrote book and lyrics, "The Nina, the Pinta, the Santa Maria." This, he mentioned with further pride, was the longest nondancing musical number filmed up to that time. The number begins when a mutiny erupts on the *Santa Maria*. The sailors are certain that Columbus has no idea of their destination on a flat world. Columbus defends his mission musically, invoking the royal name of Isabella, who had "hocked her every bracelet and earring" to finance the voyage. His entreaties do not convince the hostile crew, prompting Bill to come to his defense by singing of the wonders of the land they are about to discover. Ira's comic twist has Columbus acceding to the crew's demands on learning from Bill that the land he was about to discover would be named for his rival, Amerigo Vespucci. But it is too late to turn back when the cry "Land Ho!" ends the scene.

This parody of traditional Italian opera might tweak today's sensibilities with its stereotyping and broad humor (*Time*'s 1945 critic called it a "wopera"), but in wartime such sentiments were "politically correct." Another example is the "contrapuntal aria" sung by, in Ira's script note, "a terrific tenor":

> I miss my bambino,
> My vino,
> And "Sole Mia,"
> And the sextet from Lucia.

Another arm of the Axis is burlesqued in "Song of the Rhineland," rendered by a group of mercenary Hessians ("in waltz time") exalting their homeland in a Trenton Bierstube:

> Where the heart is mellower
> And the hair is yellower
> And the girls is juicier
> And the goose-step goosier!

Another anti-Nazi quatrain goes:

> Where the wine is winier
> And the Rhine is Rhinier
> And the Heinie is Heinier
> And what's yours is minier!

Ira enjoyed working in such an unusual form of musical film—long sequences in which, as Weill said, "the music and lyrics are integrated with the story, advancing it rather than retarding it as is the case with most musical films. . . . I have turned out a job here which I can be proud of."[16] But virtually no one else noticed, neither film critics nor filmgoers—and servicemen laughed at MacMurray's yearning for a uniform. The experiment was ignored, and its innovations were lost in the final months of World War II (when *Where Do We Go from Here?* was released in early July 1945, the war in Europe was over). The public was tried of patriotism, and the films that succeeded in 1945 were the quasi-Gershwin biography *Rhapsody in Blue*, *Anchors Aweigh* (whose action occurs in Hollywood, not at sea), and the rural-folksy Rodgers and Hammerstein *State Fair*.

Ira's flop show period ensued (*The Firebrand of Florence* and *Park Avenue*), and then he returned to California to stay and to work on another film, *The Shocking Miss Pilgrim*, which initiated the Gershwin Melody Collection. When asked to do the film, Gershwin had hoped to work with either Harold Arlen or Harry Warren, but both were on other projects at the time. *Pilgrim*, to a large degree, was an exercise in what might be called un-Gershwin activity. Instead of the usual Gershwinesque Jazz-Age-in-Gotham song-and-dance romantic fluff, the film was to be, as Ira described it, "a musical-technicolor-Boston-1870-Betty Grable-women's rights, etc." entertainment. And since it was in period, he couldn't "use some of the rhythmic and modern stuff [from the Melody trove] and have to go in more for charm, etc."[17] In fact, the most distinctive rhythm numbers are an Old World polka—a satirical view, with a jaundiced eye, of Boston—and the waltz "One, Two, Three (Waltzing Is Better Sitting Down)."

More pointed social commentary appears in "Demon Rum" (no. 48, "Blue Hullabaloo") and notably in the prescient—for 1946—feminist statement "Stand Up and Fight" (no number):

Like it or not,
Men have got
To take the view
That women are people, too!
Why can't we be judges judging evildoers?
Why can't we be engineers and book reviewers?
Why can't we be Chief Commissioners of Sewers?
Butchers? Bakers?
Undertakers?
Next November's
Cabinet members?
Aren't women human beings?

No one caught the message; nor were there excitement and clamor over the "discovery" of nearly a dozen unknown Gershwin songs. Not even "For You, for Me, for Evermore" (nos. 51 and 52), which Kay Swift was certain would prove to be "a gold mine," achieved popularity. *The Shocking*

Miss Pilgrim was indifferently received by the critics and was a box office failure.

That was a significant disappointment to Ira after so many years of wariness about the use of the unpublished songs, even on Broadway (in 1942 Samuel and Bella Spewack were reportedly working on such a musical, *Birds of a Feather*, but Ira and the estate decided against releasing the songs). Another source of frustration to Ira was the cutting from the film of "Tour of the Town," a musical excursion through Boston to such historic sites as Faneuil Hall, Harvard, Old North Church, and so on, and a special house:

> That, Miss Pilgrim, is the one house
> We do not have to peep in.
> That's the one George Washington
> Did not sleep in.

This elaborate and lengthy lyrical exercise, though recorded and probably filmed, was eliminated from the final print. Frankly, the melody sounds more Swiftian than Gershwinesque except for a short musical phrase that appears throughout linking the ten sections together. The surviving audio soundtrack sounds listless and protracted as sung by the bland Dick Haymes. Indeed, the entire film lacked the anticipated Gershwin vivacity and presented the audience with an out-of-character Betty Grable; all in all, it was pleasant but unexciting.

The Shocking Miss Pilgrim's reception and failure induced a more guarded response to requests for tunes from the Gershwin Melody cache. Ten years passed before Ira released three songs as a favor to his friend, producer-writer Billy Wilder, for an alleged comedy, *Kiss Me, Stupid* (1964). When he began work on the songs, this time aided by composer-arranger Roger Edens, he was disturbed because Wilder had no script and Gershwin preferred fitting songs into appropriate "spots" in a screenplay. Since the film was to star Dean Martin, Wilder suggested an Italianate song along the lines of Martin's hit record "That's Amore." That suggestion was readily fulfilled when Ira recalled a song he and George had written for *Shall We Dance*, "Wake Up, Brother, and Dance," which had not been used in the film or published. At that time he had felt the song had a Neapolitan flavor, so with a new lyric and a switch in meter from 4/4 to 3/4, it became "Sophia." Once the screenplay for *Kiss Me, Stupid*, by Wilder and I. A. L. Diamond, was ready, Ira was relieved to learn that only two more songs, "novelty numbers," were required.

Here's the rub: the film, an adaptation of a French farce, features two amateur songwriters who trap a Dean Martin–like singer in their small town overnight so that they can sell their songs to him. A further trap is a local call girl (Kim Novak) who impersonates the wife of the composer of the team (the real wife having once headed the singer's fan club). The singer was a notorious womanizer, and the ambitious composer did not want his true wife to come into his ken. (Ira, who did not like the project's title, was even more unhappy with the finished film, which he suggested would have been better titled *Lust Horizon* or *Lust for Lust*, among others.)

Plot aside, and with "Sophia" attended to, Ira's patchwork song writing for the film is illuminating. When Wilder asked for a "nutty" number, Ira recalled a song he and his brother had written for no special spot, "I'm a Poached Egg" (no. 105 of the Melody Collection). Wilder liked it, but there were only eight bars, so to them Ira added the release of "Are You Dancing?" (not on the Melody Collection list), which had been prepared for, but not used in, *Girl Crazy* (1930).

This was no amateur's effort but the kind of "laundry-list" lyric associated with Cole Porter ("You're the Top," for example), a form Ira enjoyed:

I'm a poached egg
Without a piece of toast,
Yorkshire pudding
Without a beef to roast
A haunted house
That hasn't got a ghost—
When I'm without you.

That he enjoyed this wordplay is evident in the pages of additional lyrics written for the song, plus one specially composed for Ella Fitzgerald when she recorded her *Gershwin Song Book* for Verve Records. Among the unused lines were:

I'm a Porgy
Who'll never find his Bess,
A sinking ship
Without an SOS,
I'm a tenant,
The kind they dispossess—
Can't sleep without you.

The final song, "All the Livelong Day (and the Long, Long Night)," had a longer history. The verse was taken from a song entitled "Phoebe" (no. 89), written in 1921 while he, his brother, and colyricist Lou Paley were vacationing in the Adirondacks. The chorus was based on a bluesy melody (no. 57) also dating from the 1920s. In notating it, Kay Swift wrote on the manuscript "figure need," sensing that it needed a bit more to be complete. Roger Edens complied with her suggestion by using a phrase from the verse. Except for the slight concession to the film's protagonists—the amateurish use of "do-oo-oo" and "you-oo-oo" at the beginning of the chorus —it is an admirable Gershwin ballad. But none of the songs amounted to anything so far as popularity was concerned, and film itself was properly maligned.

That settled it for Ira—there would be no more Gershwin Melodies wasted on another film.

After the *Miss Pilgrim* misfortune, Ira was happy to be teamed with veteran composer Harry Warren early in 1948 for what appeared to be a promising film. Warren had been the undisputed, if uncrowned, "King of the Melody Makers" at Warner Brothers during the 1930s in the heyday of the *Gold Digger* musicals. By 1948 Warren had made the transition from backstage musicals through the big bands ("I've Got a Gal in Kalamazoo" and others) at Twentieth-Century Fox and into the Metro-Goldwyn-Mayer extravaganzas under the aegis of Arthur Freed.

Freed was a former songwriter ("Singin' in the Rain" and others) turned producer and a longtime friend of Gershwin. He and Ira often clashed across Ira's pool table and talked about songs and films. Freed believed Fred Astaire and Judy Garland could repeat the great success of their *Easter Parade*, this time as a married, often bickering musical comedy team. Would Ira write the songs with Harry Warren? By May 1948 Warren and Gershwin began writing songs for Garland and Astaire.

Several songs for the stars were completed, including the impressive "There Is No Music" for Garland, when her emotional and physical breakdown forced her out of the film, by then titled *The Barkleys of Broadway*. Her replacement was Ginger Rogers, which caused the jettisoning of several songs fashioned to the Garland voice and style of delivery. New songs were written for the smaller Rogers voice, and, to mark the reunion of Rogers and Astaire on screen after a decade, Freed decided to interpolate "They Can't Take That Away from Me" (from *Shall We Dance*) as a nostalgic reminder of their golden years at RKO. (The Gershwins, George especially, felt that this fine song did not get its due in the original film.) Freed's gentle nod to the past did not please Harry Warren. "I did not take kindly to this," he told his biographer Tony Thomas, "not that I didn't like the song, but there isn't a composer alive who likes having a song by someone else interpolated into his score."[18]

Happily, this melodic intrusion did not cause any friction in the collaboration—theirs was a mutual admiration association dating back to 1930, when they first collaborated on such songs as "Cheerful Little Earful" and "The Merry Month of Maybe." They were also longtime golfing adversaries. Still, the years had gone by, and *The Barkleys* lacked the old Fred and Ginger scintillation. "It may not be the most robust musical ever made," Ira acknowledged, "but it has enough novelty and charm to make it entertaining."[19]

By "novelty," Ira clearly meant the rhythm numbers that gave the lyricist the opportunity to excel. One was Astaire's "one-man ballet in a shoe shop" (as Ira saw it), an Astaire solo in which he dances with a shopful of shoes—all his, by the way. The song's title, "Shoes with Wings On," was suggested by a drawing of Mercury and the story of *The Sorcerer's Apprentice*. Warren's tune, Gershwin found, was "tricky"; moreover, it was "tough to get a title for a song about a dance" without being obvious or trite. Mercury solved the problem of title, but setting Warren's tune was more difficult. "There was much juggling and switching and throwing out of line and phrase and rhyme," he wrote in *Lyrics*, "—maybe ten day's

worth—before the words made some singable sort of sense."[20] His "greatest challenge" was to invent three successive double rhymes (in the first
three lines of the refrain):

When I've got shoes with wings on—
The Winter's gone, the Spring's on.
When I've got shoes with wings on—
The town is full of rhythm and the world's in rhyme.

Another novelty, kin to the tongue-in-cheek satirical songs Ira had written with his brother ("The Babbitt and the Bromide" or "These Charming
People"), is "Weekend in the Country," a trio for Rogers, Astaire, and city
boy Oscar Levant, portraying himself, as usual, under the name "Ezra":

They: A weekend gets you sunburnt—
    Vitamin A you win.
Ezra: I'd rather get back unburnt
    With my original skin.

"My One and Only Highland Fling," warbled by Rogers and Astaire in
Scottish brogue, presented no language problems for Ira, and he enjoyed the
exercise. But when advance copies of the published songs arrived, he found
that someone "in the New York publishing house had undialected the lyric."
("Hame" had been corrected to "home," for example.) Such tampering in-
cited a note of protest, reading in part: "How in the world idiomatic Brook-
lynese like 'spoke real soft' got into the song where 'spoke me soft' was
indicated I'll never understand." With dispatch, "Highland Fling" was
reprinted as written.[21]

Harry Warren, like Irving Berlin, was a master balladeer and since *The
Barkleys of Broadway* was a romantic musical there was no way Ira could
avoid writing a lyric to one of Warren's ballads. One which remained in the
film was the haunting "You'd Be Hard to Replace." But there was another
ballad, "There Is No Music," unfortunately unsung after Judy Garland was
"released" from the picture:

Stars without glitter,
Sun without gold;
Nightfall is bitter,
Endless, and cold.
Silent the city,
Silent the sea—
There is no music for me.

Even without music, this lyric sings like the poetry Ira maintained he never
wrote. Incidentally, he retrieved some of the imagery and rhyme from
"There Is No Music"—"glitter" and "bitter"—for the later Garland big ballad "The Man That Got Away."

Youthful sparkle was abundant in Ira's next film, *Give a Girl a Break*
(1953), in which he collaborated with the gifted Burton Lane. This project

came after an interval devoted to Gershwin estate matters (including the knotty legalities of clearing Gershwin songs for the cornucopian *An American in Paris*) and a European junket that Leonore Gershwin cajoled him into.

After the resplendent *An American in Paris* was released—launching a resurgence of the popularity of several songs, and recordings, including a sound track album and Academy Awards—Ira developed a warm spot in his heart for MGM (producers of the movie, with Arthur Freed at the helm). Realizing that he had been idle for three or so years, Ira was delighted for the chance to work with Burton Lane at MGM on *Give a Girl a Break*. Lane, too, was free, having just competed the successful *Royal Wedding* (also MGM) with lyricist Alan Jay Lerner. MGM, on its part, had fond feelings toward Lane and Lerner and hoped to put them back to work in the afterglow of the *Wedding* profits. But Lerner was not available, having renewed his contentious collaboration with Frederick Loewe.

Enter "Swifty"—Irving P. Lazar—the agent who represented both Gershwin and Lane. He called Lane, who was willing to work, and then inquired about his preferred lyricist. Half in jest, Lane came up with a wild suggestion, "Ira Gershwin," suspecting that Ira would find some way "to get out of it." Lazar called Ira and got a yes instead. In due time Ira and Lane would wish they had replied in the negative.

Lane, who had known Ira for almost a quarter of a century, had never worked with him before and was as much in awe of him as he had been as a teenager in 1927. Once recovered from that, he found that "working with Ira . . . one of the most pleasant experiences of my creative life. Ira is an impeccable workman. Once a title has been selected, he will offer four, or five, or six, or even more, if necessary, alternate lines for each eight bar phrase until he and his collaborator are satisfied."[22]

Working with Lane was equally relaxed and pleasurable for Ira, and he even pronounced their work "good," a rare assessment for him. He was so pleased with their efforts that when he came to New York to look in on the 1952 revival of *Of Thee I Sing*, he brought a set of demonstration records with him that he and Lane had made of the *Give a Girl a Break* score. Some coaxing by family and friends persuaded him to drop by with the discs under his arm. The recordings confirm Lane as a fine pianist and vocalist, and Ira's singing, while, in Lane's word, "impeccable"—precise rhymes, rhymes on the beat, melodic integrity and faultless pronunciation—is best described as endearing.

Ira's favorite song of the score was "In Our United State," an example of the Gershwin affinity for the oblique in expressing eternal devotion in a ballad. In the film, with the United Nations building as a backdrop strikingly lighted at night, a very young Debbie Reynolds and Bob Fosse declare their feelings, employing language appropriate to the setting: "Fooling around will be unconstitutional," "annual budget," "permanent policy," "the state of our union," and so on.

Another of Ira's favorites, "Applause, Applause," is a rarity: a song for which the words came first. Its subject is the need for handmade approbation among show people. The lyric pleased Gershwin, and he was happy with Lane's setting. "Ira," Lane warmly recalled, "is one of the most appreciative partners I have ever worked with. I remember one day he gave me a lyric to set. The next day we met and I played what I had written. He stood behind me as I played my melody and sang his lyric. Suddenly, I became aware that he had placed his arm around my shoulder. Without saying a word I knew I had pleased him, and when I looked up his beaming face confirmed what I had felt."[23]

In the category of the ballad, Ira's bête noir, he set, with grace and skill, Lane's unconventional back-beat melody "It Happens Ev'ry Time":

I look and see the stormy skies,
You look at me with laughing eyes—
December days are like July's;
It happens ev'ry time.

Another equally intricate and distinctive ballad, "Dreamworld," was eliminated from the film. Like "Applause, Applause," it was germane to the plot evidenced by Ira's several allusions to show business terminology. The opening quatrain of the verse has a sly, Gershwinesque inner rhyme in the first line:

This mundane life of Mondays
Is suddenly looking up—
With a calendar full of Sundays
And joy brimming my cup.

Also dropped from the film was the whimsically witty dialect piece, "Ach, du lieber Oom-Pah-Pah," the theme song of a backyard brass band:

For schmaltziness our band cannot be matched.
Ve string along without a fiddle player—
Ve are a band that has no strings attached!
No strings attached! Holy smoke!
Dot's a joke!

The mutilation to their score hit home when, accompanied by Leonore Gershwin, they were invited to a preview screening. Besides the excised and abridged songs (about half of "In Our United State" was eliminated), some songs were poorly staged, and the finale was hopelessly abominable. As the stunned trio drove back to the Gershwin home, Leonore broke the silence by asking Ira if he had any stock in MGM. He did. "Sell it!" she said. He did.[24]

Lane drily suggested that the film should have been entitled *Give a Song a Break*.[25]

Ira's final film collaborations were with Harold Arlen, the other unavailable composer at the time of the making of *The Shocking Miss Pilgrim*. Though these collaborations were not free of the usual moviemaking turmoil, they fostered Ira's masterly, if flawed (predominantly by others), swan songs. Gershwin and Arlen worked concurrently on a Bing Crosby dramatic film, *The Country Girl* (which Ira considered a "strong psychological study" rather than a musical), and the Judy Garland classic *A Star Is Born* (both 1954). George Seaton wrote the screenplay for the first, Moss Hart the screenplay for the latter. Hart, who had provided the text for Ira's return to Broadway (*Lady in the Dark*), would do the same for Ira's retirement from the musical scene with *A Star Is Born*.

A Star Is Born was to be Judy Garland's comeback film after four years of exile from Hollywood. Several skirmishes with directors and psychological problems aggravated by drugs forced a cancellation of her MGM contract. But her several successful recitals in New York and London boded well, and Warner Brothers, through the efforts of her current husband, Sid Luft, signed her on for a film, with Luft as the producer. During the protracted shooting of *A Star Is Born*, Luft and especially Warner Brothers probably wondered if MGM had been right all along.

But Judy Garland's pitiable emotional and physical highs and lows during the making of the film never handicapped the songwriters. The collaboration was relaxed, productive, and fast—a little over three months— with time out for television sports and news, the racetrack, and other diversions. Ira and Arlen completed their work in April 1953; the film was not released until September of the next year.

Ira was pleased with their contribution, especially with "The Man That Got Away": a ballad, and a typically bluesy Arlenesque "tapeworm" (that is, longer than the conventional thirty-two bar form—sixty-two bars, in fact, and with a pulsating beat that immediately captured Ira's interest). In retrospect, Arlen composed the music for the two classic songs most intimately associated with Judy Garland: "Over the Rainbow" (with lyric by E. Y. Harburg) and "The Man That Got Away." Many believed that Ira's lyric alluded to Vincente Minnelli, Garland's previous husband. Ira had served as his best man at the wedding (their daughter is named for the Gershwin song "Liza"). If the gossip was true about the theme of the song's lyric, Ira never mentioned it.

Ira first realized the film was in trouble when, eleven months after he and Arlen had finished their score (five songs plus a throwaway calypso in the form of a commercial), Luft telephoned asking for a dramatic musical conclusion for the first half before an intermission for the now ambitious enterprise. By this time Arlen had left for New York to write the score for *House of Flowers* and was seriously ill and in the hospital. Nevertheless, he recovered sufficiently to supply the producers (plural, for Ira detected the heavy hand of the Brothers Warner in this) with the music to what Ira wrote up as "I'm Off the Downbeat," an outstanding blues-rhythm number. But it was rejected because, as Ira informed a friend, Warners and Luft had "decided that any one new number wouldn't be socky enough. . . . They feel it's some kind of insurance and with 4½ mill invested so far I hope these additional costs [to be expended on an elaborate production number] worthwhile."[26] That production number was "Born in a Trunk," a medley of old tunes by other songwriters. He was more critical in an annotation prepared for, but deleted from, *Lyrics on Several Occasions*. The comment is felicitously restored in the Kimball compilation: "It added fifteen minutes to a three-hour film, held up the show, and cost $300,000. Big mistake (but all none of my business)."[27] (Two earlier songs written for this spot had also been rejected, but jettisoning "I'm Off the Downbeat" was another mistake.)

There was more. Soon after the film's release—to rave reviews—more than twenty-five minutes were slashed from the prints of *A Star Is Born* in the wake of outcries from theater owners. The complaints were about how the film's length (vide "Born in a Trunk") precluded two screenings per evening and meant a consequent loss in revenue even with higher ticket prices. In the trimming, pieces of the plot were lost and, needless to say, three songs were eliminated. The plot tampering infuriated director George Cukor, who refused to see the mutilated film. The Arlen-Gershwin songs were restored twenty-nine years later (1983), but it was too late—both Arlen and Gershwin were ill, and Judy Garland was dead. Ira, at the time, had been gracefully resigned to the initial mangling, saying with characteristic equanimity, "I'm not going to lose any sleep over it; there's too little sleep left as is."[28] Still, such editing of a well-received film *after* its premiere was unconscionable, but nothing could be done once the songs came under studio control.

Three months after *A Star Is Born*, *The Country Girl* was released, prompting minimal musical interest (Arlen felt that neither he nor Gershwin was in top form on their songs for the film). But its star, Grace Kelly, won the Academy Award many believed should have gone to Judy Garland. And "The Man That Got Away," nominated as one of the year's best film songs, was overshadowed by the commonplace "Three Coins in the Fountain."

Except for the insignificant *Kiss Me, Stupid*, a decade later, Ira was as finished with Hollywood as he was with Broadway. Between the releases of the two Arlen-scored films, he announced in December 1954, "Am thinking of having a go at a book of lyrics."[29] True to form, he did not actually begin until August of the next year, aided in the work by his secretary, Lawrence D. Stewart. Not only did these efforts materialize in the erudite, informative, and charming *Lyrics on Several Occasions* (finally published by Knopf in 1959, after much polishing and fretting), but also, again with Stewart, the preparation of his brother's papers (and eventually his own) for deposit in the Music Division of the Library of Congress.

Sibling rivalry? Hardly. From beginning to end, Ira believed that George was the greater Gershwin. "Always Ira had preferred to walk in the shadow of George, turning the applause over to him," according to E. Y. Harburg, who had known both since their childhoods on the Lower East Side. "But it was Ira's light which shone over George's shoulder, guiding him through those tragically brief but incandescent years, that burst upon the music world with lightning boldness, lifting the art of song writing to historic new heights."[30]

Even a cursory study of the Gershwin oeuvre reveals that the George Gershwin songs that live today are graced with lyrics by Ira. In other words, George needed Ira. (Some exceptions: "Swanee," lyric by Irving Caesar; "Somebody Loves Me," lyric by B. G. DeSylva and Ballard MacDonald; and, most notably, "Summertime" and all of the first act of *Porgy and Bess*, by DuBose Heyward.) During and before their collaboration, Ira worked with other composers. In the early period, Ira's most gifted collaborator was Vincent Youmans, with whom, as "Arthur Francis," he wrote songs for *Two Little Girls in Blue* (1921). From this musical came such moderately successful songs as "Oh Me! Oh My!" and "Who's Who with You." The production ran for a respectable 135 performances—one more, incidentally, than George's most successful show up to that time, *George White's Scandals of 1921*.

During the Gershwin-Gershwin collaboration, Ira branched out now and then with happy results: with Harry Warren, and Billy Rose (arguably) as colyricist, "Cheerful Little Earful" (1930); several songs with Harold Arlen, and colyricist Yip Harburg (no argument), for the score of *Life Begins at 8:40* (1934); and, of course, with Vernon Duke, the standard "I Can't Get Started" (1936). Interspersed between the first and last of these, Ira worked with his brother on two musical comedies, three operettas, a film, and an opera: *Strike Up the Band* (1930), *Girl Crazy* (1930), the film *Delicious* (1931), the Pulitzer Prize–winning *Of Thee I Sing* (1931), *Pardon My English* (1933), *Let 'Em Eat Cake* (1933), and *Porgy and Bess* (1935).

Yip Harburg, who was there, described Ira, even as a teenager, as

> the shyest, most diffident boy [as a teenager in high school] we ever knew. In a class of lower east side raucous rapscallions, his soft-spoken gentleness and low-keyed personality made him a lovable incongruity. . . .
>
> Ira had a kid brother who was a source of embarrassment to him. He wore stiff collars, shirts and cuffs and went out with girls. Like George B. Shaw, George Gershwin found school an institution to be avoided at all costs. His brother was "my brother Ira the scholar." This admiration for Ira the scholar was lifelong, profound and of the greatest significance in the growth, development and evolvement of George's creative genius.[31]

Ira's was a unique blend of scholarly craftsmanship, gentle whimsy, a sharp eye and ear, and, yes, though he perpetually disclaimed it, poetry.

Notes

1. Kay Swift remembered that the introductory verse to "Dawn of a New Day" had been borrowed from an unused spiritual-like song titled "Come, Come, Come to Jesus," dating from 1930. The main section of the song, the chorus, and the middle release were unlyricized song ideas among the Gershwin papers. The early Gershwin Tune Books contained Gershwin's ideas for songs, most merely melodic lines without harmonization or titles. Many are carefully dated, some are fragments of a few bars. By the mid-1920s Gershwin put his ideas down in larger notebooks—the Tune Books were small enough to carry around in his pocket.

2. Ira Gershwin, *Lyrics on Several Occasions* (New York: Knopf, 1959), 70.

3. Ibid.

4. What is now known as the George and Ira Gershwin Collection, in the Library of Congress, was initiated after the death of Rose Gershwin (George and Ira Gershwin's mother) in December 1948. (Because George Gershwin died intestate, his mother inherited his estate.) In her will she left Gershwin's bound manuscripts of *Rhapsody in Blue*, Concerto in F, *An American in Paris*, Second Rhapsody, *Cuban Overture (Rhumba)*, and *Porgy and Bess* to the Library. In the 1950s Kay Swift presented her manuscript copy of *George Gershwin's Song-Book* (dedicated to her), and Ira Gershwin gave the manuscript of the *Variations on "I Got Rhythm"* (dedicated to him). Thus, the original holographs of Gershwin's major works formed the base of the archive.

Beginning in the early 1950s Ira Gershwin began adding to the collection annually (for tax purposes as well as for preserving the material): scores in his brother's hand (*Of Thee I Sing, Let 'Em Eat Cake*, etc.) and songs, including pencil sketches from *Porgy and Bess*. His other contributions ranged from Gershwin's portrait of Schoenberg to Gershwin's desk, which George himself designed, as well as notebooks, study sheets, scrapbooks, etc. Later additions were a *Blue Monday* score in the original Will Vodery orchestration and Gershwin's two-piano manuscript of *An American in Paris*. Gershwin had assumed that the Vodery manuscript had been lost since around 1922; its appearance decades later remains cloaked in mystery. As for the *American in Paris*, its manuscript was purchased by Leonore Gershwin and presented to the Library; Ira had refused to buy the valuable manuscript because he was suspicious about how the "owner" had acquired it.

As for the Secaucus "finds" over the past several years, while they are neither hoax nor fraud, a plethora of hype envelopes these findings that were never truly lost. For example, early in 1952 the late David Baker and David Craig, respectively the dance arranger and vocal director for the revival of *Of Thee I Sing*, searched through several boxes in the Gershwin publisher's warehouse (this was pre-Secaucus) and to their surprise found not only the scores but orchestrations and even songs in manuscript. In other words, Ira Gershwin knew about the trove as early as 1952.

Ten years later Don Rose, musician, arranger, and Gershwin enthusiast, hoped to find the "lost" *Let 'Em Eat Cake* score for a production at Miami University with which he was associated. When he got nowhere with the publishers, he enlisted the aid of Kay Swift. The publisher was not interested in a college production of a flop show; the argument about its "historic" nature did not help. When Kay Swift offered to do the job, since said publisher did not wish to waste the time on it, she too was rejected. (Rose soon after found the score where Ira Gershwin had placed it in the Library of Congress.)

The fruits of Rose's research and enthusiasm for Gershwin rarities was his gathering together a group of Gershwin overtures that were recorded by the Buffalo Philharmonic and released in 1977 under the title *Gershwin on Broadway* (Columbia 34542). The recording held six overtures in all, including the one to the elusive *Cake*; Rose based his orchestrations of them on the originals. The album was a success, and Woody Allen used portions of it in the film *Manhattan*.

Such harvests encouraged the publishers (by now a new and more enlightened regime) to be more cooperative. Besides, Ira Gershwin had smiled upon the project and had lent a hand—more show overtures and a suite from the Gershwin film scores followed.

Rose became ambitious and hoped next to revive another Gershwin failure, *Pardon My English*. Accompanied by musical theater scholar Robert Kimball, Rose found the score, a good deal of which was in the composer's writing, and in addition, he and Kimball found cartons of Porter, Rodgers, and others. This discovery made the front page of the *New York Times* in November 1982 and opened a can of worms for Don Rose. Ira

Gershwin dispatched Michael Feinstein, then Gershwin's assistant—before his cabaret debut—to snatch away the *English* materials because he believed the score inferior and, except for a few songs, did not want it performed or recorded. (He was wrong about the score's quality; happily, this music was recorded and released in the summer of 1994.) To go into the legalities that followed in the wake of this 1982 Secaucus find, as well as Rose's woes, are fortunately beyond the scope of this prolix footnote.

Five years later, in March 1987, the "find" made the *Times* first page again, proclaiming the discovery of "about 70 . . . lost songs by George Gershwin, many with lyrics by his brother Ira." These "lost" songs, then, are in addition to those of the Ira Gershwin–Kay Swift Gershwin Melody Collection of about 125, with perhaps three dozen or so of the seventy complete.

What these "lost" songs in Secaucus might be were not spelled out, but they are undoubtedly manuscripts, piano copies, or excerpts from a conductor's score of *unpublished* songs from the shows. At the time it was not a practice to publish complete scores. The hoped-for hits, usually a half dozen or so, were published, and the rest of the score—patter songs, choral pieces, dances, minor songs—were packed into boxes and stored. They were not lost; they were merely ignored. (For the record, during Gershwin's lifetime he saw the publication of the full scores to, in England, *Primrose*, and in the United States, *Strike Up the Band*, *Girl Crazy*, *Of Thee I Sing*, and *Porgy and Bess*.)

In time all of the Secaucus Gershwin materials will find their proper niche in the George and Ira Gershwin Collection, Library of Congress. Other collections of Gershwiniana are in the George Gershwin Memorial Collection, Fisk University Library, Nashville, Tennessee (very scanty Gershwin: a scrap of manuscript marked "Sportin' Life"; a signed photo to Carl Van Vechten, who established the collection; printed music, etc.) The collection is mainly devoted to books on music, autograph letters, musical biographies, opera scores, programs, etc., and manuscripts by Samuel Barber, Victor Herbert, Leonard Bernstein, and Aaron Copland.

The Gershwin archive at the Academic Center Library, Humanities Research Center, University of Texas, Austin, has some George Gershwin manuscripts and paintings, Ira Gershwin's drafts to lyrics for *A Star Is Born*, some of his paintings, etc.

The Museum of the City of New York houses Gershwin memorabilia: Gershwin's portable silent piano keyboard, sheet music, photographs, and a cigarette lighter—a gift from George to Ira marking the opening of *Girl Crazy*.

But the Library of Congress has the richest collection of all.

5. Pianist-musicologist Alicia Zizzo has been editing George Gershwin's solo piano works in his original conceptions for publication by Warner Brothers Music. Working from his manuscripts, she has published *Lullaby* (an early piano piece that Gershwin transcribed for string quartet) and a suite from the one-act opera *Blue Monday* based on Gershwin's manuscript piano-vocal score and Will Vodery's original orchestration. Ready also are all six of the Preludes, plus a fragment of a seventh that served as the opening of the third movement of the Concerto in F. Near publication, too, is a solo piano version of *Rhapsody in Blue* based on no less than three copies in Gershwin's hand. Smaller piano pieces are also being edited, and in time all this work will richly expand the Gershwin solo piano repertory.

6. "Notes and Quotes from Ira's Friends," *ASCAP Today* 5 (January 1972): 7.

7. See a slightly different version of the story in Leonard Lyons, "New York Is a Great Place to Be . . . ," *Saturday Review* 41 (18 October 1958): 26.

8. Robert Kimball, ed., *The Complete Lyrics of Ira Gershwin* (New York: Knopf, 1993).

9. Ira Gershwin, *Lyrics on Several Occasions*, 187.

10. Ibid.

11. Letter from Ira Gershwin to Edward Jablonski, January 1945.

12. Ira Gershwin, *Lyrics on Several Occasions*, 349.

13. Letter from Ira Gershwin to Edward Jablonski, November 1946.

14. Kern, too, remembered a tune he had liked by George Gershwin. This was "Put Me to the Test," used instrumentally but not sung in *A Damsel in Distress*. "Test" is the sprightliest rhythm number in *Cover Girl*, and its kinship with the Gershwin tune is noteworthy.

15. Letter from Ira Gershwin to Edward Jablonski, early 1945.

16. Letter from Kurt Weill to Leah Salisbury (his agent), quoted in Ronald Sanders, *The Days Grow Short: The Life and Music of Kurt Weill* (New York: Holt, Rinehart, and Winston, 1980). 334.

17. Letter from Ira Gershwin to Edward Jablonski, 5 July 1945.

18. Tony Thomas, *Harry Warren and the Hollywood Musical* (Secaucus, N.J.: Citadel, 1975), 250.

19. Letter from Ira Gershwin to Edward Jablonski, spring 1948.

20. Ira Gershwin, *Lyrics on Several Occasions*, 290.

21. Ibid., 62.

22. "Notes and Quotes from Ira's Friends," 8.

23. Ibid.

24. Ira Gershwin, *Lyrics on Several Occasions*, 256.

25. "Notes and Quotes from Ira's Friends," 8.

26. Letter from Ira Gershwin to Edward Jablonski, ca. April 1954.

27. Kimball, *The Complete Lyrics of Ira Gershwin*, 376.

28. Letter from Ira Gershwin to Edward Jablonski, April 1954.

29. Letter from Ira Gershwin to Edward Jablonski, December 1954.

30. "Notes and Quotes from Ira's Friends," 7.

31. Ibid.

Index